EXPLORING RELATIONSHIPS IN BUSINESS AND PROFESSIONAL COMMUNICATION

EXPLORING RELATIONSHIPS IN BUSINESS AND PROFESSIONAL COMMUNICATION

AN ANTHOLOGY

FIRST EDITION

Edited by William J. Taylor

Kansas State University

cognella®
SAN DIEGO

Bassim Hamadeh, CEO and Publisher
Angela Schultz, Senior Field Acquisitions Editor
Alisa Munoz, Project Editor
Alia Bales, Production Editor
Emely Villavicencio, Senior Graphic Designer
Greg Isales, Licensing Associate
Natalie Piccotti, Director of Marketing
Kassie Graves, Vice President of Editorial
Jamie Giganti, Director of Academic Publishing

Printed in the United States of America.

3970 Sorrento Valley Blvd., Ste. 500, San Diego, CA 92121

CONTENTS

ACKNOWLEDGMENTS

Thanks to Cognella Academic Publishing for this tremendous opportunity. Composing a textbook requires a ton of advice and support. I would like to thank all of my students, whose insights, questions, and suggestions provided the primary motivation and basis for this book. Thank you to all of my friends, family, and colleagues too numerous to mention in their entirety here for their support and encouragement over the years. Special thanks to my mother, Doris, and Kenna Reeves, Toya Green, Irene Fowler, and Cindy Myler for ... everything.

EDITOR'S INTRODUCTION

"Employers and college students both agree that soft skills are import-ant to obtain jobs post-graduation. Employers hire college graduates expecting some level of expertise in applied soft skills, but then often complain the new hires lack these soft skills or have overstated their level of competency."

—Carol Stewart, Alison Wall, Sheryl Marciniec (2016)

Business and professional environments represent unique areas of commu-nication that intersect with the growing trends of diversity, globalization, and technological change. Many businesses actively seek out diversity in hiring practices to obtain top talent. Small-town storeowners interact with customers, suppliers, and vendors on the other side of the world with ease. New graduates and students reading this text embody the most technologically proficient gener-ation in history, as they begin filling vacancies created by retiring baby boomers. As industries and workplaces change, so too should our understanding of how we communicate within those environments.

Business communication generally refers to all forms of communicative interactions that take place within business and other professional environments. It constitutes a broad area of study and practice that encompasses every aspect of the business world, from the boardroom to the break room and beyond. This book attempts to distill some of the most important topics and lessons for successfully navigating business and professional environments. These pages explore business commu-nication as a tie that binds us in relationships with bosses, clients, and coworkers.

Motivation and Design

As a young instructor assigned to teach a class in business communication, I reviewed a number of textbooks and settled on one I felt gave the students the most reference material and practical examples. After the first semester, it became apparent that this approach did not meet the needs of my students. Not all students will write memos or draft quarterly sales reports, nor will they all go to work only in corporate offices or cubicles. Yet I felt as though those were the future employees most traditional textbooks targeted. The sheer diversity of majors taking my classes demanded a different approach. Finally, one student asked why he needed to know proper typesetting for memos and reports, considering that his business goal was to take over his family farm. Given the material in the textbook, that was a difficult question to answer.

Recognizing that each student will interact with different workplaces in different ways, my task then was to discover some element of business communication that would maintain relevance to students with diverse futures. What connects the future workplaces of students majoring in business, communication studies, food science, park management, gender studies, animal science, computer programming, chemical engineering, theater, history, and so forth? To find this answer, I dived into various industry journals. What I discovered seemed such an obvious answer: *relationships*.

Relationships constitute a single element connecting all peoples in all professions across industries. We do not generally work in strict isolation. In every industry, we communicate with coworkers, bosses, clients, suppliers, vendors, and government representatives. At the same time, we *communicate* our relationships. In fact, when communication occurs, there is always and already a relationship between the two or more parties. When we say or type "Hello," we are automatically in a relationship. When we ask for directions on a street corner, regardless of the response, we enter into a relationship with that person. If this is true, just think about the hundreds or thousands of relationships in our lives, experienced every day.

As an instructor, I struggled to meet the diverse needs of all students. Focusing on relationships as the essential connective element across business communication allowed me to contextualize class material in such a way that it became much more relevant to all students. Moreover, employers agree that the ability to maintain and cultivate positive relationships is important not only for good working environments but also for the success of the business. Employers want new employees that have strong transferable skills and come equipped with an understanding of communication and relationships. They call these the "soft skills." Therefore, this book works to satisfy the needs of both students and employers.

Of course, no one book can comprehensively cover the broad array of topics within business communication. Borrowing primarily from relational and interpersonal communication perspectives, this book seeks to cultivate these "soft skills" in students. Cultivating and managing a complex set of business and professional relationships requires competency in a variety of areas. In this volume, I tried to include articles and essays that address transferable skills for a diversity of students and majors. Within certain limitations, broad applicability guided my selection of the articles presented herein. Many additional areas merit serious attention and remain under consideration for future volumes. Those topics include, but are not limited to, LGBTQ+ discrimination, disability, transnational workers, listening, and customer relations. I have tried to maintain the integrity of the original texts included in this volume, with minimal alterations.

Given the diversity of topics and nontraditional approach to business communication, this book has several potential audiences. Students and instructors will appreciate the flexible design and engaging articles. Lessons gleaned from these readings offer guidance for everyday communication in the workplace and other professional environments. Approaching business communication through the lens of relationships will benefit the full range of business personnel, including management, employees, and human resources associates.

Organization

To accomplish the objectives and goals of this volume in an orderly fashion, I arranged its contents into eight sections. Each section contains several articles and essays under a unifying theme. Chapter introductions preview contents and draw out the significance of the works to provide guidance for the reader. Keywords and discussion questions follow each entry.

Section 1 introduces the concept of business and professional communication. Snyder and Frank provide an overview of business communication and its major elements. The authors make an initial connection between communication and relationships by describing our daily communicative interactions as essentially negotiations in relationship development. Hynes continues this discussion by emphasizing the roles of trust, job satisfaction, and culture in shaping interpersonal communication in the workplace. Both articles draw attention to the strong interplay between communication and interpersonal relationships.

Section 2 applies the knowledge of section 1 to the specific skills most desired in today's workplace. Stewart, Wall, and Marciniec introduce the reader to the "soft skills," those relational skills that foster productive workplace relationships. Perhaps most striking, the authors discuss discrepancies between the interpersonal skills competencies that employers desire and the perceived level of competency among recent graduates. Jones, Baldi, Phillips, and Waikar go further in explicating the specific skills demanded by employers and offer advice for improving competency.

Section 3 examines four factors that influence the interplay between workplace communication and relationships. Each article functions as a standalone lesson, but the topics converge as a set of primary influencers. These articles also serve as compliments to those in sections 4–8. DuBrin explains the concept and importance of impression management. While students intuitively know that impressions matter, DuBrin reveals the historical basis of this thought and describes how impressions can change to accomplish particular goals. Winters addresses everyday communication in professional environments and workplaces concerning polarized topics, such as race or politics. Such everyday conversations are both inevitable and important influences in professional relationships. Warburton and Warburton dive into the role of nonverbal cues in influencing workplace relationships. Finally, Hynes describes the layered influence of culture in workplace relationships with managers and coworkers. According to Hynes, cultivating an understanding of culture allows us to confront difference productively.

Section 4 explores two additional fundamental factors that influence both communication and relationships: race and gender. I have elected to present these factors in a separate category for two reasons. First, both factors affect some more prominently than others. For example, impression management cuts across race and gender lines. Second, both race and gender shatter the preceding assumption. Both systemically influence communication and the ways in which people relate to one another. Each factor operates in both explicit and subtle ways that are often underemphasized. Both articles draw on the notion of power relations as structural forces that shape how race and gender operate. Allen's discussion of racial harassment centers on the role of communication as a conduit for power relations in pursuit of oppression and liberation. The time we spend in the workplace makes it a unique site for researchers to apply critical race theorization to unsettle dominant power relations. Joyce draws attention to the gendered experience women commonly face in the workplace and other professional environments. Discrimination and stereotypes represent prevalent forces of inequality. We can decry them as injustices, but they are real. Each of us must decide how to navigate these difficult waters in our own way. That path begins with a deep awareness of the problem.

Section 5 contains essential advice for living socially in business and professional environments, in recognition of the fact that at the same time we exist as employees in a workplace, we are also social beings. Outside of offices and meetings, we talk and interact with one another in social situations, such as hallways, cocktail parties, and meals. Fleming's contributions focus on such everyday communicative interactions in business and professional situations. "Eating, Drinking, and Walking Around" offers scenario-based discussions that provide additional context to the broad lessons described in sections 1–3. "What Is Small Talk For?" continues this discussion by delving into several aspects of everyday communication that serve to either divide or unite relationships. Medved spotlights the communicative elements associated with the struggle to maintain a work-life balance. Specifically, the author discusses the role of human resources managers in assisting employees in navigating the complicated conditions of living across the work-life divide.

Section 6 addresses the difficult topic of conflict, an inherent feature of all relationships. In the workplace, conflict often produces destructive relationships and undermines success. Wiedmer explores workplace bullying as a specific and prevalent form of conflict. As social disavowal of bullying becomes more prominent, researchers are beginning to uncover trends that undermine workplace relationships. Hynes describes five strategies for managing conflict. Porath, Foulk, and Erez contextualize negative forms of conflict as "incivility." The authors describe the often-unnoticed harm associated with everyday acts of incivility in the workplace and professional organizations, as well as several methods to address these concerns.

Section 7 follows with a discussion of leadership and communication in three areas. Straus offers a perspective on leadership that departs from traditional models, in which power and decision-making flow from the top down. Instead, Straus advocates a facilitative model of decision-making to foster a climate of collaboration. Booher continues the theme of facilitative leadership in the context of meetings to manage participation difficulties. Viator, Dalton and Harp conclude this section on leadership by exploring the role of mentoring. The authors provide useful assistance in understanding the roles, benefits, and challenges mentors face in creating a productive relationship.

Section 8 offers invaluable lessons for every student who will participate in a job interview. Students should understand that a job interview has two parts: while students will answer questions, someone composes those questions with agendas in mind. The more students understand what employers *really* want to know, the better they may answer the questions and stand out against their competitors. Davis and Herrera offer a glimpse into the responsibilities of the interviewer. Including this article may be particularly helpful for students preparing for interviews. Berk describes different types of questions and offers tips on how to give the *best* answers.

Utility for Students

Exploring business communication through relationship-based perspectives should appeal to students. In contrast to traditional business communication textbooks, the articles and essays here offer engaging perspectives that examine both principles and real-world applications. I hope students will appreciate the diverse professional backgrounds of the authors, including university deans, engineering professionals, human resources consultants, diversity administrators, and professors in business, communication studies, accounting, finance, and education, to name a few. The book begins with introductory material for the topic of business communication, following with sections that present a variety of perspectives on issues that can and will affect students in their professional lives.

Understanding that communication establishes the basis for relationships, students may take the lessons included here beyond the classroom. Having a broader base of knowledge in relational and interpersonal communication can benefit students in their daily lives. This book offers lessons that extend beyond the traditional business workplace. Other professional environments also require attention to nonverbal cues, gender, and impression management, to name a few of the relevant topics included. Such professional environments may include academic conferences, product pitches, civic engagement forums, and more.

Students are encouraged to define keywords and address discussion questions at the conclusion of each section. Many find it useful to identify these elements before reading the articles. This allows students to generate study sheets for future quizzes and examinations. Moreover, thinking about the discussion questions prior to reading often provokes a deeper understanding of the text.

Utility for Instructors

For instructors, this book might offer a refreshing take on business and professional communication. It departs from traditional textbooks in both form and content. As an anthology, it does not *seem* like a textbook. Students read from a diverse set of texts ripe for in-class discussion, reading quizzes, roleplaying, and other learning activities. Because no anthology can be comprehensive, instructors may prompt students to explore unique areas of interest not included in this text.

Instructors may capitalize on the flexible format to explore supplemental texts and videos. The initial three sections provide a strong foundation and justification for the class. Instructors may assign the remaining sections and individual readings in a nonsequential manner to accommodate and customize their teaching plans. Utilizing combinations of readings within and between sections adds depth and texture to instruction. Moreover, assignments and activities geared toward drawing connections throughout the various sections not only stimulate critical thinking but also inspire students to see applicability in their own lives. Keywords and discussion questions provide a basis for examination questions and in-class activities.

Primary readings from the first three sections, such as DuBrin's article on impression management, serve as platforms to explore intersections with each of the issues represented in other sections. For example, impression management bears particular importance for persons in leadership positions (section 7) and interviewing (section 8). In section 4, Allen and Joyce discuss gender and race discrimination in the workplace. Discussing the intersections between race and gender in the workplace can illuminate new perspectives to address the needs of all persons. Combining readings within sections can show commonalities among topics and foster new ways of understanding individual topics.

SECTION ONE

MAXIMIZING WORKPLACE RELATIONSHIPS THROUGH BETTER COMMUNICATION

Many students initially conceptualize "business communication" in terms of giving sales presentations, meetings, and preparing reports. These activities represent only a small part of business communication, which covers a wide range of activities, including web conferencing, emails, formal reports, small talk, contracts, meetings, sales presentations, and customer relations, just to name a few. Section 1 provides an overview of the text and business communication. In the first article, Snyder and Frank introduce readers to business communication and make primary connections to relationship-based communication. The authors draw attention to the everyday communicative interactions experienced in business and professional environments, which can serve as conduits for the building and maintenance of relationships. Hynes builds on this work by discussing the role of interpersonal communication in the workplace. Hynes analyzes how communicating factors like trust, empathy, job satisfaction, and culture influence how we relate to one another in business and professional environments.

Consider the following questions when reading this section:

1. Based on the various descriptions and definitions, how would *you* define *communication*? Can you justify this definition in contrast to the others?
2. Why do the authors describe communication as an ongoing process? What does it mean for communication to be "interdependent"?
3. Can you think of your own examples that might illustrate the ten secrets of business communication?

4. How do cultural differences and workplace relationships interact? How might these differences manifest themselves through day-to-day workplace interactions?
5. How would you describe "loyalty," "trust," "commitment," and "job satisfaction" in the context of coworkers or bosses?

Key Terms and Concepts

- Effective business communication
- Symbolic communication
- Interpersonal communication
- Communication competence
- New Golden Rule
- Empathy
- Employee engagement
- Trust
- Generational differences

Using the Secrets of Effective Business Communication

Jason L. Snyder and Lisa A.C. Frank

What separates the best communicators from the rest of us? This question was posed by Anne Grinols, a nationally recognized professor of business communication, at a discussion during the 2010 convention of the Association for Business Communication.[1] Those in attendance, including Jason, discussed what they'd observed and what they'd learned from research. As a result, Jason crafted a lecture that he calls the secrets of effective business communication. He's delivered the lecture for his students as well as during a number of invited presentations. In this chapter, we share with you the ten secrets and how they can be applied to your professional life.

Before diving into the secrets, however, we should tell you what we mean when we talk about effective business communication. Effective business communication must accomplish two goals: (1) Your audience must understand your message, and (2) your audience must respond the way you want them to respond. Both of these goals matter and they should be accomplished while fulfilling the ABCs of effective business communication: accuracy, brevity, and clarity (we address the ABCs later in the book). For instance, it's not enough for your employer to understand you when you ask for a raise and then not give it to you. In addition to meeting these two goals, effective business communicators practice the following ten secrets.

Secret 1: Communication = Relationships

We thought an equation might get your attention. One of the first secrets of effective business communicators is that they understand the principle that communication is about relationships. In order to help you arrive at that conclusion, we need to first discuss what we mean by communication. Although what we're about to discuss will sound like definitions, it's important to remember that there are no right or wrong definitions. One of Jason's professors used to say that some definitions are more useful than others. Definitions provide limits and frame our ways of thinking about a subject.

Many books begin their discussion of communication by providing readers with a picture of the basic process. In that process, person A sends a message to person B, who then responds in some way. Those models, which we discuss later in the book, are a great way to learn about how communication works and what kinds of barriers communicators confront. They help us think about the nuts and bolts of communication. For now, however, we want you to think beyond the communication model.

There are literally hundreds of definitions for communication. Rather than get into the weeds, we direct you to a few resources.[2,3] We point out, however, some important distinctions about how communication is defined.

The first distinction is between definitions that describe communication as purely symbolic and definitions that include spontaneous and pseudo-spontaneous signs. Symbolic communication is intentional and is usually associated with written and oral communication. The words and numbers we use are symbols that we put to intentional use. The e-mail that a financial planner sends to a client contains symbols and is intended to send a specific message. Communicators intentionally construct messages to be conveyed to their audiences. Definitions focused on symbolic interaction describe communication as discrete.[4]

Other definitions of communication move beyond symbolic interaction to include spontaneous and pseudo-spontaneous messages.[5] Spontaneous messages include emotional responses to stimuli, for example, the stunned look on a stockholder's face when he learns of a sudden and precipitous drop in stock price. Pseudo-spontaneous communication includes false and intentional representations of emotion. An employee is taking part in pseudo-spontaneous communication when the boss fires her but she doesn't show any visible emotional reaction. She is intentionally displaying (or not displaying) an emotional reaction to send a specific message. In this case, she's trying to send the message that she's unaffected.

We prefer the definitions that include symbolic, spontaneous, and pseudo-spontaneous messages. Symbolic communication is important, especially in the United States where business is conducted in a low-context culture that wants everything in writing. The symbolic message is really important. However, we believe that spontaneous and pseudo-spontaneous messages influence the nature of what is being communicated symbolically. For example, consider that employee we mentioned in the preceding text who has been fired. Does the nature of that message change if the person doing the firing has a giant grin on his face while delivering this sobering news? The spontaneous and pseudo-spontaneous messages matter. And they affect the nature of the relationship. Effective business communicators are aware of all three messages and how they impact their business relationships.

The other important distinction between communication definitions is whether communication is viewed as an event or a process. We follow the definition that communication is processual in nature.[6] Our messages don't take place in a vacuum. The last e-mail you sent at work or school was an event in a much larger process. You were responding to something.

Communication is patterned over space and time.[7] As an example, we all follow basic social scripts. We all say good morning to our coworkers and customers. The situation may vary (e.g., the words we use, the gestures we use), but the basic pattern stays the same. We were recently at a presentation where the speaker played a YouTube video of the many different versions of the song "Besame Mucho." The notes followed the same pattern between versions, but the arrangement changed. Similarly, communication follows patterns but can still be different from one situation to the next.

Thinking about communication as an ongoing process also acknowledges the role communication plays in building and maintaining healthy relationships. The process approach recognizes the interdependent nature of communication. This approach allows us to avoid dehumanizing our audiences, acknowledge the important role of relationships in our professional lives, and understand the interdependence and mutual influence that truly characterize our dealings with others.[8]

Imagine that you are trying to sell a product to your customer and that customer frowns, leans back in her chair, and crosses her arms. Do you think, "This is going great; I won't change a thing"? Probably not. You're more likely to think that things aren't going so well and it's time to change the pitch. But what if you've worked with this customer for years and happen to know that this customer is quiet, thoughtful, and rarely smiles? Your history with that person may, in fact, lead you to an entirely different interpretation of the communication episode.

Another common example is the business colleague who always tries to dominate discussion during meetings. Each time this person acts in a domineering way, you can either submit to that style or push back. Your choice will be affected by your past experiences in meetings and with this colleague. In turn, these factors and your choice to use a one up (push back) or one down (submit) tactic in response to domineering behavior will influence how your colleague responds. In both of these examples, the relationship has influenced the communication process and vice versa.

TRY THIS AT HOME

Another fun way to test the interdependent nature of communication is to take a friend to dinner. During the course of your conversation, hold a particular posture, such as elbows on table and fingers interlocked in front of your face. By the end of dinner, your friend will likely mimic that behavior.

So, communication is a process including symbolic, spontaneous, and pseudo-spontaneous messages in which the parties involved are interdependent and able to influence one another. What does that imply? Why does it matter?

The great communicators have come to understand that communication is really about the building and maintaining of relationships. In other words, communication is the sine qua non of relationships. Expressed another way, relationships do not exist without communication.

Edna Rogers put it best, "The concept of a relationship implies some form of interconnection between different sets of events, individuals, or entities; in essence it refers to an interconnectedness of differences."[9] Your reputation, your history with others, the things you have done in the past, and many other factors impact your relationships with others. Relationships exist only if we first communicate.

Think about your own industry. Do you think relationships are important? How do you build and maintain relationships that will help you succeed in your career? The first step is understanding that communication matters. You can't have relationships without communication, and the quality of your communication translates to the quality of your relationships. Vincent Finelli put it nicely, "Professional relationships are everything in a corporate environment. You need to be a hard worker, but most importantly you need to fit in with your colleagues."

So, it's important to understand that in a world where relationships matter, your communication skills will largely determine the quality of those relationships. We understand that you won't always have good news to share with those you encounter in your professional lives, and some people will test the limits of your grace and good nature. We are not suggesting that you have to be a 24-hour-a-day ray of sunshine, but that you need to be aware of how your communication behaviors affect your professional relationships. You can deliver bad news without being bad. The person you say no to today may be the person from whom you need help tomorrow.

Secret 2: People Are Busy

Effective business communicators understand that other people are busy, and it's important to respect others' time. We all are bombarded by messages and information that are demanding of our attention. E-mails, voice mails, phone calls, instant messages, reports, memos, meetings, and other communications beckon our attention. We simply can't keep up. As a result, we ignore some things and pay attention to others.

According to a recent study, new MBA hires send and receive approximately 200 e-mail messages each day.[10] A 2014 *Harvard Business Review* article stated the typical executive receives 30,000 e-mails per year.[11] The average worker in the United States spends 650 hours writing more than 41,000 words in e-mails each year.[12] In addition, the average worker attends 62 meetings per month.[13] A 2016 study of one large organization concluded that one weekly meeting of midlevel managers resulted in a $15 million per year cost to the organization.[14] And sometimes we check e-mail while attending meetings, which is also a waste of time because multitasking decreases our productivity.[15] So much of our work time is not seen as a resource, and much of it is wasted as a result. The authors of a recent article in the *Harvard Business Review* expressed the problem this way:

> Most companies have no clear understanding of how their leaders and employees are spending their collective time. Not surprisingly, that time is often squandered—on long e-mail chains, needless conference calls, and countless unproductive meetings.

This takes a heavy toll. Time devoted to internal meetings detracts from time spent with customers. Organizations become bloated, bureaucratic, and slow, and their financial performance suffers. Employees spend an ever-increasing number of hours away from their families and friends, with little to show for it.[16]

We recently interviewed Ms. Connie Myles who has 26 years of experience in finance and currently works as a Director of Financial Planning and Analysis for a major telecommunications firm. She told us that in her experience:

> Respecting people's time is a message that really resonates with me. I never take my cell phone into a meeting. Yet, in almost every meeting I attend, as I look around the room, there are many individuals skimming their emails during a colleague's presentation. It sends the message that their time is more important than that of the presenter.[17]

Every piece of communication impinges on our senses, like any other stimulus that impinges on our senses. If we tried to keep up with every piece of information communicated to us, we would go insane! To highlight this point, think about all of your senses. At any given moment, all of those senses are being impinged upon. Do you pay attention to every little stimulus? Of course not; your body would freak out.

For example, think about the socks on your feet. They impinge upon your senses every second of the day. Does that mean you are constantly and consciously aware of how they feel at all times? No. You do not pay attention to that information. It is usually unimportant and not salient. Except for right now. We bet you can feel those socks at this very moment. Our point is that just as your body can't consciously think about those socks all of the time, your mind can't process all of the information that is being communicated to you. As a result, we all use selective perception processes to help us pay attention to important information and filter out everything else.

Great business communicators know they have to make a choice to either (a) find a way to make messages stand out or (b) risk having communications ignored, like the socks of the communication world. Great communicators understand that people are busy, place a value on time, and find ways to respect time and get attention. Ms. Myles put it best when she told us:

> People with good communication skills will excel in comparison to those with poor communication skills. If one tends to fly below the radar, no matter how smart he may be, he will never be recognized for his efforts. One needs to be able to present their findings whether written or verbally. Great leaders are great communicators. They connect with their teams. They keep their teams engaged.[18]

Communicating concisely is important to respecting people's time. It's important to be clear and brief. Every word we use takes time. Every time we make an error in communication, we lose time in correcting that error and we waste our audience's time by creating confusion. Although there are a number of ways that we can respect others' time and get attention, we offer some advice you can follow in two areas: meetings and e-mails.

Effective meetings are all about the planning. We like to listen to the advice of efficiency and productivity guru Merlin Mann when it comes to meetings. From his speeches, we can take away a few simple lessons.[19]

- *Hold meetings only when necessary.* We shouldn't hold a meeting simply because our team traditionally meets on the first Wednesday of the month. Have a purpose.
- *Invite to meetings only those who need attend.* Again, we tend to invite people out of tradition. Think about the agenda and who *really* needs to be in attendance. Consider how you would respond to each person on the guest list if he or she asked, "Why should I be there?"
- *Let people know what they should do to be prepared for the meeting.*
- *Show up prepared.* Think about how annoying it is to sit in a meeting and wait while an unprepared colleague shuffles through notes or can't find information that would have been readily available with a little preparation.
- *Stay on task and stay on time.* If you schedule a meeting to conclude at 10 a.m., then finish at 10 a.m. Be thorough in how you plan out the time.

Beyond face-to-face communication, research and (too much) experience tells us that e-mail is the preferred channel of communication in the modern work environment. As noted already, this leads to abusive e-mail behavior. Here are some rules to improve your use of e-mail that respects others' time and gets your communications noticed.

- *Write short, actionable subject lines.* Consider using two words at the beginning of the subject line that tell the reader some action is required. For example, "Please Advise." Such subject lines let the reader know he or she must do something other than simply read the message. You know you delete e-mails without opening them. If you don't believe you have a reason to open an e-mail, you won't. It may be a dirty little communication secret, but there's no reason to pretend that other people won't delete your messages if they aren't compelled to read them.
- *Use the top-of-screen test.* Newspapers put their best headlines above the fold on the first page, because that gets people's attention. We should practice the same principle in our e-mails. Try to put your request and the most vital pieces of information at the top of your message, preferably in an area that covers less than half the computer—or mobile device—screen (see Figure 1.1.1). Due to common e-mail interfaces that default to providing e-mail content on only half the screen, readers often skim messages and move on without looking past that first half screen unless they feel compelled to do so. If you don't make your point in the first few lines, it will likely be overlooked.
- *Use bulleted and numbered lists.* Another way to make important pieces of information stand out in an e-mail is to offset it in a bulleted or numbered list. Use lists only for important pieces of information. Remember the following rule about lists: *If everything is important, then nothing is important.*
- *Pick unique times to send messages, when possible.* Think about a time when you might send the message and have it appear at the top of the receiver's inbox—like sending it at 8:30

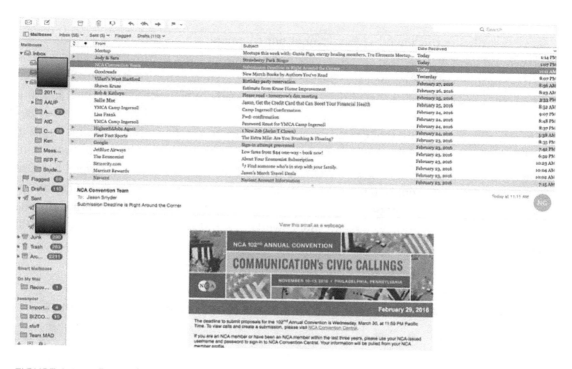

FIGURE 1.1.1   Busy Inbox Requiring You to Pass Top of Screen Test

a.m. if the person arrives at work at 9 a.m. A colleague of Jason's recently commented that he was surprised to see that Jason sends him e-mails at 4 a.m. Jason may not sleep much, but his colleague reads those messages.

- *Don't hide behind your e-mail.* Sometimes an e-mail simply isn't an effective means for communicating your message. Great communicators understand that point. Relationships often require you to get out from behind the monitor and interact with the people around you. Remember Secret #1? At times, e-mail can damage a professional relationship. E-mail is inappropriate when you need to consider others' feelings, when you are angry, or when you need to make sure you are understood.[20]

- *Avoid overusing "cc" and "bcc."* Just as with meetings, please send information only to people who need that information. Wasting others' time by copying them unnecessarily is a sin to the effective business communicator.

Secret 3: Each Communication Carries Two Messages

When we communicate with others, we are implicitly negotiating the nature of our relationship (Secret #1) with others. It's a truism of communication and completely unavoidable. In their famous (in communication nerd circles, anyway) 1967 book, Paul Watzlawick, Janet Beavin, and Don Jackson discussed five rules of communication that are always true (see Box 1). As you can see, we have already discussed Rules 4 and 5. In this section, we address Rules 1 and 2.

Let's first discuss this idea that "one cannot not communicate." Ignore the grammar in that sentence and focus on what that sentence means. Any behavior that can be perceived by someone else has the potential to communicate. Therefore, we can't avoid communicating with others when we find ourselves in the same social space. We are continually communicating information about ourselves, our reaction to others, our reaction to the situation, and our intentional messages.

For example, think about that coworker who walks past you in the hallway, puts his hands in his pockets, looks at the floor, and doesn't say a word. That person may be trying to avoid communicating with you, but that doesn't mean he hasn't communicated with you. In fact, because you perceived this behavior, you have drawn conclusions about what your coworker is "saying" to you. Depending on the context and your history with that coworker, you may draw any one of several different conclusions. Despite your coworker's efforts to avoid it, communication still occurred. So, why does this matter?

BOX 1 WATZLAWICK, BEAVIN, AND JACKSON'S (1967) COMMUNICATION RULES

1. One cannot not communicate.
2. Your communications carry both content and relational messages.
3. Verbal communication has punctuation similar to nonverbal communication.
4. You communicate verbally and nonverbally.
5. The nature of the relationship you have with others influences your communication behavior.

This rule matters because the message you received was probably not the message that was intended. In fact, the message you received was likely more than what your coworker intended. People assign meaning to stimuli. They use whatever information they have available to draw conclusions about you, the situation, the relationship, and the intentional message.[21] Great business communicators understand that they are always communicating. Everything we do that can be perceived by others sends all sorts of information that can be interpreted in many ways. It's important to understand that something as simple as how you dress communicates something about you. And that leads us to Rule #2—your communications carry both content and relational messages.

In business, we tend to believe that we make rational decisions and act rationally. We underestimate the importance of emotion. We focus on the written word. Our organizations comprise people who have emotions, and those emotions matter. The words we use make up the content message we send with every communication. However, every communication carries a relational message, a message about the nature of the relationship and the relative status of those involved. These relational messages matter as much as—and sometimes more than—the content messages. Great business communicators pay careful attention to both the words they use and the context in which they're used.

For example, a colleague who is a member of a financial advisory board for a small business attends board meetings on a regular basis at which dinner and beverages are usually served. Board advisors offer their expertise to the small business during the meeting, and this has historically been viewed as a benefit to the business. However, the most recent meeting was held earlier than usual and food was not served. Clearly there is a nonverbal message here, whether intentional or not, indicating that the business no longer values the expertise of the members enough to indulge them with dinner and drinks.

Secret 4: Nonverbal Communication Needs to Complement Verbal Communication

What we say and how we say it need to complement one another. Secret #4 is closely related to Secret #3. Effective business communicators understand that when verbal and nonverbal communication do not complement or reinforce one another, greater weight is usually given to the nonverbal communication. In other words, if you say during a conversation that you're passionate about your job, but you say it in a whisper while staring at your shoes, your verbal and nonverbal behavior are not saying the same thing. The person you're talking to will be more likely to believe the nonverbal message.

Effective business communicators understand this principle and pay attention to it for a handful of reasons. First, when what we say and how we say it don't align, our messages lose clarity and can create confusion. Second, when what we say and how we say it don't line up, we lose control over our communications. The audience draws its own, often inappropriate, conclusions about the intended message.

A vice president shared the following insights from his own experience.

> When a verbal/non-verbal communication is aligned (i.e., "You did a great job" accompanied by a smile), the verbal cue is dominant and supported by the nonverbal cue. However, it's been my experience that when verbal and nonverbal communication are misaligned, (i.e., "You did a great job" accompanied by rolling one's eyes), the nonverbal cue becomes dominant and the verbal cue is almost dismissive. Key to anyone's career is genuine verbal face-to-face communication that delivers both key facts/information and portrays sincerity to the message receiver. This is critical to building relationships, trust and loyalty among colleagues. Once such verbal based relationship is established, written and other forms of communication are more important and actionable to the message receiver.[22]

Those insights are accurate and supported by research. Research in deception detection tells us that when we believe a coworker is being dishonest, we pay closer attention to the coworker's nonverbal behaviors. As we learned from Secret #1, our interpretation is colored by our past experiences with the coworker (among other things). Although that seems reasonable, the research tells us that we pay attention to the wrong nonverbal behaviors.[23] As a result, we are not good at detecting lies.

To be fair, benign fabrications can be used to help others save face (e.g., when your supervisor asks if you like his tie). But, by and large, we want our nonverbal communication to complement or reinforce our verbal messages.

Secret 5: You Are Not Your Audience

Are you passionate about your career in finance? Do you love numbers? Too often, you may be alone. You should not assume that the things you care about are the things your audience cares about. Our audience members' perspective just doesn't line up with our own. Even when our audience members are similar to us, they don't always necessarily see issues and problems from the same perspective. To demonstrate this concept, try playing the following game.

TRY THIS AT HOME

Identify a common object, such as a pick-up truck. Ask a group of people to write down the first five things they think of when they think about pick-up trucks. Once they are done, compare lists. You're likely to see that no two lists are the same.

In finance, you talk about things like present values, future values, return on investment, and cash flows. These are fairly common concepts to you and when you talk with other finance professionals, they know what you're talking about. However, you will often have to share this "simple" information with people who do not have a background in finance. They do not share your perspective on these topics. Therefore, you will have to understand their perspective and talk about these matters from their perspective.

If you're going to be an effective communicator, you will have to learn the lesson that your perspective does not matter as much as your audience's perspective. Effective business communicators think from their audience's perspective and then write and speak about their own ideas from that perspective. What if you don't have a great deal of information about your audience? In that case, you have to approach the communication situation the way many great leaders do. A 2016 *Forbes* article argued that great leaders, such as Steve Jobs, communicate using the language of third graders. In other words, they simplify their language to the point that a third grader could comprehend most, if not all, of the content.[24]

One thing we know about all audiences is that they care about themselves more than anything else. When crafting messages, always try to answer the WIIFM question—What's In It For Me? Audiences will invariably, and often subconsciously, ask themselves the WIIFM question. So, always try to answer it.

Great business communicators understand that the more they know about their audience members' backgrounds, beliefs, and attitudes, the more successful they will be in engaging that audience. Learn to put your own perspective in the background and your audience's perspective in the foreground. Not only will it keep your audience engaged, it will also enhance their perception of your goodwill.

Secret 6: Communication Breakdown Does Not Exist

What does the bearded fellow in Figure 1.1.2 have in common with communication breakdown? Don't tell our kids, but neither really exists, and it would really upset them to know that communication breakdown isn't real. You probably hear the term communication breakdown all the time, but we implore you to purge it from your vocabulary. After all, as we learned earlier in this chapter, communication is a process. It's a made-up word with hundreds of definitions. It is not tangible.

FIGURE 1.1.2   A Child Posing with a Model of Communication Breakdown

It's our opinion that the phrase communication breakdown is commonly used to deflect blame when things go wrong. Even effective business communicators make mistakes. They encounter barriers to communication that they fail to overcome. It happens all the time. The major difference between effective business communicators and the rest of us is that they accept personal responsibility for their failures and learn from them. We advocate for an approach to communication that embraces accountability. Don't blame your failures on a thing that isn't tangible. Be accountable and learn from your errors.

Secret 7: Your Written Messages Are Permanent

As we mentioned earlier, we live in a low-context culture that places a great deal of weight on those things we write. In fact, e-mail has become one of the most preferred channels in the modern workplace because of corporate cultures that value the channel.[25] According to the Pew Internet & American Life Project, e-mail usage has become so commonplace that all four generations in the current workplace have reported usage rates of 90% or greater![26]

Effective business communicators know that the things we put into writing carry legal weight. And as important, the things you put in writing almost never go away entirely. So, you should get into the habit of approaching your written communications from the perspective of the effective business communicator. Treat your written communications as permanent and legally binding.

As of the writing of this book, the 2016 presidential primary season is underway. One problem for Democratic candidate Hillary Clinton is the fact that while acting as secretary of state, she allegedly sent official e-mails using an unsecure, private server and e-mail account. According to some accounts, a number of the e-mails she sent through that server contained national defense information. As a result, she is accused by her political opponents and some in the media of conducting government business via private e-mail and putting national security at risk.[27] Whether this issue goes away or leads to legal problems—as in the case of former CIA Director David Petraeus—remains to be seen. However, a more professional handling of her work communications would have helped her avoid these issues.

In another interesting example of this permanency secret, parents of children attending Brandywine Elementary School were outraged when a satirical form was inadvertently sent with an e-mail advertising events at the school. The bullying report form, titled *Hurt Feelings Report*, mocked children who are victims of bullying and offended many of the families who received the e-mail. Although the school apologized for the error, the e-mail and its ramifications are permanent. The things you put in writing simply don't go away.[28]

Secret 8: Credibility Fuels Communication

How people feel and think about you is largely determined by your credibility, a characteristic comprising trustworthiness and expertise.[29] Think of trustworthiness as the degree to which other people believe that you have their best interests in mind. Expertise has to do with the degree to which people believe you know what you're talking about. Studies show that business professionals with high credibility are better liked and are more persuasive.[30] If you were a financial services customer, wouldn't you rather take advice and purchase products from a professional who is knowledgeable and looks out for your best interest? Effective business communicators understand that credibility is one of the most important factors in shaping their reputations and that they are not naturally endowed with credibility.

Almost anyone in finance would rather do business with Warren Buffet than Tom Hayes. Tom Hayes is a former employee of UBS and Citigroup who is spending 14 years in jail for his role in conspiring to rig the London Interbank Borrowed Rate (LIBOR) interest rate, which is used globally to price financial products. That scandal cost banks billions of dollars to settle with regulators in the United States and Europe.[31] This scandal will cost far more in the long run and will very likely destroy the credibility and careers of some senior banking officials.

Former bank chairman Gianni Zonin is another example of this credibility secret. He was the head of an Italian bank that made it through the most recent recession. The bank was part of the local community. It provided sponsorship to local sports teams and paid for the construction of a theater. But the bank fell on hard times due to bad loans and questions about its business practices. While an investigation is ongoing as of the writing of this book, Mr. Zonin stepped down amid the allegations and his credibility has been destroyed. A recent Morningstar story reported that Mr. Zonin, once a local hero, has become a pariah:

Mr. Zonin, a 78-year-old wine producer, has gone from respected leader to pariah, banned from a half-dozen restaurants and heckled at his church, residents say. "If I see Mr. Zonin on the street, I take a side street," said Luigi Ugone, a bank shareholder who was recently part of a protest against the bank in the center of Vicenza. "I don't even want to see him."[32]

Credibility is what we in the social sciences call a perceiver construct. In other words, none of us actually has credibility, because it resides in the minds of our audience. We "have" credibility only to the extent that others see us that way. As you've probably heard before, credibility can take a lifetime to build and a minute to destroy. Effective business communicators shape others' perceptions of their credibility by keeping their promises, delivering results for their business partners, communicating in a way that respects others, finding common ground with others, and acting ethically.

Secret 9: Keep It Short

We discussed earlier in this chapter the need to put your audience first. You need to communicate from their perspective. That means you must understand that your audience rarely cares about the same things you do. Even if they care about the same things, they may not care as deeply as you. Keep your messages clear and short. We have never heard anyone say, "I wish that meeting took up more time." Keep it short.

Secret 10: You Are the Message

Just as important as what you say and how you say it is the fact that you are the one saying it. Effective communicators understand that how the world perceives them has a direct influence on how their behaviors are perceived.[33] In other words, you are the message.

One important takeaway from this secret is that you may not always be the best communicator of your own ideas. Sometimes if you want your idea to be approved or the customer to say yes, then you have to allow someone else to deliver the message. One of our authors—the bald one—holds an administrative position at his university. Faculty members have a natural and healthy skepticism for proposals made by administrators. So, sometimes our bald author will enlist the help of faculty members to make proposals on his behalf. He understands that his messages will be better received by faculty members if they are delivered by faculty members.

You may be familiar with the Volkswagen (VW) emissions scandal that broke in September 2015. A U.S. Environmental Protection Agency investigation concluded that VW installed "defeat devices" on diesel-engined cars. These defeat devices could tell when the cars' emissions were being tested and enhance the cars' performance so that carbon dioxide output would decrease during testing. The findings and eventual admission by VW has led to the recall of millions of vehicles and the company's first quarterly loss in 15 years.[34] A bigger long-term problem may be that VW cannot be taken at its word. Assurances from the company that it will work to fix the problem are being met with harsh skepticism.

> Rep. Jan Schakowsky, an Illinois Democrat, said that Volkswagen should buy back the diesel cars at the original purchase price. "If they want it, every VW clean diesel owner should be able to get their money back," she said. ... Schakowsky said assurances from the company that the cars will eventually be fixed, perhaps by the end of next year, are not enough. "Volkswagen's word isn't worth a dime," she said. "To find a company that deliberately cheated asking customers for patience, is not acceptable."[35]

Effective business communicators understand that they are their messages. Once your reputation has been tarnished, it is far more difficult to get others to "take your word." Your audience always considers the source.

Conclusion

In this chapter, we hope to have convinced you that following the lessons learned from these ten secrets of effective business communication—summarized in Table 1.1.1—will help to separate you from the crowd. Many of these lessons are common sense. Despite this fact, too many professionals fail to put the secrets into practice. Being an effective business communicator is

TABLE 1.1.1   Chapter 1 Takeaways

Secret	Easy application
Communication = relationships	Deliver bad news without being bad.
People are busy	Respect people's time.
Each communication carries two messages	Pay attention to context.
Nonverbal communication needs to complement verbal communication	Be authentic.
You are not your audience	Put your audience's wants and needs ahead of your own.
Communication breakdown does not exist	Take responsibility for your actions, and learn from your failures.
Your written messages are permanent	Think before you send.
Credibility fuels communication	Keep your promises, deliver results, respect others, find common ground, and act ethically.
Keep it short	Understand that your audience does not care about the same things as you.
You are the message	Act in a way consistent with how you want the world to see you.

hard work. Only those who are willing to put in the effort required to establish and maintain healthy relationships will realize the career-enhancing benefits of the ten secrets.

Notes

1   Grinols (2010).
2   Littlejohn and Foss (2011).
3   Buck and VanLear (2002).
4   Barnlund (1968).
5   Buck and VanLear (2002).
6   Berlo (1960).
7   Watt and VanLear (1996).
8   Rogers (1993).
9   Rogers (1993).
10 Middleton (2011).
11 Mankins, Brahm, and Caimi (2014).
12 Garber (2013).
13 *Effectivemeetings.com* (2013).
14 *Harvard Business Review* (2016).
15 Merrill (2012).
16 *Harvard Business Review* (2016).
17 C. Myles, personal communication, February 3, 2016.
18 Connie Myles (2016).
19 Mann (2006).
20 Warrell (2012).
21 Lindsay and Norman (1977).
22 Anonymous, personal communication, February 18, 2016.
23 Neiva and Hickson, III (2003).
24 Gallo (2016).
25 Snyder and Lee-Partridge (2013).
26 Purcell (2011).
27 McCarthy (2016).
28 Cline-Tomas and Chang (2016).
29 Hamilton and Hunter (1998).
30 Priester and Petty (2003).
31 Harrison (2015).
32 Sloat (2016).
33 Bolino, Varela, Bande, and Turnley (2006).
34 Hotten (2015).
35 Isidore (2015).

References

Barnlund, D. C. (1968). *Interpersonal communication: Survey and studies*. New York: Houghton Mifflin.

Berlo, D. (1960). *The process of communication: An introduction to theory and practice*. New York: Holt, Reinhart, and Winston.

Bolino, M. C., Varela, J. A., Bande, B., & Turnley, W. H. (2006). The impact of impression-management tactics on supervisor ratings of organizational citizenship behavior. *Journal of Organizational Behavior, 27*(3), 281–297. doi:10.1002/job.379

Buck, R., & VanLear, C. A. (2002). Verbal and nonverbal communication: Distinguishing symbolic, spontaneous, and pseudo-spontaneous nonverbal behavior. *Journal of Communication, 52*(3), 522–541. doi:10.1111/j.1460-2466.2002.tb02560.x

Cline-Thomas, A., & Chang, D. (2016, February 17). Elementary school accidentally sends "Hurt Feelings Report" to parents. *NBC Philadelphia*. Retrieved from http://www.nbcphiladelphia.com/news/local/Hurt-Feelings-Report-Lombardy-Elementary-School-Brandywine-School-District-Email-Delaware-369189861.html

Gallo, C. (2016, March 31). 40 years later, Steve Jobs' success secrets still apply to aspiring leaders. *Forbes*. Retrieved from http://www.forbes.com/sites/carminegallo/2016/03/31/40-years-later-steve-jobs-success-secrets-stillapply-to-aspiring-leaders/#3ab97e029b75

Garber, M. (2013, February 10). You probably write a novel's worth of e-mail every year. *The Atlantic*. Retrieved from http://www.theatlantic.com/technology/archive/2013/01/you-probably-write-a-novels-worth-of-emailevery-year/266942/

Grinols, A. (2010). *The last lecture: 7 values of effective communicators*. Presented at the 2010 Convention of the Association for Business Communication, Chicago, IL.

Hamilton, M. A., & Hunter, J. E. (1998). The effect of language intensity on receiver evaluations of message, source, and topic. In M. Allen, & R. W. Preiss (Eds.), *Persuasion: Advances through meta-analysis* (pp. 99–138). Cresskill, NJ: Hampton Press.

Harrison, V. (2015, August 3). Libor scandal trader Tom Hayes jailed for 14 years. *CNN Money*. Retrieved from http://money.cnn.com/2015/08/03/news/libor-scandal-tom-hayes-jail/

Hotten, R. (2015, December 10). Volkswagen: The scandal explained. *BBC News*. Retrieved from http://www.bbc.com/news/business-34324772

Isidore, C. (2015, December 10). VW chief: Scandal is "hard to believe." *CNN Money*. Retrieved from http://www.bbc.com/news/business-34324772

Lindsay, P., & Norman, D. A. (1977). *Human information processing: An introduction to psychology* (2nd ed.). New York: Academic Press.

Littlejohn, S. W., & Foss, K. A. (2011). *Theories of human communication* (10th ed.). Belmont, CA: Wadsworth.

Mankins, M. C., Brahm, C., & Caimi, G. (2014, May). Your scarcest resource. *Harvard Business Review*. Retrieved from https://hbr.org/2014/05/your-scarcest-resource

Mann, M. (2006, February 21). Running more productive meetings. *43 Folders*. Retrieved from http://www.43folders.com/2006/02/21/meetings

McCarthy, A. (2016, February 6). Hillary's e-mail recklessness compromised our national security. *National Review*. Retrieved from http://www.nationalreview.com/article/430879/ hillary-clinton-email-scandal-assume-intelligence-compromised?target=topic&tid=4571

Merrill, D. (2012, August 17). Why multitasking doesn't work. *Forbes*. Retrieved from http://www. forbes.com/sites/douglasmerrill/2012/08/17/why-multitasking-doesnt-work/

Middleton, D. (2011, March 3). Students struggle for words: Business schools put more emphasis on writing amid employer complaints. *Wall Street Journal Online*. Retrieved from http://online. wsj.com/article/SB10001424052748703409904576174651780110970.html

Neiva, E., & Hickson III, M. (2003). Deception and honesty in animal and human communication: A new look at communicative interaction. *Journal of Intercultural Research, 32*(1), 23–45.

Priester, J. R., & Petty, R. E. (2003). The influence of spokesperson trustworthiness on message elaboration, attitude strength, and advertising effectiveness. *Journal of Consumer Psychology, 13*(4), 408–421. doi: 10.1207/S15327663JCP1304_08

Purcell, K. (2011). Search and email still top the list of most popular online activities. *Pew Internet and American Life Project*. Retrieved from http://www.pewinternet.org/Reports/2011/Search-and-email/Report.aspx

Rogers, E. (1993). *A history of communication study: A biographical approach*. New York: Free Press.

Sloat, S. (2016, April 22). Volkswagen posts deep loss after taking $18.28 billion hit on emissions scandal. *Morningstar*. Retrieved from https://www.morningstar.com/news/dow-jones/ TDJNDN_201604227225/volkswagenposts-deep-loss-after-taking-1828-billion-hit-on-emissions-scandal.html

Snyder, J. L., & Lee-Partridge, J. (2011). Employee media choices when sharing knowledge in work teams: A test of the layered model. Manuscript published in the *Proceedings of the Association for Business Communication*. Available at: http://businesscommunication.org/conventions/ abc-convention-proceedings/2011-annual-convention-proceedings/

Warrell, M. (2012, August). Hiding behind email? Four times you should never use email. *Forbes*. Retrieved from http://www.forbes.com/sites/margiewarrell/2012/08/27/ do-you-hide-behind-email/

Watt, J. H., & VanLear, C. A. (1996). *Dynamic patterns in communication processes*. Thousand Oaks, CA: Sage.

Strategies for Strengthening Work Relationships

Geraldine Hynes

"Getting along" on the job means developing and maintaining strong work relationships. In the previous chapter, we saw that relationships are built on communication—if there is no communication, there is no relationship. Think of someone you see around your worksite from time to time but you haven't ever talked with. Do you have a relationship with that person? No. Now think of someone at work that you do engage with—a boss, a subordinate, or a peer. Do you have a relationship with that person? Yes, of course. Whether the relationship is negative or positive, whether you like or dislike that person, your relationship is the result of interpersonal communication.

These strategies for listening, checking understanding, and responding are invaluable communication competencies. As the Sequence for Success model (Figure 1.2.1) shows, interpersonal communication leads to interpersonal relationships.

Now that we have explored the connection between communication competence and interpersonal relationships, we are ready to move further along the Sequence for Success and explore the connection between interpersonal relationships and several other important elements—loyalty, commitment, job satisfaction, and trust. When those emotional conditions are present, people are more productive because they can work together more smoothly. In Part Three of this book we will describe how "getting along" leads to "getting it done."

The New Golden Rule

As a child, you probably were taught to "do unto others as you would have them do unto you." This maxim is based on the ethic of reciprocity, and its roots can be traced

FIGURE 1.2.1   Sequence for Success

back over 4,000 years. Variations of the Golden Rule are found in writings from ancient Egypt, Greece, China, and other cultures, as well as all major religions of the world.

In the workplace, it makes some sense to treat others as you would like to be treated. However, as a manager, you need to do better. When building relationships, try treating others as *they* want to be treated, not the way *you* want to be treated. Sharon Sloane, CEO of Will Interactive, a maker of training videos, calls this version of the Golden Rule the "Platinum Rule: Do unto others as they would have you do unto them."[1] She explains that this ethic recognizes that not everybody is motivated by the same thing that motivates you. In short, leaders should figure out what makes their people tick.

> **New Golden Rule:** Treat others as they want to be treated, not the way you want to be treated.

Managing by the new Golden Rule starts with using your communication competencies to learn about your people and what's going on with them, then building a relationship based on that knowledge. Briefly, the strategies that will help you understand people at work are:

1. Observe their verbal and nonverbal behavior
2. Ask questions to test the accuracy of your observations
3. Walk in their shoes to gain understanding and empathy

Ask yourself, "If I were this person, how would I feel? What would I say? How would I react?" Developing empathy is particularly important—and difficult—in a culturally diverse workplace. However, conflict management, decision making, problem solving, and other leadership activities are much easier and more effective when "dynamic connectedness" among workers is present.[2] No longer do people work alone; 100 percent of the Fortune 500 companies and 90 percent of all U.S. companies implement some form of group decision process. Teamwork demands strong interdependent relationships.

Empathy

Having close relationships with colleagues—even just one—makes a difference in personal and organizational growth. Bridges are built across cultural divides one person at a time. Researchers at the University of Chicago provide evidence for this claim. They studied hundreds of teenagers from cultures that are historically in conflict (Israelis and Palestinians, Catholics and Protestants in Northern Ireland, rural whites and urban blacks in the United States). For several years the Seeds for Peace program has brought teenagers together for a three-week summer camp in Maine, sleeping, eating, playing games, and participating in discussions. The University of Chicago researchers measured how the relationships that the students developed with each other changed their attitudes.

The results are striking. Regardless of their initial attitudes, the teens who formed just one close relationship with someone from the other group were the ones who developed the most positive attitudes toward the other group. The conclusion is that forming just one friendship was as good or better a predictor of future attitudes toward the conflicting group than the total number of friendships that a person formed.[3]

Creating opportunities for coworkers and subordinates to interact informally fosters empathy.

As a manager, you can foster the development of empathy among your subordinates by forming them into teams or workgroups and assigning them a project. The proximity and forced interaction will pave the way toward empathic relationships. That's because the group members will have to find common ground. Further, as the employees engage with each other, they will become more emotionally invested in the organization. Ultimately, the organization will become smarter and more effective because the work of the organization is done through person-to-person relationships.

These strategies apply to horizontal as well as vertical work relationships. Just as you can influence subordinates to develop empathy, there are ways to encourage empathy among your coworkers. For instance, you can gather everyone to celebrate an achievement, a holiday, or even a birthday. That will give everyone an opportunity to exchange perceptions and learn about each other in a low-stress environment. Informal, face-to-face interactions work best for developing empathy because both verbal and nonverbal cues are exchanged; the combination gives a more complete understanding of the information being shared.

"Lean" communication channels such as virtual meetings, text messages, and email exchanges are a poor substitute for face-to-face interactions. If your people are scattered in the field or telecommuting from remote locations, it's much more difficult for them to develop empathic relationships. Be creative and try to get everyone together from time to time. The benefits will be worth the cost.

Loyalty, Commitment, and Job Satisfaction

A study by the Great Place to Work Institute found that employees enjoy working where they "trust the people they work for, have pride in what they do, and enjoy the people they work with."[4] Open, two-way communication is a hallmark of such workplaces.

Employee loyalty and commitment to an organization increase when they "feel a strong emotional bond to their employer, recommending it to others and committing time and effort to help the organization succeed."[5] Committed employees have been linked to important organizational outcomes such as higher retention, fewer safety violations, reduced absenteeism, and perhaps most importantly, higher productivity.[6]

Supervisory communication has consistently been identified as a key factor in employee commitment. As discussed in Chapter 4, honest, frequent communication keeps workers informed about the organization's goals and how they can contribute to reaching the goals. One company I worked with found that the need for periodic employee meetings with the CEO became unnecessary when they built communication into the culture of their organization. As routine communication improved, attendance at the meetings with the CEO dwindled to nothing. "We already know what's going on" was the employees' explanation.

An additional benefit of consistent, honest, and frequent communication is that it makes workers feel appreciated and respected. When employees believe their supervisor supports them, they respond by becoming more committed and engaged in their job. Engaged employees have a strong, positive relationship with their supervisor. Putting it another way, employees don't quit their job; they quit their boss.

> **Employees don't quit their job; they quit their boss.**

Employee engagement has become a major theme in current management literature. In a recent Gallup poll, a startling 70 percent of American workers said they were not engaged with their jobs, or were actively disengaged. When asked why, the workers complained about the lack of opportunity for self-expression, personal growth, and meaningful work. Finding meaning is about being engaged. It's about feeling important, feeling recognized, and feeling informed.

Employee engagement levels are down all across the United States, but they appear to be particularly weak among Millennials. In a 2011 Harris Interactive report commissioned by the Career Advisory Board, "meaning" was the top career priority for those between the ages of 21 and 31. If you are from a previous generation, like me, you are more likely to value loyalty to the company above meaningful work. You may even be willing to admit that you've complained about younger employees' lack of commitment to their organization. But it's risky for managers to ignore such generational differences in priorities, whether real or imagined, because they may affect morale, retention, and even productivity.

The single best tool to enhance engagement is face-to-face, one-to-one communication between you and your subordinate. As a manager, you can increase your employees' level of engagement by making small but key changes in your daily workplace interactions. You can talk to your people more often than emailing them. You can notice their contributions more often than their mistakes. You can simply ask your employees whether they had a good day and what moments made it so.[7] Then listen. Try to adjust the work environment to make those moments happen more frequently.

To keep your workers from going elsewhere, find out why they are unhappy. To keep your workers happy, find out why they stay. Conducting an exit survey may reveal the working conditions—or people—that drove someone away, but it's too late at that point to impact the leaver's attitudes. Instead, conduct a retention survey among current employees. A retention survey can make people feel valued and will determine what the company can do to improve employee satisfaction, whether it's training, benefits, improved communication channels, or recognition programs. Sometimes you can even redesign the individual's job to make it more closely align with personal strengths and passions.

An engaged workforce is a happier workforce and a more productive workforce.

For maximum impact, responsibility for employee engagement should be corporate wide. Indeed, in the best companies, a culture of open communication begins with the CEO and other top executives, who know that employees must be engaged so they will contribute to the company's goals. Internal communication processes are in place in these companies to ensure that employees understand the company's mission and how they fit into it.

Companies with an open communication culture invest in a range of platforms to support employee dialogue and promote engagement. Meetings, web casts, executive presentations, newsletters, feedback mechanisms, forums, company blogs, and other interactive media are examples of formal internal channels designed to build engagement. As a vice president of an energy company said, "The more employees understand and feel like they're contributing or in line with the company strategy, the more productive they are and the higher the morale and [the] lower [the] turnover."[8]

Trust

Putting your employees first, helping them to feel engaged and committed, is a matter of trust above all else. Employees who are not engaged in what they do don't trust their supervisors or their companies. Today's employees are looking for a place where they can do their best work. They are looking for cultural fit and trusting relationships on the job.

Trusting Them

If you want your employees to trust you, then you must trust them. Remember Sharon Sloane, CEO of Will Interactive? Here's the extent to which she trusts her people:

> "We give what we call mission-type orders here. I will be very clear with what the goal is, what the objective is. Then I'm basically going to give you the latitude to do it. If you need my help or have a problem, come see me. Otherwise, I bless you."[9]

Trusting your employees means nurturing their independence, allowing workers freedom to express their opinions and follow preferred work styles without denying those of others. This willingness to let people approach the work their preferred way—so long as the goal is achieved—is particularly important if you have a culturally diverse workforce. Diverse environments call for a high tolerance for disagreement. Ask yourself, "Which is more important—that things get done my way, or that things get done?"

A healthy work climate is a trusting climate. Douglas McGregor, a famous expert in organizational communication, summarized the optimal characteristics of a work climate:

1. The atmosphere is informal, relaxed, and comfortable.
2. Everyone participates in discussion about the work at hand.
3. Everyone is committed to the task and the objective.
4. Everyone listens to each other. Every idea is given a fair hearing.
5. Disagreement is not suppressed. Rather than silencing dissent, the reasons are examined, and the group seeks rational solutions.
6. Important decisions are reached by consensus.
7. Criticism is frequent, frank, and relatively comfortable, but not personal.
8. People freely express their feelings.
9. The leader does not dominate.
10. The group monitors itself.[10]

Do these characteristics sound like the characteristics of your work group? If you are comfortable hearing differences expressed, if you trust people to find their own way to reach the performance goal, the result will be relational satisfaction, commitment to excellence, and organizational success.

Trusting You

Of course, if you want your employees to trust you, you need to be trustworthy, yourself. The following paragraphs present ways to develop trust. Briefly, trust is developed when:

1. Your words, nonverbals, and actions are consistent.
2. Your behaviors are predictable.
3. You explain what is going on and why (transparency).

Elements of trust:

- **Consistency**
- **Predictability**
- **Transparency**

Let's take a closer look at these factors. First, make your words, nonverbals, and actions consistent. As you read in Chapter 4, when what you say is inconsistent with how you look and sound, people believe how you look and sound. If you say, "These procedural changes are going to be an improvement," while looking glum, your people won't believe the changes will be beneficial, and they will resist adopting them.

Appropriate nonverbal behaviors for managers can be summarized as those demonstrating a confident manner. Confidence builds trust. Stand and sit straight, keep your head balanced on your neck, and be aware of eye contact patterns. Use a clear, pleasant but strong tone of voice and minimize disfluencies ("uh," "um," "you know," "like").

Appropriate verbal behaviors for managers who want to build trust include using inclusive words to indicate that both you and your listeners belong to a group. Words such as "we," "us," and "our" rather than "I" and "my" signal a social category that will increase loyalty and trust for members of the in-group. Another verbal tool is to disclose more frequently, sharing information as much and as often as you can. This will reduce uncertainty and increase trust, even if your people won't like what they hear. Telling people more about what's going on will also increase predictability. A third verbal tool is to use concrete language—facts and words with clear meanings—rather than abstract or vague terms. Speaking conceptually or with lofty, vague expressions causes doubt and distrust.

Trustworthy talk is:

- **Inclusive**
- **Frequent**
- **Complete**
- **Concrete**

Finally, trustworthy talk is honest. The 2012 Edelman Trust Barometer calls for companies to "practice radical transparency," which means telling employees the truth about what's going on.[11] If a company shares information, employees feel a sense of belonging and a part of a shared mission. This develops a bond of trust between employees and the company. Leaders who are transparent, who openly share truthful information with their people, retain credibility.

Cultural Differences and Work Relationships

So far, we have focused on ways to strengthen work relationships in a democratic, egalitarian culture. However, the contemporary work environment requires recognizing that there are significant differences in what people of other cultures think are appropriate supervisor–subordinate and peer relationships.

Cultures that value authoritarian leadership reward managers who are directive, prescriptive, and judgmental. The boss's word is not to be questioned. Subordinates are expected to be dependent and submissive, suppressing their opinions. An example of such a culture is Korea. In his best-selling book, *Outliers*, Malcolm Gladwell described Korean national airlines as once having the worst accident record of all. Careful investigation of the reasons for the alarming frequency of plane crashes revealed that the crashes were often due to pilot error. Apparently even when crew members perceived their captain making mistakes, they didn't try to correct the captain, because they believed it was not their place to question authority. Once training programs incorporated the notion that calling attention to potential errors was a crewmember's duty, the airline's record of accidents improved significantly.

In authoritarian cultures where leaders are expected to be dominant (and some U.S. companies are still like that), the strategies emphasized in this chapter will fail, and managers who apply them will be considered weak. For example, companies in Spain and Portugal are more likely to stress the importance of interpersonal communication and employee satisfaction than are companies in Germany and France.

Generational differences regarding the importance of solid workplace relationships have also been noted. While stereotyping is risky because it doesn't account for individual differences, there is ample evidence that many Boomers are loyal to their employers and exhibit long-term commitment, to the point of refusing to retire when eligible. Gen-Xers are known to be more individualistic, skeptical of authority, and think of themselves as free agents; they seek more work-life balance than their workaholic parents do. Millennials are reputed to feel special, entitled, and approval seeking; they are group-oriented and achievement-motivated, but they will leave employment if they feel unappreciated.[12]

To become a culturally sensitive manager, you need to assess your employees' personal achievement needs and relationship expectations and create a work environment that maximizes everyone's comfort level. Look for possible cultural, generational, even gender-based differences among your coworkers and subordinates that might influence the development of work relationships. If you're not sure about the implications of what you are observing, ask questions. The goal is to gain communication competence across contexts.

Summary

Getting along at work involves building and maintaining relationships. This chapter presents a range of communication strategies that will strengthen relationships among workers and between workers and their managers so they can "get along." First, the new Golden Rule is to treat others as they want to be treated. Foster dynamic connectedness by creating opportunities for formal and informal get-togethers so workers can form empathic relationships.

Loyalty, commitment, and job satisfaction will grow when employees feel engaged in meaningful work. Trust will develop when managers are consistent and predictable in their verbal and nonverbal behavior. Communication that is frequent, true, and comprehensive will also contribute to trustworthiness.

Managers should be sensitive to differing perceptions of the importance of work relationships and interpersonal communication among cultures, generations, and genders.

Notes

1   A. Bryant (2014, August 3). "See Yourself as Others See You: Interview with Sharon Sloane," *New York Times*, p. 2.

2   P.M. Sias, K.J. Krone, F.M. Jablin (2002). "An Ecological Systems Perspective on Workplace Relationships," in *Handbook of Interpersonal Communication*, 3rd ed., eds. M.L. Knapp, J.A. Daly (Thousand Oaks, CA: Sage Publications), pp. 615–42.

3   J. Schroeder, J.L. Risen (2014, July 28). "Befriending the Enemy: Outgroup Friendship Longitudinally Predicts Intergroup Attitudes in a Coexistence Program for Israelis and Palestinians," *Group Processes and Intergroup Relations Journal,* doi: 10.1177/1368430214542257.

4   A.B. Carroll (2006, July 29). "Trust Is the Key When Rating Great Workplaces," Retrieved from http://onlineathens.com/stories/073006/business_20060730047.shtml, p. 1.

5   B. Quirk (2008). *Making the Connections: Using Internal Communication to Turn Strategy Into Action* (Burlington, VT: Gower), p. 102.

6   J. Robison (2012, January 5). "Boosting Engagement at Stryker," *Gallup Management Journal,* Retrieved from http://gmj.gallup.com/content/150956/Boosting-Engagement-Stryker.aspx, p. 1.

7   A. Hurst (2014, April 20). "Being 'Good' Isn't the Only Way to Go," *Houston Chronicle,* p. B2.

8   K. Mishra, L. Boynton, A. Mishra (2014). "Driving Employee Engagement: the Expanded Role of Internal Communications," *International Journal of Business Communication* 51, no. 2, p. 191.

9   A. Bryant.

10 D. McGregor (1960). *The Human Side of Enterprise* (New York, NY: McGraw-Hill).

11 Edelman (2012). "Edelman Trust Barometer: Executive Summary," Retrieved from http://www.scribd.com/doc/79026497/2012-Edelman-Trust-Barometer-Executive-Summary

12 G. Hammill (2005). "Mixing and Managing Four Generations of Employees," *FDR Magazine Online*, Retrieved from http://www.fdu.edu/newspubs/magazine/05ws/generations.htm

SECTION TWO

WHAT EMPLOYERS WANT— THE "SOFT SKILLS"

Understanding the importance of interpersonal skills in the workplace broadly, readers will now explore differences in how students and potential employers perceive interpersonal communication competency. This bears direct importance for those about to graduate and enter (or re-enter) the workforce. Many employers refer to the so-called soft skills as among the most important skills in business. Beyond impressive degrees and letters of recommendation, employers increasingly desire new applicants possessing competency in relating to coworkers productively. Stewart, Wall, and Marciniec discuss the differences between "hard" and "soft" skills before diving into their study on the discrepancies between student and employer perspectives on interpersonal competency levels of graduates. Their work uncovers those skills most desired by employers and lacked by graduates, such as teamwork, relationship-building, and verbal communication. Jones, Baldi, Phillips, and Waikar continue the discussion with a different study to identify the particular skills for which employers are looking. They analyze perspectives from job recruiters, who consistently rank a range of soft skills as most desired. Together, these essays help establish the central rationale for this book. Both articles underscore the importance of mastering interpersonal communication skills for success in business and professional environments.

Consider the following questions when reading this section:

1. As an employer, what skills might you value most in potential employees?
2. How good are your interpersonal skills? What areas might you improve on?

3. How might signaling theory explain the differences in perception between college graduates and employers?
4. What soft skills might an employer in your field find most attractive?
5. What might we learn from understanding these differences in perception between college students and recruiters?
6. What are the implications for colleges and universities charged with educating students in business communication?

Key Terms and Concepts

- Soft skills
- Hard skills
- Signaling theory
- Competency
- Grade point average (GPA)
- Face-to-face communication
- Computer-mediated communication (CMC)
- Brick-and-mortar universities

Mixed Signals

Do College Graduates Have the Soft Skills That Employers Want?

Carol Stewart, Alison Wall, and Sheryl Marciniec

Introduction

Entering the job market as a new college graduate is a daunting yet exciting prospect. Fresh from the higher-education buffet of learning, college grads seek employment opportunities to capitalize upon their academic knowledge and inherent talents. Even those with lingering doubts as to their true professional calling tend to believe they "have what it takes" upon graduating to succeed in the global market. Employers have a different perspective: The majority of college graduates are confident in the level of their abilities, while in reality their skills fall short of employer expectations.

Recent studies reflect this dichotomy of evaluation. College graduates are highly confident of their abilities in both traditional "hard" and "soft" skill areas (Twenge, Campbell, & Gentile, 2012). Employers, on the other hand, are increasingly frustrated at what they see as a growing problem with graduates' soft skills, or rather, *lack* thereof (St. Louis Community College & Workforce Solutions Group, 2013). **Soft skills**—those non-technical competencies associated with one's personality, attitude, and ability to interact effectively with others (i.e., to be optimally employable)— are believed to be as valuable in the workplace as **hard skills**—technical, tangible, measurable competencies. Soft skills' interpersonal relations focus is especially important in our global marketplace (Nunn, 2013), where sensitivity to potential individual and/or collective diversity can tip the scale toward being hired or passed over. Despite college graduates' belief in the strength of their abilities, however, employers report a dearth of basic soft skills such as communication, critical thinking, and problem solving within this very group of potential job candidates (Hart Research Associates, 2015).

What accounts for this disconnect of perception, this "gap" between college graduate and employer perspectives? Acknowledging the gap leads to further reflection: Do college graduates understand the soft skills employers seek? What method or "yardstick" is used for self-evaluation of these competencies? Are colleges providing adequate opportunity to learn and develop soft skills? Do employers appropriately recruit for these desired skills? These questions, along with many others, can help clarify the origin of the perceived soft skills gap and how to address it.

To get to the root cause, we need to first determine what employers consider to be top soft skills. Research shows use of varied terminology, with most skills falling into broad categories of communication, interpersonal relationships, professionalism, teamwork, problem-solving/critical-thinking, ethical behavior, flexibility, leadership, and diversity awareness/sensitivity. These soft skills, and/or subsets of these skills, are deemed essential for professional success and so should appear alongside required hard skills, education, and other relevant candidate qualifications.

In this paper, we explore the soft skills considered most valuable in today's job market, as well as the level of preparedness in recent college graduates, from the perspective of both employer and college student.

Literature Review

As previously mentioned, soft skills are non-technical, applied skills that employees are expected to possess and are oftentimes difficult to measure. Soft skills such as communication, problem solving, and critical thinking are important skills to have in any industry but are especially important in a global environment. With advances in technology and the ever-changing scope of business competition, the need for soft skill sets has changed (Deepa & Seth, 2013). Employers are looking for people with a cross-cultural literacy with experience in areas such as global awareness, communication, economics and the knowledge of the cost of doing business globally (Gore, 2013).

Most soft skills cannot be learned in a classroom setting or by reading a textbook. People learn soft skills by doing them. Managers need to learn how to manage competencies and the most cost-effective way is through soft skills development training. This training would focus on building "essential skills and confidence in performance management, managing difficult conversations, effective team meetings, delegation and communication skills" (Jain & Anjuman, 2013, p. 35). The training should be focused on changing behaviors especially with managers who are newly hired or promoted. It should include activities that involve training of hands-on skills that are used with performance management and are evident. However, oftentimes this training is difficult to measure return on investment and is the first to be cut from the budget.

When faced with deciding between two candidates with similar backgrounds, hiring managers agree that the candidate with soft skills experience would have an edge over the other candidate with little to no soft skills competencies. From an employer perspective, soft skills competencies are necessary in order to remain competitive especially in a global world. Employers want

TABLE 2.1.1   Top 10 Soft Skills Employers Seek in College Graduates

Skill	Employer %	% Employers feel college grads well prepared	% College grads feel well prepared	% Students surveyed feel well prepared
Hart Research Associates:				
Verbal communication	85	28	62	72.4
Teamwork	83	37	64	83.6
Written communication	82	27	65	84.1
Ethical judgment/decision making	81	30	62	65.4
Critical/analytical thinking	81	26	66	86.9
Applying knowledge & skills to real world	80	23	59	—
Problem-solving	70	24	59	87.9
Locating, organizing, and evaluating info	68	29	64	—
Innovation/creativity	65	25	57	—
Staying current on changing technologies	60	37	46	—
NACE:				
Leadership	80.1			
Teamwork	78.9			
Written communication	70.2			
Problem-solving	70.2			
Verbal communication	68.9			
Work ethic	68.9			
Initiative	65.8			
Analytical/quantitative	62.7			
Flexibility/adaptability	60.9			
Technical	59.6			

Hart Research Associates. (2015, January). "Falling Short? College Learning and Career Success." National Association of Colleges and Employers (NACE). (2015, November). "Job Outlook 2016."

those employees who have soft skills that are easily transferable from the classroom to the work place (Deepa & Seth, 2013).

A review of the literature reveals strong communication ability, in both written and verbal form, to be a valued soft skill in new hires by employers (Hart Research Associates, 2015). In this day and age of technology and auto-correction tools, poor spelling and improper grammar are prevalent. Employers are looking for employees who master the English language well enough to maintain and nurture business relationships that focus on excellent communication skills. They do not want employees to ruin a business relationship simply because of poor communication skills (Deepa & Seth, 2013).

Accompanying communication skills as commonly desired attributes in job candidates are teamwork and critical/analytical thinking. In a survey conducted by the National Association of College and Educators (NACE), the top five soft skills employers *look for* on a candidate's resume are: Leadership (80.1%), teamwork (78.9%), written communication (70.2%), problem-solving (70.2%), and verbal communication (68.9%) (NACE, 2016, p. 31). Hart Research Associates found employers believe the following to be the top five most *important* skills when hiring college grads: Verbal communication (85%), teamwork (83%), written communication (82%), ethical judgment and decision making (81%), and critical/analytical thinking/reasoning (81%) (Hart Research Associates, 2015, p. 4). A similar survey conducted by the Society of Human Resources Management (SHRM) lists the top five applied skills employers believe college graduates *lack* as: Professionalism/work ethic (43%), relationship building/soft skills (29%), business acumen (28%), written communications (26%), and critical thinking/problem-solving (26%). Leadership came in at number six (18%), with teamwork/collaboration number eight (12%) (SHRM, 2015, p. 24) (Tables 2.1.1–2.1.3).

TABLE 2.1.2   Top 10 Soft Skills Employers Believe College Graduates Lack

Skill	% Employers
Professionalism/work ethic	43
Relationship building/soft skills	29
Business acumen	28
Written communications	26
Critical thinking/problem-solving	26
Leadership	18
Lifelong learning/self-direction	16
Teamwork/collaboration	12
Coaching skills	9
Flexibility/openness to new experience	9

Source: Society for Human Resource Management (SHRM). (2015). "The Hiring of 2015 College Graduates."

TABLE 2.1.3   Students Surveyed Top Soft Skills

Students soft skills survey—April 2016*

Communication (written, verbal, active listening)	*Teamwork*
Flexibility/openness	*Work ethic*
Ethical behavior	*Intellect/reasoning/problem-solving*
Interpersonal skills	Social/diversity awareness and sensitivity
Professionalism	Work experience

*Italics = Top soft skills in both SHRM–Students studies

Along with the acknowledgment among employers of these top soft skills' value is growing recognition of the dearth of these attributes among recent college graduates. The majority of employers find college graduates lacking and/or unprepared in the most desired skills (Tables 2.1.1 and 2.1.2). The majority of college students, however, feel *well* prepared for the working world in regard to top valued soft skills, including those involved in a recent survey at the four-year university selected.

Theory

There are multiple perspectives one could take to explain the gap between the levels of perceived soft skills graduating students possess. In this paper, we posit that based on signaling theory, students are adequately evaluating their level of soft skills, but are either failing to convey to employers that they possess the skills or the employers are failing to signal to the students that the skills are valued. Using signaling theory, the communication process is characterized by an informed party attempting to "signal" or convey that information to the other party in order to reduce uncertainty and improve the quality of the relationship, thereby increasing desired or favorable behaviors (Spence, 1973, 2002). Based upon the amount of information provided, the intent and quality of the relationship becomes clear as information asymmetry is reduced and the parties become aware of the characteristics, intents, and needs of the other party and are capable of engaging in appropriate responses (Stiglitz, 2002).

By obtaining a degree or other education, an applicant is attempting to signal their quality to employers and convey valued information regarding their skills and abilities (Connolly, Certo, Ireland, & Reutzel, 2011). If employers are not "signaling" to graduating applicants that certain skills are needed, then students may not realize they need to signal to the employers that they possess those skills as the relationship expectations are not clear. In this view, both students and employers function as informed parties with neither party accurately conveying the specific information needed to improve the relationship quality and reduce information asymmetry. Further, when a party is uninformed, they are likely to look to environmental or interactional cues to guide their behaviors or attitudes (Connolly et al., 2011). This is why feedback is an important part of signaling theory; it allows the uninformed party to signal that information received was appropriately interpreted and valuable. If the organization is not appropriately rewarding or clearly displaying that they value these skills or behaviors, by hiring applicants or promoting employees who do not possess or display them and/or failing to provide learning and developmental opportunities, then they may be unintentionally signaling that those skills are not valued, thereby discouraging others from displaying those skills.

Methodology

The objective of this study was to determine whether or not college students felt confident in their soft skills competencies. The survey was given to 214 college students in a four-year university in the northeast. Of those participating, 45.8% were graduating seniors, 52.8% were juniors and the remaining 0.9% being sophomores. The survey consisted of twenty questions, where the participants were asked to rank their soft skill level based upon a Likert scale where the number "1" represented those who strongly disagreed with the question up to the number "5," which represented those who strongly agreed with the question. The Likert scale is often used in surveys to determine varying degrees of opinions. The survey was given to students over a two-week period and the findings were analyzed.

Although the number of females (52%) exceeded the number of males (48%) participating in this study, gender had little to no impact on the survey results.

Findings of the Study

The study supported what employers had previously stated: The majority of college graduates are confident in their soft skills competencies. However, the soft skills in which college graduates feel competent are the same that employers feel the graduates fall short of possessing. Using the NACE, Hart Research Associates, and SHRM studies as a guide, students participating in a 2016 soft skills survey were asked to evaluate their soft skills using standard Likert Scale 1-5 ratings. Results show problem-solving to have the highest degree of confidence (87.9%), followed by written communication (84.1%), teamwork (83.6%), and verbal communication (72.4%).

Jean Twenge, a professor of psychology at San Diego University who has studied data on college students' confidence and self-perception versus reality (and compared the data from present day to prior generations), has stated, "It's not just confidence—it's overconfidence" (Irvine, 2011). Twenge points out that this level of self-confidence can lead to self-centeredness—even narcissism—that can eventually lead to problems in relationships and careers. She compared students' high level of self-confidence to "entitlement" in two ways: Students receiving good grades in school without earning them, and students being rewarded for activities regardless of performance level (Irvine, 2011).

Twenge's critics disagree. Jeffrey Arnett, a research professor of psychology at Clark University, argues against Twenge's broad statements of narcissism and classifies her comments as stereotyping all college students based solely upon their level of confidence. Arnett points out that other behavioral factors need to be taken into consideration, such as crime, substance abuse and sexual risk-taking, all of which have declined among college students in recent years. John Pryor, director of UCLA's Cooperative Institutional Research program, disagrees with Twenge's research findings as well. Pryor points out that confidence is only one trait students possess—there are other traits that impact their confidence. His research included students' participation in providing community service, which studies show has increased over the past decade (Irvine, 2011), a possible correlation with the increase in student self-confidence.

Limitations of the Study

While our study revealed the majority of college students are indeed confident in their level of soft skills, it did not explain how or what tool (criteria) students use to measure their competencies. For example, when asked to rate their written communication skills, do students equate getting an "A" in a college writing course as an indicator of their above-average communication competency? Or do they base their apparent self-satisfaction on something else entirely? Further research is needed to determine what criteria or tools are used for soft skill self-ratings.

Conclusion

The study found that the majority of college students rate highly their levels of soft skill competencies. Employers and college students both agree that soft skills are important to obtain jobs post-graduation. Employers hire college graduates expecting some level of expertise in applied soft skills, but then often complain the new hires lack these soft skills or have overstated their level of competency. More research is needed to determine the criteria students use to measure their abilities in order to offer a solution to close this "soft skills gap."

References

Chakraborty, M. (2009). Impact of soft skills in the professional domain. *The Icfai University Journal of Soft Skills,* 3(1), 25–27.

Connolly, B. L., Certo, S. T., Ireland, R. D., & Reutzel, C. R. (2011). Signaling theory: A review and assessment. *Journal of Management,* 37, 39–67.

Deepa, S., & Seth, M. (2013). Do soft skills matter? *The IUP Journal of Soft Skills,* 7(1), 7–20.

Gore, V. (2013). 21st century skills and prospective job challenges. *IUP Journal of Soft Skills,* 7(4), 7–14.

Hart Research Associates (2015). Falling short? College learning and career success [Electronic version]. Selected findings from online surveys of employers and college students conducted on behalf of the association of American colleges & universities. Retrieved from https://www.aacu.org/sites/default/files/files/LEAP/2015employerstudentsurvey.pdf

Irvine, M. (2011, June 16). New data on college students and overconfidence. *USA Today*. Retrieved from http://usatoday30.usatoday.com/yourlife/parenting-family/teen-ya/2011-06-16-college-freshmen-highly_n.htm

Jain, S., & Anjuman, A.S. (2013). Facilitating the acquisition of soft skills through training. *The IUP Journal of Soft Skills*, 7(2).

National Association of College and Educators. (2016). *Job outlook 2016*. Bethlehem, PA.

Nunn, R. (2013). More on the soft skill deficiencies of college graduates. Workforce Solutions Group; St. Louis Community College. Retrieved from http://workforcesolutions.stlcc.edu/2013/time-soft-skill-deficiencies-college-graduates/

Society of Human Resources Management. (2015). SHRM survey findings: The hiring of 2015 college graduates. Retrieved from https://www.shrm.org/hr-today/trends-and-forecasting/research-and-surveys/pages/shrm-hiring-college-graduates-2015.aspx

Spence, M. (1973). Job market signaling. *Quarterly Journal of Economics,* 87, 355–374.

Spence, M. (2002). Signaling in retrospect and the informational structure of markets. *American Economic Review,* 92,434–459.

Stiglitz, J. E. (2002). Information and the change in the paradigm in economics. *American Economic Review,* 92, 460–501.

St. Louis Community College & Workforce Solutions Group. (2013). State of St. Louis workforce 2013. Retrieved from http://www.stlcc.edu/Workforce-Solutions/St-Louis-Workforce/Reports/State-of-St-Louis-Workforce-Report-2013.pdf

Twenge, J. M., Campbell, W. K., & Gentile, B. (2012). Generational increases in agentic self-evaluations among American College Students, 1966-2009. *Self and Identity*, *11*(4), 409–427.

White, M. (2013). The real reason new college grads can't get hired. Retrieved from *Business.Time.com; http://business.time.com/2013/11/10/the-real-reason-new-college-grads-cant-get-hired/*

The Hard Truth about Soft Skills

What Recruiters Look for in Business Graduates

Michael Jones, Cindi Baldi, Carl Phillips, and Avinash Waikar

We have entered a new age—the age of communication. This is probably not new news but like every era, the change brought about oftentimes has unintended consequences. In this case, thinking through the unintended consequences of this communication revolution may mean reexamining the kind of characteristics organizations might be seeking in new hires, and thus mean changes in how business schools prepare students to obtain jobs. For example, a quirk of the communication revolution is that the proliferation of quick ways to communicate has potentially made us worse communicators. While we may have become experts at texting, our reliance on easy, lower-order communication may have eroded our higher-order communication skills, such as negotiation and conflict resolution—two skills necessary for successfully working well with others (Tumlin, 2013). As a result, we may be seeing the beginning of a paradigm shift, where in the past academic achievement was the key to landing a job (e.g., Werbel, Phillips and Carney, 1989), and now recruiters are becoming more concerned about hiring people who can communicate and work well with others (Alsop, 2006; Colvin, 2014; Taylor, K. A., 2003; Taylor, W. C., 2011; White, 2013).

Many new studies have come forth discounting the importance of grade point average and lifting the relevance of social skills in obtaining a job (Bryant, 2013; Nisen, 2015; Schramm, 2013). This study will contribute to this research in three ways. First, while many associations (e.g., Schramm, 2013), magazines (e.g., Adams, 2014) and companies (e.g., Bryant, 2013) have posted their recent research findings that companies are placing a high preference on candidates who can communicate and work well with others, it has not been entirely clear where academic success falls in their preferences. Many of these studies do not appear to include academic success in their lists of applicant qualities. Second, these previous studies have primarily focused on organizations (e.g., Google) that heavily recruit from Ivy League schools, where recruiters may be able to uniquely disregard academic success because entrance into these universities may be enough of an intellectual indicator. Potentially, this suggests that recruiters actively seeking job candidates from universities that serve a wider public might place more importance on academic success than recruiters focused on the Ivy Leagues. This study addresses this issue by surveying recruiters at a university career fair where student capabilities are far more diverse than those found in the Ivy Leagues. Third, many of these studies examine the recruitment needs of large, national organizations—those primarily found in the Fortune 500—that can overlook functional knowledge because they often offer extensive training of potential employees upon entry into the organization. As a consequence, the Fortune 500 recruiter's needs may place less importance on some characteristics that might be quite valuable to a non-Fortune 500 recruiter. This study mitigates this bias by surveying recruiters from a more diverse set of organizations, including those employers that are less likely to be able to offer this level of training to new recruits.

This article is structured in the following manner; first, the authors discuss the skills which were rated most and least important in this sample; then we make suggestions for business faculty regarding the training of these attributes and skills to students.

Method

Participants

Data was collected through personal interview (mall-intercept) of recruiters at a career fair at a regional state university of 15,000 students in a southeastern US state. Participants were 51 recruiters from 37 organizations. Examples of the types of industries represented include banking and financial services, the beverage industry, the insurance industry, the retail industry, distribution services, and computer and software services. Eleven of the companies are listed in the Fortune 500 for 2014. The university has an acceptance rate of 87% and caters to a wide range of students.

Materials

Participants were asked to rate on a scale of one to five (one being the least important and five very important) the importance of 21 job candidate characteristics (e.g., high grades, good communicator). The list was derived through interviews with 10 human resource professionals and their internal rating systems of candidates during interviews.

Results

We first examined the results across all types of recruiters. The results indicate that the following factors, in order of importance from highest to lowest, were the characteristics recruiters most valued in potential job candidates: positive attitude, respectful of others, trustworthy, takes

TABLE 2.2.1   Factors, Means, Standard Deviations

Factors	Mean	SD
1. Positive Attitude	4.83	0.48
2. Respectful of Others	4.8	0.49
3. Trustworthy, Honest and Ethical	4.76	0.69
4. Takes Initiative	4.72	0.61
5. Takes Responsibility	4.72	0.53
6. Cooperative/Team Player	4.61	0.64
7. Good Communicator/Interpersonal Skills	4.6	0.72
8. Ambitious	4.39	0.85
9. Self-Confident	4.36	0.73
10. Critical Thinker	4.27	0.81
11. Dress/Demeanor/Personal Appearance	4.2	0.77
12. Leadership Ability	4.19	0.89
13. Good Sense of Humor	4.02	0.99
14. Good Writing Skills	3.6	0.94
15. Knowledge of Major Field	3.5	1.11
16. Computer Software Skills	3.39	0.92
17. Work Experience	3.16	0.91
18. Quantitative/Statistical/Math Skills	3.1	1.3
19. High Grades	3.04	0.83
20. Active in Student Professional Organizations	2.78	1.2
21. Knowledge of Global or International Business	2.52	1.24

initiative, takes responsibility, team player, good communicator, ambitious, self-confident, critical thinker, appearance, leadership ability, good sense of humor, good writing skills, knowledge of major field, computer software skills, work experience, math skills, high grades, active in student professional organizations, and knowledge of global business. See Table 2.2.1 for a complete list of items with their means and standard deviations.

Most important factors

When examining the top four characteristics in the list, the top desired characteristics primarily come down to soft skills—will this candidate be someone others will want to work with and will this candidate be able to successfully work with others? Having a positive attitude was the most important factor to recruiters. Having a positive attitude may be important in terms of attracting help from others, coordinating work, working on teams, and having the mental resilience to overcome obstacles. Respectful and trustworthy, similarly, are beneficial for team environments, coordinating efforts, and building long-term work relationships (Erdem and Ozen, 2003; Jones and George, 1998; Pullon, 2008). The fourth factor was takes initiative. This indicates that employers want to hire students who are self-starters that can analyze situations, diagnose problems, and work toward solutions without a lot of reliance on others.

Least important factors

The least important factors in potential candidates were fairly surprising and are in order of least importance as follows; knowledge of global business, active in student professional organizations, high grades, math skills, and work experience. In particular, while the knowledge of global business and math skills might be more or less desirable depending on the type of job a candidate was applying for, the lack of value recruiters placed on participation in student professional organizations, grades and work experience seems to contradict conventional thinking and supports Google's position on the matter—grades are not a marker of future success in a job and experience oftentimes just creates bad habits (Nisen, 2015).

Comparison between Fortune 500 and non-Fortune 500 recruiters

To further investigate these findings, we wanted to see if perhaps Fortune 500 recruiters had different preferences from non-Fortune 500 recruiters. For example, Fortune 500 companies have the kinds of resources to customize training and shape employees in such a way that past experience and academic success might be less important to them than for recruiters from companies without these resources at their ready. To examine these differences, recruiters were divided into two groups (Fortune 500, non-Fortune 500). T-tests were then conducted using Welch's t-test in SPSS 23 to look for differences in preferences. Welch's t-test was used because the sample sizes in each group were substantially unbalanced (16 recruiters from 11 Fortune 500 companies versus 35 recruiters from 26 non-Fortune 500 companies). See Table 2.2.2 for a complete breakdown between recruiters representing Fortune 500 companies and recruiters representing non-Fortune 500 companies.

Remarkably, the results of the top and bottom four remain largely unchanged, even after the two groups are broken apart. Regardless of whether or not the recruiter was representing a Fortune 500 company or not, both types of recruiters most valued candidates with a positive attitude, respectful of others, and who take initiative. The only difference between groups is that Fortune 500 recruiters place a greater importance on self-confidence in their candidates than non-Fortune 500 recruiters. The difference in recruiter's preference for self-confidence in candidates between the groups was significant ($p = 0.01$). Fortune 500 recruiters have a stronger preference for candidates with self-confidence and self-confidence would be in their top four preferences. In contrast, non-Fortune 500 recruiters placed trustworthiness in the top four characteristics. While there was no significant difference between groups on how they rated trustworthiness ($p = 0.55$), the difference in the ranking between groups is due to the differing levels of importance each group places on self-confidence.

The least desirable characteristics, while the exact order fluctuates, remain the same across groups. Recruiters least value knowledge of global business, activity in student professional

TABLE 2.2.2   Mean Differences and T-Tests between Recruiter Groups

Factor	Fortune 500		Non-Fortune 500		p value
	Mean	Rank	Mean	Rank	
Positive Attitude	4.94	1	4.74	3	0.11
Respectful of Others	4.81	2	4.77	1	0.78
Trustworthy, Honest and Ethical	4.63	5	4.77	2	0.55
Takes Initiative	4.81	3	4.69	4	0.43
Takes Responsibility	4.56	7	4.11	10	0.03
Cooperative/Team Player	4.56	8	4.51	5	0.81
Good Communicator/Interpersonal Skills	4.63	6	4.43	6	0.37
Ambitious	4.06	12	4.34	7	0.4
Self-Confident	4.69	4	4.14	9	0.01
Critical Thinker	4.44	9	4.17	8	0.27
Dress/Demeanor/Personal Appearance	4.31	11	4.06	11	0.23
Leadership Ability	4.38	10	3.93	12	0.14
Good Sense of Humor	4.06	13	3.71	13	0.26
Good Writing Skills	3.56	14	3.49	14	0.78
Knowledge of Major Field	3.38	16	3.46	15	0.79
Computer Software Skills	3.38	17	3.31	16	0.85
Work Experience	3.41	15	3.06	17	0.16
Quantitative/Statistical/Math Skills	3.19	19	2.89	18	0.4
High Grades	3.19	20	2.89	19	1.76
Active in Student Professional Organizations	3.31	18	2.43	20	0.01
Knowledge of Global or International Business	2.63	21	2.43	21	0.61

organizations, high grades and math skills. Based on these results, recruiters from Fortune 500 companies do place a higher value (mean = 3.31) on activities in student professional organizations than non-Fortune 500 recruiters (mean = 2.43), but even with this difference, the characteristic is still in the bottom four least preferred characteristics in both groups.

Discussion and Suggestions

In summary, the findings in this study suggest that, more than grade point average, recruiters are seeking potential employees with soft skills, and that this trend is reflected in preferences of recruiters from both Fortune 500 and non-Fortune 500 companies, with only some minor fluctuations between the two groups. In addition, this study reflects the preferences of recruiters seeking applicants from a regional school that serves a broad student base rather than an Ivy League university where the students have previously been sorted based on academic ability by the university prior to admissions.

The implications of this study are not straightforward. For example, a surface analysis of these results might suggest that recruiters do not value college educations. However, these recruiters are still choosing to recruit on university campuses, which suggests that they perceive some benefit in doing so. One possibility is that, while a more straightforward indicator of academic success is intellectual capacity, pursuing a university degree may just as likely be an indicator of motivation, willingness to learn, and perseverance and that a university degree is a bar that separates those who are willing to voluntarily sacrifice to obtain a degree (and therefore indicate motivation, willingness to learn and perseverance) from those who are not. In this regard, the findings of this study need to be considered carefully because it would probably be a mistake to disregard the importance of academic rigor and excellence as these are what set the bar between the two groups.

Another important consideration is the impact of these results on brick and mortar universities and online education. There is external pressure on universities to compete and therefore match online institutions in their offerings. The results of this study would suggest a viable, valuable means by which brick and mortar universities can outshine their online competitors—an opportunity to develop students' soft/social skills. More so than any other age cohort, 18- to 29-year-olds have been harmed (in terms of developing social skills) by the proliferation of communication devices in ways that are just beginning to emerge (Turkle, 2011). For example, face-to-face communication teaches individuals how to respond in situations that are not fully under their control. In contrast, texting enables users to have full control over when and how they respond, as well as time to think over their response (Turkle, 2011). Yet, the work environment, at least currently, is still mainly a face-to-face, real-time venue that requires individuals to be able to handle the uncertainty of conversations, the lack of control, and to do so instantly. These are skills that are not being fully developed in a generation of people who have substantially substituted face-to-face communication with computer-mediated communication (Newport, 2014). While this shift in communication from real-time to controlled, delayed communication (computer-mediated communication) is happening across all age groups, a key distinction between young adults and older generations is the shift has occurred in young adults before they had a chance to fully develop their social skills. This suggests that having social skills today is actually a positive differentiator in the age group currently attending college.

This is an opportunity for brick and mortar universities that will be difficult for online universities to compete with because, at present, there does not appear to be a good way in which students can learn to physically interact with one another in real-time that online universities can duplicate. Many online programs try to overcome the sense of distance and disconnect an online education can create with video conferencing with students, but previous research has shown that a real sense of connection is best fostered when individuals are physically present with one another (Fredrickson, 2013). Physical proximity enables individuals to synchronize their biochemistry and behaviors, which is critical for connections between people to be made.

Video conferencing does not enable this synchronicity to occur because in a video conference each participant is looking at their own camera and not the individual on the other side of the conversation. In addition, for young adults who have grown up primarily relying upon computer-mediated communication, even when physically present with others, they may not have learned how to adapt and respond to these physical cues, but with training, they could develop these skills.

Brick and mortar universities, and even university hybrids (part physical–part online), can help students overcome this gap in their development by building into the curriculum opportunities to develop these skills. This is especially important in business schools. The essence of management requires the ability to build and maintain interpersonal relationships, yet most classrooms are still lecture-based and the primary communication assignments are public speaking, which is important but requires a different set of skills than interpersonal skills. Classes and seminars that are focused on developing interpersonal skills, such as negotiation, mediation, conflict management, and group brainstorming, where the class is designed to give students experiences in engaging in these activities (rather than merely learning the theory), coupled with opportunities to improve might be immensely helpful to students. Opportunities to practice these skills with individuals of different generations, who might be inherently better at these skills, might also be a type of learning experience that could better prepare students for building relationships in the workforce. For instance, competitions that incorporate current and past students to engage in exercises that develop interpersonal skills might be one way in which students can be developed. Lastly, colleges can institutionalize a code of conduct (e.g., no cell phones allowed to ring in class, no texting in class, tardiness not allowed, students must speak one at a time) that raises awareness of what it means to engage in professional behavior.

References

Adams, S. (2014). The 10 skills employers most want in 2015 graduates. Retrieved from http://www.forbes.com/sites/susanadams/2014/11/12/the-10-skills-employers-most-want-in-2015-graduates/

Alsop, R. (2006). M.B.A. survey: Something old, something new. Retrieved from http://www.wsj.com/articles/SB115860376846766495

Bryant, A. (2013). In head-hunting, big data may not be such a big deal. Retrieved from http://www.nytimes.com/2013/06/20/business/in-head-hunting-big-datamay-not-be-such-a-big-deal.html?_r=0

Colvin G. (2014). Employers are looking for new hires with something extra: Empathy. Retrieved from http://fortune.com/2014/09/04/employers-new-hires-empathy/

Erdem, F., and Ozen, J. (2003). Cognitive and affective dimensions of trust in developing team performance. *Team Performance Management: An International Journal, 9.5*(6), 131–135.

Fredrickson, B. L. (2013). *Love 2.0.* Hudson Street Press, New York.

Jones, G. R., and George, J. M. (1998). The experience and evolution of trust: Implications for cooperation and teamwork. *Academy of Management Review, 23*(3), 531–546.

Newport, F. (2014). The new era of communication among Americans. Retrieved from http://www.gallup.com/poll/179288/new-era-communication-americans.aspx

Nisen, M. (2015). Do grades matter? Depends if you're asking Google or Goldman Sachs. Retrieved from http://qz.com/382570/goldman-sachs-actually-google-gpas-arent-worthless/

Pullon, S. (2008). Competence, respect and trust: Key features of successful interprofessional nurse-doctor relationships. *Journal of Interprofessional Care, 22*(2), 133–147.

Schramm, J. (2013). Skills gap holds back some grads. *HR Magazine, 58*(8), 104.

Taylor, K. A., (2003). Marketing yourself in the competitive job market: An innovative course preparing undergraduates for marketing careers. *Journal of Marketing Education, 25*(2), 97–107.

Taylor, W. C. (2011). Hire for attitude, train for skill. Retrieved from https://hbr.org/2011/02/hire-for-attitude-train-for-sk

Tumlin, G. R. (2013). *Stop Talking, Start Communicating: Counterintuitive Secrets to Success in Business and in Life.* McGraw Hill, New York City.

Turkle, S. (2011). *Alone Together.* Basic Books, Philadelphia.

Werbel, J. D., Phillips, C. R., and Carney, F. (1989). Is Prescreening Biased? *Journal of Career Planning and Employment, 49*(2), 41–43.

White, M. (2013). The real reason some grads can't get hired. Retrieved from http://business.time.com/2013/11/10/the-real-reason-new-college-grads-cant-get-hired/

SECTION THREE

COMMUNICATION INFLUENCES THAT SHAPE RELATIONAL INTERACTIONS IN THE WORKPLACE

Several of the articles in this volume discuss the broad influences on interpersonal interactions in the workplace. The articles in this section represent a collection of unique influences, most of which deserve greater attention than a standard discussion would allot. Students should consider these topics influential variables as they read later articles. DuBrin explains the concept and importance of impression management. While students know that "impressions matter," DuBrin reveals the historical basis of this thought and describes how impressions can change to accomplish particular goals. Winters addresses the difficulty of everyday communication over polarizing topics to productively manage relationships. Warburton and Warburton offer a broad description of the role nonverbal cues play in communication. They divide their discussion into five broad areas: kinesics, proxemics, territoriality, chronemics, haptics. Finally, Hynes describes the role of culture in professional relationships and steps to maximize those relationships.

Consider the following questions when reading this section:

1. What are the key factors to consider in making a good first impression?
2. What steps can you take to improve your impressions in the workplace?
3. What topics do you find to be inappropriate or "out of bounds" in the workplace?

4. Which channel of nonverbal communication do you find to be most important in your current or probable future workplace?
5. In what ways do acts of incivility undermine productivity?
6. How might cultural considerations interact with impression management in business?

Key Terms and Concepts

- Impression management
- Impression motivation
- Impression construction
- Polarization
- Nonverbal communication
- Nonverbal channels
- Kinesics
- Proxemics
- Territoriality
- Chronemics
- Haptics
- Cultural competence
- High-context cultures
- Low-context cultures

The Meaning and Nature of Impression Management

Andrew J. DuBrin

Wanting to create a favorable impression on others is a basic part of human nature in both work and personal life. In meeting with the public, the chief executive officer (CEO) wants to convince others that he or she is wise, hardworking, and trustworthy. When exiting from the cockpit to greet the passengers, the commercial airline pilot wants to project the impression of self-confidence, being in control, and exercising good judgment. The customer service representative listening to the problem you are having with an electronic device wants to project the feeling that he or she is a friendly, competent person who will take care of your problem. And, of course, some scammers want to convey the false impression that they have your best interests in mind while really trying to steal from you.

In fitting with the theme of this book, an instructive definition of **impression management** is the process by which people control the impression others form of them.[1] *Control* in this sense refers to managing, shaping, or adjusting. For example, a certified financial planner wants to ensure that clients and potential clients perceive her to be a trustworthy and knowledgeable person. Toward this end she might engage in such activities as referring to the large portfolios she has managed, and the fact that she holds office in an association of certified professional planners.

People in the workplace are particularly eager to create a positive impression because they want to attain such outcomes as developing allies, getting a raise, getting promoted, receiving a bonus, making a sale, avoiding being placed on the downsizing list, and being hired in the first place. Impression management is such a natural part of organizational life that it is considered to be a major component of organizational politics.[2] Furthermore, Edward J. Hegarty wrote many years ago that impressing important people is the objective of all company politics.[3]

Impression management often connotes creating a false impression, or hiding deficiencies. In contrast, the thrust of this book will be to focus on research, theory, and practice about creating impressions that help a person emphasize legitimate positive qualities. Another misperception about impression management is that it is largely aimed at superficial aspects of a person's impression, such as wearing expensive clothing and accessories, having their teeth whitened, and facial wrinkles removed. A more rigorous study of impression management suggests that deeper aspects of behavior, including logical thinking and persuasive skills, are part of managing your impression.

We begin our study of impression management by describing the modern origins of its study, representative definitions, along with the motivation behind creating impressions and how they are constructed. We also describe some of the ethical considerations associated with impression management. As with other chapters in this book, we also devote a separate section to applying knowledge about impression management.

The Origins of the Modern Study of Impression Management

The idea of people using conscious or pre-conscious techniques to facilitate others thinking positively of them probably goes back thousands of years. (*Conscious* in this context refers to being fully aware of what you are doing. *Pre-conscious* refers to almost automatic behavior not requiring much thought, such as braking when you see a red light.) Survival in prehistoric times might have been partially dependent on other prehistoric people thinking kindly of you. Projecting too strong a negative image might have resulted in being stoned. In approximately 1600, impression management became better known with the famous statement of William Shakespeare, written in *As You Like It*: "All the world's a stage, and all the men and women are merely players. They have their exits and entrances, and one man in his time plays many parts." Shakespeare's famous words are still quoted frequently in books and articles about impression management.

The modern-day roots of the scientific study of impression management are frequently attributed to sociologist Erving Goffman, who framed impression management with his dramaturgical model of social interaction.[4] In overview, Goffman views people as "actors" engaging in "performances" in various "settings" before audiences. The key task of actors or performers is to construct an identity. The impression a person creates is a major part of his or her identity.

The actors and the audiences interact to develop a definition of the situation which guides their behavior. Although not mentioned specifically by Goffman, much of this behavior takes place without much conscious awareness by participants. Imagine a CEO holding a town-hall meeting with hundreds of employees. The CEO appears somber and dignified because he has to announce further cost reductions, including worker layoffs, eliminating jobs, and closing several offices and plants. The image the CEO projects helps define the situation as quite serious. As a result, the usual joking and kidding that might occur at a town-hall meeting do not appear.

Goffman reasoned that the performance of people functioning as actors depends upon the characteristics of both the situations and the audiences present. Performing as actors on the stage of life, people attempt to control the images or identities they portray to relevant people in their environment. The end-states the actors hope to attain could be social, psychological, or material. Being perceived in a particular way could therefore lead to better interpersonal relationships, feeling better about yourself, or receiving higher compensation on the job.

Goffman, as well as other researchers, believed that controlling one's identity as it is portrayed to others can influence how situations are defined, and thereby establish expected norms, roles, and behaviors. (Goffman evidently credits most people with a high degree of insight into human behavior and political skill.) By interacting with and influencing situations and audiences (or the environment) actors can better position themselves to achieve their desired ends. Impression management is therefore goal-directed behavior.

Goffman also described the importance of self-presentation for defining the individual's place in the social environment, for establishing the tone and direction of an interaction, and for defining how roles influence performance. According to Goffman, self-presentation is influential in the construction of social reality. For example, if a person projects himself or herself as being intelligent and well informed during a meeting, a social reality of being given a key follow-up assignment to the meeting might be forthcoming.

Perhaps the most useful point of Goffman's complex analysis is that even seemingly innocuous actions might be aimed at showing a person in a favorable light. For example, an electronics repair technician might scratch the back of his head during a discussion of a customer problem. The head scratching is aimed at creating the impression that the technician is thinking deeply about the customer's problem.

In practice, Goffman's analysis would include a mutual funds sales representative dressing elegantly, and making reference to her MBA from an elite school during an investment seminar. Many members of the audience might be persuaded to believe that a credible mutual funds sales representative is therefore a wealthy and well-educated person, prompting them to invest in the funds she represents.

A Variety of Definitions of Impression Management

As mentioned above, impression management refers generally to the process by which individuals attempt to control the impressions others form of them. The object of an individual engaging in impression management is generally to have others form a positive impression of him or her. Yet some people are looking to form a negative impression. A soldier attempting to avoid combat duty, or who is seeking a medical discharge, might want to project the image of an emotionally unstable person, and therefore not suited for combat. A prison inmate might have been incarcerated for so long that when the time comes for parole or release he fears competing in the outside world. With the prospects of no employment, no housing, and no food, he decides to form the impression that he will return quickly to crime if released. So he makes statements to the prison officials and parole board about his likelihood of returning to crime.

Creating a negative impression can also take place within a work organization, in the form of *strategic incompetence*. The actor projects the impression of being incompetent with respect to a task in order to avoid being assigned the task. A person asked to take notes at a meeting might declare, "I am terrible at note taking," in order to avoid the responsibility.

Steven Crawley, a human resources executive, says the inability to perform certain tasks can be very helpful in avoiding the tasks a person does not want to perform. He claims that his proudest moment of strategic incompetence took place when the president of an automotive-parts manufacturer asked Crawley to organize the company picnic. Not liking to do party planning, he responded to inquiries with comments such as "How do you do that?" The responsibility for the picnic was soon assigned to another worker.[5] The link to impression management is that Crawley created a negative impression about his competence by pretending not to understand the task. (You might not think highly of Crawley's ethics.)

As explained by Mark R. Leary and Robin M. Kowalski, most scholars in the field have used the terms *impression management* and *self-presentation* interchangeably, yet some have distinguished between the terms.[6] For example, Barry Schlenker defined impression management as the "attempt to control images that are projected in real or imagined social interactions." He reserved the term *self-presentation* for images that are "self-relevant."[7]

The distinction between impression management and self-presentation can be important. A person might enhance the image of another person, such as through flattery. The flattered person then develops a more positive impression of the flatterer. Another consideration is that images may be managed by methods other than self-presentation. A person intent on developing a good reputation might ask somebody else in his or her network to *good mouth* him or her.

In general, the term impression management is broader and more encompassing than self-presentation. Given that most research on the topic has dealt with how people control the impression others form of them, it is difficult to avoid using the terms interchangeably.[8] Chapter 6 in this book focuses on techniques of impression management designed to enhance the status or good feelings of others, thereby facilitating a positive impression of the enhancer.

Figure 3.1.1 presents ten representative definitions of impression management. Enough consistency among these definitions exists to make the formal study of impression management viable. At the same time, the term *impression management* conveys enough meaning to facilitate communication about the topic. The common meaning is that the person takes action so that the target person or persons perceive him or her positively. (The slight exceptions about creating a negative impression are mentioned above.)

Impression Motivation and Impression Construction

Impression management is sufficiently complex to be described and analyzed in a variety of ways. Here we examine a two-component model of impression management developed by Mark K. Leary and Robin M. Kowalski that offers two major advantages.[9] The model provides a solid base for understanding other frameworks for impression management. The same model

1. The attempt to control the image that others form about an individual.[10]
2. *Impression management* (also called *self-presentation*) refers to the process by which individuals attempt to control the impressions others form of them.[11]
3. Impression management involves what we do to create and maintain the desired impression in others about ourselves.[12]
4. A person's systematic attempt to behave in ways that will create and maintain desired impressions in the eyes of others.[13]
5. Behaviors designed to influence the way in which a person is perceived by others.[14]
6. Impression management in organizations consists of strategic communications designed to establish, maintain, or protect desired identities.[15]
7. The activity of controlling information in order to steer others' opinions in the service of personal or social goals.[16]
8. A new form of social competence in organizations, which individuals employ to master organizational politics, facilitate better work relationships, increase group cohesiveness, avoid offending coworkers, and create a more pleasant organizational climate.[17]
9. Impression management is concerned with the behaviors people direct toward others to create and maintain desired perceptions of themselves.[18]
10. *Image management* is a leader's ability to project an image that is consistent with observers' expectations.[19]

FIGURE 3.1.1   Ten of Definitions of Impression Management

offers insights into what makes for successful management of the image a person projects. The model is based on a synthesis of dozens of research studies as well as theorizing about impression management.

The general point of the model under consideration is that impression management involves two discrete processes: impression motivation and impression construction. Under certain circumstances, people become motivated to control how others see them. At a business networking gathering, for example, many people are motivated to project the image of a successful person whom other people would consider to be a valuable network member. Upon being motivated to create certain impressions, people may alter their behaviors to affect others' impressions of them. Altering behavior includes choosing the type of impression to create, and also deciding whether to create the desired impression through such means as self-description, nonverbal behavior, or props.

The person engaged in networking who is motivated to create a successful impression might then rehearse certain scenarios about how well connected he or she is to venture capitalists.

As outlined in Figure 3.1.2, the process of impression motivation is influenced by three primary factors: the goal relevance of the impression, the value of the desired goals, and the discrepancy between the desired and the current image. The process of impression construction is influenced by five factors: the person's self-concept, his or her desired and undesired identity images, role

Impression Motivation	Impression Construction
• Goal relevance of impressions • Value of desired goals • Discrepancy between desired and current image	• Self-concept • Desired and undesired identity images • Role constraints • Target values • Current or potential social image

Source: Mark R. Leary and Robin M. Kowalski, "Impression Management: A Literature Review and Two-Component Model," *Psychological Bulletin*, No. 1, 1990, p. 36.

FIGURE 3.1.2   The Two Components of Impression Management

constraints in which the person is placed, the target's values, and the actor's perceptions of his or her current or potential social image.

Impression Motivation

People vary as to how much they are concerned about how others view them. Also, the same person does not always have the same level of concern about how he or she is viewed. A person waiting in line at a fast-food restaurant might be less concerned about the impression he or she creates than during an in-person tax audit or a job interview. Most of the time, people operate between these two extremes. According to Leary and Kowalski, people process others' reactions to them at a pre-attentive or non-conscious level. As a consequence, impression management for most people in most situations occurs automatically without much deliberate thought. Yet, as will be described throughout this book, there are many ways in which people deliberately go about managing their impressions to succeed in a given situation.

Motives for Impression Management and Self-Presentation

Before looking at the antecedents of impression motivation listed in Figure 3.1.2, it is helpful to examine several of the motives behind managing one's impression.

1. *Maximizing rewards and minimizing punishments.* A primary consideration is that people manage their impression for the same reason they engage in many other behaviors—to maximize expected rewards and minimize expected punishments. For example, during a meeting with potential investors the aspiring entrepreneur wants to make a positive self-presentation in order to attract investors. Not receiving funding would be a punishment because the entrepreneur's efforts at launching the new company could be blocked without funding.

2. *Gaining power over others.* Self-presentation is also based on the desire to gain power over others. By creating a positive impression, it is possible to control the actions of others toward you in a favorable direction. The supervisor who creates a favorable impression will have an easier time inducing subordinates to work extra hard than a supervisor who creates a negative impression.

3. *Creating a public self in accord with the ideal self.* A subtle reason for impression management is to create a public self that is consistent with the ideal self. Many people have ideal images that go beyond their typical behavior. The ideal image might include believing that one is trustworthy, moral, and highly intelligent. To make others believe that this ideal image is valid, the person constructs a public image that might include references to trustworthy activities such as being a treasurer for a church or an executor of an estate.

4. *Self-esteem maintenance.* Self-esteem maintenance can be a strong motive for positive self-presentation. Regulation of self-esteem through impression management works in two ways. First, the reaction of others to the individual may raise or deflate self-esteem. Self-esteem is elevated via compliments, praise, and other indicators of positive attitudes toward the person. As a result, many people attempt to create impressions that will bring about the types of positive feedback just mentioned. For example, an engineer having lunch with colleagues in the company cafeteria might casually mention that he just was granted a patent for a technology that supports a major company product. The positive feedback he receives will boost his self-esteem—at least temporarily.

   Second, self-esteem is affected by self-evaluation of performance and others' imagined reactions to the person. Even without explicit feedback from others, the person's subjective self-evaluation of performance can influence self-esteem. Assume that a marketing specialist makes a PowerPoint presentation about sales forecasts for her company's new noncarbonated beverage. Her evaluation is that the presentation was captivating, even if the people present offered no evaluation of her performance. Believing that she did a wonderful job, she gains in self-esteem. The reverse is also true—if the marketing specialist believes that her presentation was flawed, she might suffer a drop in self-esteem.

5. *Creating an identity.* Self-presentation is also a means of creating an identity. The person may engage in public behaviors that symbolize group membership. A person wanting to appear like a young business professional might walk through the office and streets occupied with a cell phone and personal digital assistant, and quite often carrying a bottle of water. The same person would most likely wear business attire typical of business professionals in his or her field. Although the stereotyped behaviors just mentioned are superficial, they contribute heavily to identity creation.

The different motives for engaging in impression management described above will sometimes be satisfied by the same behavior. For example, documenting one's job successes to other people might (1) enhance rewards, (2) gain power over others, (3) create a positive public self, (4) boost self-esteem, and (5) create an identity.

Antecedents of Impression Motivation
Three central factors that determine impression motivation are outlined in Figure 3.1.1 and described next: the goal relevance of the impressions, the value of the desired outcomes, and the discrepancy between the person's desired and current social image.

Goal Relevance of Impressions   The more the managed impression is perceived to be relevant to attaining a person's goals, the more strongly the person will be motivated to manage his or her impression. The goals in question relate to the motives described above, such as gaining power over others and boosting self-esteem. One factor determining whether a given impression management behavior is relevant is how public the behavior will be, including the probability that the behavior will be observed by others and the size of the audience. A worker seeking more self-esteem would be strongly motivated to impress others via a description of her work presented on a company blog because so many other employees would see the blog.

Another factor enhancing goal relevance is the extent of dependency on the target. When the person is dependent on others for valued outcomes, such as receiving a bonus, the impressions he or she creates are more important. The individual will therefore be more motivated to manage his or her impression. If a person's immediate manager has the authority to make bonus recommendations, he or she will be the recipient of considerable ingratiation.

The anticipated frequency of contact with the target will also help shape the relevance of impression management to attaining a goal. When people expect future interactions with another person, they are more likely to attempt to control how that person perceives them. A middle manager who anticipates periodic contact with the company CEO is likely to work hard at creating a good impression in his or her presence.

Personal characteristics can also influence how relevant impression management appears to be in attaining positive outcomes. A person with strong Machiavellian tendencies (a propensity to manipulate others) is likely to perceive creating the right impression as essential in attaining goals.

The characteristics of the target also influence how relevant impression management might be to attaining certain goals. In general, people are more motivated to manage their impressions for people who are powerful because the powerful person can help the actor attain an important goal, such as being promoted. A small-business owner would be more motivated to manage his impression for a loan officer in a bank than for a vendor, such as the manager of an employment agency for temporary workers. Correctly or incorrectly, the small-business owner reasons that the loan officer has a greater impact on the viability of his or her business. The goal in this situation is to raise enough capital to expand the business.

Value of Desired Goals   A principle of motivation is that the more value a person places on a goal, the stronger will be his or her effort to pursue that goal. Effort invested in impression management will therefore increase with the value of the goals the individual hopes to attain. If a person believes that becoming a corporate executive is an ideal career outcome, and also believes that appearing charismatic will facilitate attaining the goal of becoming an executive, he or she will work hard at appearing charismatic.

Leary and Kowalski note that because the value of outcomes increases as their availability decreases, the motivation to engage in impression management is stronger when the desired resources are scarce. A CEO position is a scarce resource (only one per company), which triggers a higher frequency of impression management to work toward becoming a CEO.

Discrepancy between Desired and Current Image   Impression management is also motivated by the person's real and ideal image, or the image that one would like to hold of oneself and the image one believes that others already hold. Most people have a range of images that they regard as acceptable to project. When the image falls outside that range, the person might be motivated to fine-tune the image. When the image falls within the range of acceptability, the person is less likely to be motivated to manage his or her impression.

People who believe they have failed in the eyes of others, as well as those who have been embarrassed, are more likely to want to change the image they project. A case in point was an executive who received feedback from the human resources director, as well as an office assistant, that he had developed a reputation for being too flirtatious toward young women employees. Two women had even complained that some of the executive's comments about their appearance constituted sexual harassment. The executive worked quickly to change the impression he created in respect to his interaction with women. His most effective tactic was to stop commenting on the appearance of women, except for the occasional comment, "You are dressed for success today." He would also make the same comment to men, when appropriate.

Impression Construction

The construction of an image is not simply based on making a handful of positive statements about yourself to others. Following the synthesis developed by Leary and Kowalski, we look at five determinants of impression content, or how images are constructed.

Self-Concept   Many impressions that people attempt to create of themselves are accurate impressions that fit their self-concept. Furthermore, the self-concept is the primary determinant of the impressions people attempt to project to others for several reasons. First, most people are proud of certain aspects of their self-concept and therefore eagerly display these aspects at appropriate times. Also, impression management may be used to ensure that people are perceived accurately, such as a software engineer wanting to emphasize to coworkers that she has good interpersonal skills, and is not exclusively a technical person.

Second, self-beliefs serve to limit self-presentations by providing information regarding the probability that they can project particular impressions. If the software engineer just mentioned perceives herself as having good interpersonal skills, she might attempt to project the image of a person who gets along well with people. (A caution is that irrational people may not be constrained by their self-concept because it might be distorted.) Most people are hesitant to attempt to project images that are inconsistent with their self-concept because of concern about being able to pull it off.

Third, people who are uncomfortable with lying are hesitant to make claims about themselves, or project images that are blatantly inconsistent with their self-concepts. The same people might be willing to stretch their self-concept a little before believing they are lying. Job applicants, for example, will often project an image of capabilities that are a little beyond their true expertise. Personal websites are one job-related domain related to work life where positively distorted self-presentations are likely to occur. Exaggerating one's accomplishments on these websites is almost expected.

Desired and Undesired Identity Images   Image construction is also based on how people would like to be and not be seen. People often convey impressions that are biased in the direction of their desired identities. A manager who wants to see himself as a good coach will frequently engage in behaviors that show an interest in helping others, such as asking subordinates questions about their progress, and making encouraging statements to them. People also manage their impressions to avoid fitting an *undesired* identity image—something a person does not want to be. The manager in question might avoid statements and behaviors that suggest he or she does not really care about the welfare of subordinates. For example, even when work pressures are high the manager would take the time to listen to subordinates.

Role Constraints   The roles we occupy are typically a powerful force in establishing limits to the impressions we create. In addition to specific prescriptions for behavior, most roles demand that the role occupants appear to be a particular kind of person or possess certain characteristics. To illustrate, a chief financial officer (CFO) is supposed to be a person of high integrity who manages money prudently. It would be inconsistent with the CFO's role to brag about junkets to gambling casinos or having lost thousands of dollars in a risky investment. Executives in general who publicly deviate too far from their role expectations are subject to dismissal. Several male executives have been asked to resign in recent years because they were known to have sent romantic e-mail messages to young women employees. Similarly, when a married executive conducts an affair with a company employee, he or she might be asked to resign.

On the positive side, role constraints can propel a person into engaging in positive aspects of impression management consistent with the role. Visualize a customer service representative in a department store. Part of her role is to be helpful so she projects the image of being friendly and concerned while dealing with customer problems.

Target Values   Substantial research indicates that people modify their public images to the perceived values and preferences of key people with whom they interact. In a company where top-level management demands heavy commitment to the job as well as a strong work orientation, many employees will project the image of total company involvement. Among their behaviors would be to brag about working at nights and on weekends, and not having taken allotted vacations. Conversely, when top-level executives favor work-life balance, employees are likely to talk about leisure activities and wonderful family vacations. The people who manage the impressions in question are not necessarily being deceptive. Instead, they are emphasizing different aspects of the self in order to match the target's values. For example, the person who brags about working nights and weekends might also have outside interests and take vacations yet does not brag about these activities in the presence of company executives.

At times people will present themselves in ways that are inconsistent with the target's values. They make these self-presentations for the purpose of irritating the target or displaying independence. By emphasizing an image the target disapproves of, the person achieves his or her goal of annoying the target. Assume that a financial executive believes that the company is spending too much money on frivolous new products that ultimately consume too many company resources, as well as losing money. In contrast, the head of research and development believes that the company must invest heavily in new products in the hopes that one or two will be major successes. To irritate and antagonize the financial executive, the head of research and development talks flamboyantly about new products in her meetings with the financial executive.

Current or Potential Social Image   A final aspect of how the content of images is determined to be discussed here is how people think they are currently regarded by others and how they think they will be perceived in the future. A primary consideration is that people are reluctant to present themselves in ways that conflict with the information others have about them. To do so might arouse suspicion, and trigger being perceived as unauthentic. The knowledge others have about a person therefore constrains the image projected. A businessperson who was fined for insider trading might be reluctant to attempt to create the impression of a holier-than-thou individual. Instead, he or she might engage in impression management tactics to repair the damage, such as emphasizing that he or she has learned from the mistake in action and judgment.

Another twist on the impact of the current image on a person's style of impression management can occur when his or her accomplishments are well known. The person might feel compelled to modestly downplay the accomplishments in a show of modesty. A manager well known for having turned around a failing division of the company will often deflect personal credit and talk about the wonderful performance of the team.

Being perceived in certain ways can also make the person feel entitled to claim certain images. A person who has conformed to group norms for a long time will accumulate *idiosyncrasy credits* that allow the person to deviate a little from the norm in the future. A staid information technology specialist known for her conscientiousness might therefore return from a vacation bragging about 24 consecutive hours spent at a casino.

At times the ingredients to impression management will be influenced by how people think they will be perceived in the future. The possibility that people will learn certain information about them in the future affects the content of the self-presentation. A sales consultant might anticipate losing a major account by the end of the year. He might take a pre-emptive approach by explaining to his boss how hard he has worked with the customer to help the company avoid bankruptcy, but his efforts might not be successful.

In review, the model of impression motivation and construction developed by Leary and Kowalski identifies three central factors that determine impression motivation and five central factors that determine the mode of impression construction, as outlined in Figure 3.1.2.

Ethical Considerations Associated with Impression Management

Impression management in the workplace, as with other forms of organizational politics, often has ethical implications. An extreme example of unethical impression management would be attempting to impress others by pretending that your social network includes world-famous industrialists, athletes, and politicians. An example of ethical impression management would be keeping informed of current events and staying abreast of developments in your field in order to impress others with your knowledge and dedication. Most forms of impression management would fall between these extremes. One example would be exaggerating a little about how interested you are in marketing strategy when speaking to a marketing executive.

When evaluating the ethics of a particular approach to impression management, it is helpful to use a standard ethical screen. A representative ethical screen is the one developed by the Center for Business Ethics at Bentley University, which asks six questions to evaluate the ethics of a specific decision:[20]

- *Is it right?* This question is based on the deontological theory of ethics that there are certainly universally accepted guiding principles of rightness and wrongness, such as "thou shall not steal."
- *Is it fair?* This question is based on the deontological theory of justice that certain actions are inherently just or unjust. For example, it is unjust to fire a high-performing employee just so you can impress top management that you are cutting costs as much as possible?
- *Who gets hurt?* This question is based on the utilitarian notion of attempting to do the greatest good for the greatest number of people. If your approach to impression management hurts nobody, it is ethical from the standpoint of this question.
- *Would you be comfortable if the details of your decision or actions were made public in the media or through e-mail?* This question is based on the universalist principle of disclosure. Would you be willing to let others know that you blamed your poor performance with a client on a migraine headache you developed from drinking a contaminated energy drink?
- *What would you tell your child, sibling, or young relative to do?* This question is based on the deontological principle of reversibility, which evaluates the ethics of a decision by reversing the decision maker.
- *How does it smell?* This question is based on a person's intuition and common sense. For example, looking good by stealing someone else's innovative suggestion would "smell" bad to a sensible person.

As implied above, ethical issues that require a run through the guide are usually subtle rather than blatant, a decision that falls into the gray zone. For example, if you were applying for a position at Calvin Klein, would you purposely purchase some Calvin Klein clothing to wear to the interview?

Guidelines for Application and Practice

1. Managing your impression well at both superficial and deeper levels is a major factor in attaining career and personal success. Studying the subject of impression management and selectively applying the concepts are therefore of substantial potential benefit to your career.

2. Whether or not you believe that impression management is important, others will often judge you on the basis of the impression you create. Projecting a favorable impression, whether spontaneously or through conscious effort, is therefore to your advantage.

3. Your self-presentation is influential in creating a social reality. How you are perceived by others helps create circumstances. An example would be creating a sterling impression on a higher-level executive during a meeting, and subsequently being nominated for a new, higher-level position.

4. Almost any behavior can contribute to or detract from the image you project. Impressions of an individual can be generated by everyday, seemingly innocuous acts such as smiling at others, being helpful, and listening to another person.

5. A practical viewpoint of impression management is that you take actions to be perceived positively by the target person or persons.

6. To manage your impression effectively, it is helpful to understand the motivation behind your attempts at impression management. Among your motives might be maximizing rewards and minimizing punishments, gaining power over others, creating a public self in accord with your ideal self, maintaining your self-esteem, and creating a personal identity. The same behavior on your part, such as being an articulate speaker, might satisfy more than one of these motives.

7. As you go about constructing an image, keep in mind several determinants that may guide you in developing your image. The image should ordinarily fit your self-concept. Your self-beliefs, such as your analysis of your strengths and weaknesses, will often guide you as to the type of image you can project well. What you are the most proud of in relation to yourself should be incorporated into your self-presentation, such as taking pride in your advanced information technology skills. It is natural to incorporate into the impression you create your desired identity, or the way you would like to be known. Think through the role you occupy when creating an image. Your image works most effectively when it is consistent with your role, such as an employee assistance counselor projecting warmth and caring.

   It is also helpful to project those aspects of your personality and talents that fit the key values and preferences of your audience. For example, when dealing with cost-conscious managers, emphasize some of your frugal work practices (if true). Should your accomplishments be well known, you will be perceived positively by many audience members when you do not incorporate bragging about these accomplishments in your image.

8. Before choosing a particular approach to impression management, reflect on its ethical merits. In this way, you are likely to engage in impression management that has enduring value.

Summary

Impression management refers to the process by which people control the impression others form of them. A positive impression often leads to important work-related outcomes such as getting a raise and being promoted. Impressions can be deep as well as superficial.

The modern-day roots of the scientific study of impression management are frequently attributed to Erving Goffman, who views people as "actors" engaging in "performances" in various settings before "audiences." The actors and the audiences interact to develop a definition of the situation which guides their behavior. The performance of people functioning as actors depends upon the characteristics of both the situations and the audiences present. Controlling one's identity as it is portrayed to others can influence how situations are defined, and thereby establish expected norms, roles, and behavior. Self-presentation also defines the individual's place in the social environment. Another declaration of Goffman is that even seemingly innocuous actions might be aimed at showing a person in a favorable light.

Impression management has been defined in a variety of ways, as presented in Figure 3.1.1. Impression management is usually for the purpose of creating a positive impression, yet some people go out of their way to look bad. The terms impression management and self-presentation are often used interchangeably, yet sometimes behaviors are directed at enhancing the impression another person creates in order to be liked. The common meaning of the definitions of impression management is that the person takes action so that the target person or persons perceive him or her positively.

The two-component model of impression management developed by Leary and Kowalski is summarized here. The model states that impression management involves two discrete processes: impression motivation and impression construction. The process of impression motivation is influenced by three primary factors: the goal relevance of the impression, the value of the desired goals, and the discrepancy between the desired and current image. The process of impression construction is influenced by five factors: the person's self-concept, his or her desired and undesired identity images, role constraints in which the person is placed, the target's values, and the actor's perceptions of his or her current or potential social image.

Among the motives for engaging in impression management are (1) maximizing rewards and minimizing punishments, (2) gaining power over others, (3) creating a public self in accord with the ideal self, (4) maintaining self-esteem, and (5) creating an identity. The different motives for engaging in impression management will sometimes be satisfied by the same behavior.

Managing your impression well at both superficial and deeper levels is a major factor in attaining career and personal success. Almost any behavior can contribute to or detract from the image you project. Impressions of an individual can be generated by everyday, seemingly innocuous acts such as smiling at others, being helpful, and listening to another person.

Before reaching a decision about using an approach to impression management that is not obviously ethical or blatantly unethical, seek answers to questions such as: Is it right? Is it fair? Who gets hurt? Would you tell your child, sibling, or young relative to do it?

Notes

1 Mark R. Leary and Robin M. Kowalski, "Impression Management: A Literature Review and Two-Component Model," *Psychological Bulletin*, No. 1, 1990, p. 34.

2 Constant D. Beugré and Patrick R. Liverpool, "Politics as Determinant of Fairness Perceptions in Organizations," in Eran Vigoda-Gadot and Amos Drory, *Handbook of Organizational Politics* (Northampton, MA: Edward Elgar, 2006), p. 124.

3 Edward J. Hegarty, *How to Succeed in Company Politics*, 2nd ed. (New York: McGraw-Hill, 1976), p. 228. The same explanation was presented in the first edition of *How to Succeed in Company Politics*, 1964.

4 Erving Goffman, *The Presentation of Self in Everyday Life* (Garden City, NY: Doubleday Anchor, 1959); Robert A. Giacalone and Paul Rosenfeld, "Impression Management in Organizations: An Overview," in Giacalone and Rosenfeld (Eds.), *Impression Management in the Organization* (Hillsdale, NJ: Lawrence Erlbaum Associates, 1989), p. 2; William L. Gardner and Mark J. Martinko, "Impression Management in Organizations," *Journal of* Management, No. 2, 1988, p. 322; Dennis P. Bozeman and K. Michele Kacmar, "A Cybernetic Model of Impression Management Processes in Organizations," *Organizational Behavior and Human Decision Processes*, March 1997, p. 9.

5 Cited in Jared Sandberg, "The Art of Showing Pure Incompetence at an Unwanted Task," *The Wall Street Journal*, April 17, 2007, B1.

6 Leary and Kowalski, "Impression Management," p. 34.

7 Barry R. Schlenker, *Impression Management: The Self-Concept, Social Identity, and Interpersonal Relations* (Monterey, CA: Brooks/Cole, 1980), p. 6.

8 Leary and Kowalski, "Impression Management," p. 34.

9 Leary and Kowalski, "Impression Management," pp. 34–47.

10 Stephen B. Knouse, book review in *Personnel Psychology* of Paul Rosenfeld, Robert A. Giacalone, and Catherine A. Riordan, *Impression Management in Organizations: Theory, Measurement, Practice* (London: Routledge, 1995).

11 Leary and Kowalski, "Impression Management," p. 34.

12 Bernard M. Bass, *Bass & Stogdill's Handbook of Leadership: Theory, Research, & Managerial Applications*, 3rd ed. (New York: The Free Press, 1990), p. 210. Derived from Barry R. Schlenker, *Impression Management: The Self-Concept, Social Identity, and Interpersonal Relations* (Monterey, CA: Brooks/Cole, 1980).

13 John R. Schermerhorn, Jr., James G. Hunt, and Richard N. Osburn, *Core Concepts of Organizational Behavior* (New York: Wiley, 2004), p. 79.

14 Mark C. Bolino and William H. Turnley, "More Than One Way to Make an Impression: Exploring Profiles of Impression Management," *Journal of Management*, No. 2, 2003, p. 141.

15 Bozeman and Kacmar, "A Cybernetic Model of Impression Management Processes in Organizations," p. 9.

16 Barry R. Schlenker and B. A. Pontari, "The Strategic Control of Information: Impression Management and Self-Presentation in Daily Life," in A. Tessler, R. Felson, and J. Suls (Eds.), *Perspectives on Self and Identity* (Washington, DC: American Psychological Association, 2000), p. 199.

17 Lauren Morgan Roberts, "Changing Faces: Professional Image Construction in Diverse Organizational Settings," *Academy of Management Review*, October 2005, p. 205.

18 18. D. J. Schneider, "Tactical Self-Presentations: Toward a Broader Conception," in J. T. Tedeschi (Ed.), *Impression Management Theory and Social Psychological Research* (New York: Academic Press, 1981), pp. 23–40.

19 Martin M. Chemers, *An Integrative Theory of Leadership* (Mahwah, NJ: Erlbaum, 1997), p. 27.

20 James L. Bowditch and Anthony F. Buono, *A Primer on Organizational Behavior*, 5th ed. (New York: Wiley 2001), p. 4; www.bentley.edu/cbe/, 2009.

Why Do We Have to Talk about **THAT** at Work?

Mary-Frances Winters

> High performing leaders are able to unite diverse team members by building common goals and even shared emotions by engaging in powerful and effective dialogue.
>
> —GEORGE KOHLRIESER,
> Clinical and Organizational Psychologist[1]

Why in the world would we want to encourage employees to talk about polarizing topics in the workplace? We come to work in order to make products and provide services for our customers, members, and/or clients—not to talk about social issues. Topics such as race, politics, and religion are inappropriate and should be discouraged.

Perhaps this is how you feel. For as long as I can remember, this has been the prevailing sentiment for many organizations and corporate environments. However, there are compelling reasons why a position of avoidance is no longer the best policy.

The most persuasive reason for building the skills necessary to talk about polarizing topics at work is that they are already being talked about or thought about, more than you may think. Social media is a huge factor in the increased visibility of and exposure to these issues. And even as these topics remain top of mind for most of us, in general, we lack the skills to have effective dialogue.

The goal of this book is to help you make the conversations that are already happening more productive, supportive, and inclusive, leaving people feeling whole and ultimately resulting in better teamwork, productivity, and engagement.

A Polarized Society Leads to a Polarized Workplace

When race enters our public conversations about these important national issues, the dialogue is too often dehumanizing and racially charged. Language matters, and we need more tools to move our race conversations forward in more accurate, fair, and productive ways.

—President Barack Obama[2]

As the workforce becomes more diverse, there are more people from different racial/ethnic groups, religious affiliations, political affiliations, sexual orientations, and **disability** statuses who may be facing very different realities than ever before. We are living in times of heightened social conflict around race, religion, and politics. The last few years have been filled with instances of police brutality, the shooting and killing of police officers, immigration debates, religious intolerance against Muslims and Jews, heightened awareness of transgender rights and its backlash, terrorism, and extreme political divisions, making it impossible for many *not* to bring strong emotions about these issues into the workplace.

Social scientists contend that the more we feel threatened, the greater our tendency to be "tribal" and polarized. Tribalism is part of human nature. We've found that many people feel that their way of life is being threatened by terrorism, demographic changes, and new technology. When people are fearful, the gut level response is to blame "the other tribe(s)" for their plight. With so many complex issues facing society today, there is more polarization than ever before. Consider these realities:

- In a 2016 survey that explored the state of race relations in the United States, only 44 percent of white people were very concerned about the killings of black people at the hands of police, compared to 77 percent of black responders. However, when asked about the killings of police officers in Dallas, over 75 percent of *both* black and white people were very concerned.[3]
- In a survey on race and workplace trauma conducted by The Winters Group, six in ten whites answered that they think their organization understands the unique experiences of blacks in the workplace. In direct contrast six in ten blacks answered that they did *not* think their organization understands their unique experiences.[4]
- The vote for Britain to exit the European Union has largely been attributed to class issues and xenophobia. A headline in the *Guardian* in June 2016 read, "BREXIT is the only way the working class can change anything."[5] The results of the election showed deep class divides. Many working-class Brits blame immigration for the loss in jobs. Between 1993 and 2014, the number of immigrants into the UK surged from 3.8 million to 8.3 million.[6]
- A recent poll showed that 56 percent of Americans feel that Muslim values are at odds with US values. However, 68 percent said that they had never or seldom talked to a Muslim.[7]

- In a Pew survey on gender equality, 56 percent of men said that obstacles inhibiting women's progress are largely gone. Only 34 percent of women shared that view.[8]
- According to a global study conducted by Unilever based on interviews with 9,000 men and women across eight global markets, stereotypes and inappropriate behavior targeting women in the workplace still prevail. Sixty-seven percent of women in the study reported that they feel pressured to "get over" inappropriate behavior, and 55 percent of men and 64 percent of women believe that men do not challenge each other when they witness such behavior.[9]
- Relative to political polarization in the United States, a Pew study showed that 93 percent of Republicans are more conservative than the median Democrat, while a nearly identical share of Democrats (94 percent) is more liberal than the median Republican. Twenty years ago, there was a much smaller divide, with 64 percent of Republicans to the right of the median Democrat, and 70 percent of Democrats to the left of the median Republican.[10]
- The inauguration of Donald Trump as the 45th president of the United States drew strong protests around the world. Globally, over three million people participated in the Women's March to protest the election of President Trump, who they feel does not represent the values espoused by the United States, especially those policies geared toward gender equality, health care for women, religious freedom, and **LGBTQ** rights. Protesters said that they joined the marches because of Trump's divisive campaign and his disparagement of women, minorities, and immigrants.[11]
- The North Carolina HB2 bill, known as the "bathroom bill," requires transgender people to use public bathrooms associated with their birth sex.[12] As a result, a number of organizations cancelled high-profile events in the state, resulting in millions of dollars of lost revenue.
- Environmental justice and racism, both highly political subjects, intersected in mid-2016 when the US Army Corps of Engineers authorized the Dakota Access Pipeline project (DAPL), which threatened the safety and sanctity of the Standing Rock Sioux tribe's water and sacred cultural sites. The project sparked national protests and a grassroots movement that sought to reaffirm the humanity of indigenous people and their land. The DAPL has sparked polarization among business, political, and Native American communities.[13]
- There has been ongoing dissention around the term "Redskin" and other mascots that denigrate Native American communities. As of 2010, over 115 professional organizations—representing civil rights advocates, educational institutions, athletes, and scientific experts—have published resolutions or policies that state that the use of Native American names and/or symbols by non-native sports teams is a harmful form of ethnic stereotyping that promotes misunderstanding and prejudice, which contributes to other problems faced by Native Americans.[14] However, as of the publication date of this book, the Washington, DC, football team has not changed its name.
- We see a great deal of polarization and discourse around immigration. A range of counter-measures have been put forth—from building a wall to the more liberal proposal of the Dream Act, a multi-phased process for undocumented residents to provide conditional

residency leading to permanent status. Due in part to political dissention, the bill never passed.[15]

- While conversations about disability and people with disabilities may not be deemed as polarizing, I have found that we shy away from the subject matter, even in discussions around diversity. Perhaps this is because we do not know how to effectively have these bold conversations. In 2014, the British charity Scope conducted a survey that found two-thirds of British people feel uncomfortable or awkward talking to somebody who is disabled.[16]

Kate Vernon, director of strategy programs at Community Business and author of extensive research on diversity and inclusion in Asia, makes this observation:

It can be difficult to have open and honest conversations about race in Asia. We often talk about **culture** and the impact of different cultural profiles on communication and working styles—but we rarely address the biases and prejudices that exist about or between different ethnic groups, or openly acknowledge the power and **privilege** that certain groups enjoy. But there is no doubt that racism does exist in Asia. Whether it be India or Hong Kong, Japan or Singapore, there is an unspoken, often complex racial hierarchy that many will recognize but be wary to articulate. If we are to promote a culture of true inclusion, we need to find a way to broach this sensitive topic. Yet the Asian preference for promoting harmony, saving face, and showing respect can make having such bold conversations doubly hard.[17]

These polarized views and often-avoided topics drive attitudes, perceptions, and behaviors. If I no longer believe there are barriers for women in the workplace, I would see no need for special programs designed to bolster women's chances for advancement. If I am not concerned about the shootings of unarmed black men, then I may not be empathetic to workers who are fearful and traumatized by such events.

Polarization Thwarts Inclusion; Inclusion Drives Engagement

Polarization thwarts attempts for inclusion. Polarization is the opposite of inclusion. Polarization fosters an "us-and-them" environment, whereas inclusion attempts to create a sense of belonging and unity. Most major organizations today have a goal to create an inclusive culture because they realize that inclusion drives engagement. As reported in a 2013 Gallup study, inclusion and engagement are highly correlated.[18] The results showed that the most engaged employees rated the company high on diversity and inclusion. The least engaged employees rated the company very low on the questions related to diversity and inclusion. The Winters Group conducted a survey with a large financial institution that showed similar results. Inclusion was the highest correlated factor to engagement.

When employees feel that they are psychologically safe, they are also more engaged and innovative. According to a study by Catalyst that surveyed Australian workers, employees who experience psychological safety feel that they can freely speak up about problems and tough issues.[19] One's perception of psychological safety is based on a belief about the organization's norms or culture. The same study identified four leadership characteristics that enable psychological safety across race, gender, and other demographic variables. They are accountability, courage, humility, and empowerment.

The Impact of Social Media on Polarization

Social media outlets are exacerbating the increase in polarization. Instantaneous access to breaking news and opinions via tools such as Twitter, Facebook, Snapchat, and others has magnified opportunities to engage in contentious conversation and debate. People routinely use their smart phones to record all sorts of events that go viral for the whole world to see and comment on.

Before social media, we weren't as likely to be constantly confronted with polarizing topics such as race, religion, and politics unless we were news junkies. In the workplace, it is easy, even if against company policy, to have ongoing access to social media on our smart devices. Therefore, many people are constantly debating and sharing their opinions and beliefs on social media; and to the extent that they are virtually connected to coworkers, they are having these conversations at work, or in a workplace context. Social media makes it very easy to know the beliefs and opinions of coworkers.

The more that an individual's personal beliefs are repeated (i.e., go viral), the more they become accepted as fact. By the same token, the more an individual's or a group's beliefs are challenged, the more they are believed by that group. When beliefs are challenged, the human tendency is to become more obstinate and determined to defend the opinion. In other words, we dig our heels in deeper, as the saying goes. Any attention to the belief or opinion, positive or negative, acts as fuel for the fire.

Let's take Facebook, for example. The personal nature of this form of electronic communication can keep our emotions in high gear. We tell our Facebook friends what we like and what we don't like. When we disagree with a friend on Facebook we continue to post more rationale for our own position, and they, in turn, post more for their position, increasing the polarization. In the extreme, when a friend posts something we don't like, we can "un-friend" them. In other words, we can stay firmly rooted in our own beliefs, totally rejecting another's viewpoint. We take an "I don't want to hear it" attitude and in some cases, an "I don't like you anymore." We are often unable to separate the person from their position.

Many people today are addicted to social media. Social and behavioral scientists are busy studying the psychological ramifications of this fairly new phenomenon. I have talked with many people who say they have disconnected from social media and now feel less stressed. Some, who have not done so, bring these intense emotions and associated anxiety with them to work. And they do not stop communicating on polarizing issues just because they are at work.

The Impact on Employees, in Their Own Words

The Winters Group has conducted a number of dialogue sessions for a variety of different clients over the past year, supporting them in effectively addressing the aftermath of recent traumatic events and the polarized views that seem to always be associated with them. My first request is "Describe how you are feeling in one word." The responses range from depressed, despondent, frustrated, angry, helpless, and hopeless to encouraged, energized, hopeful, and optimistic. However, a majority of the emotions are negative.

Psychologists believe that the recurrence of unfortunate events intensifies feelings of stress and trauma. The more we see images of police shootings, terrorist attacks, and other acts of violence, the more we are likely to experience effects likened to post traumatic stress syndrome. Individuals who are most impacted by these events—for instance, black men fearful that they will be wrongly targeted by police, Muslim women in hijabs afraid they will be subject to bullying or worse, transgendered employees afraid to use the bathroom that corresponds to their gender identities—are likely distracted at work. This impacts engagement and productivity.

The Winters Group has conducted several public, free virtual learning webinars to address some of these issues. One was called Race & Workplace Trauma during the Age of #BlackLivesMatter. More than 250 people were in attendance. Another, called Let the Healing Begin: Restoring Our Quest for Inclusion, was conducted immediately following the 2016 presidential election. Over 600 registered for this 90-minute session. We polled participants during both sessions to explore the extent to which these events impacted their productivity at work. More than 60 percent admitted that there was either a "great deal" or "somewhat" of an impact.

Here are some perspectives shared during these sessions:

> "I came to work the day after the Philando Castile killing and I said to my boss that I was pretty upset, and I got nothing, not even an acknowledgment. This really shook me up and now I don't know if I can really trust her."[20]
> —African American male at large consulting company
> (I heard similar sentiments from several others from different companies.)

> "I am Muslim, gay, and from the Middle East. That is three strikes against me. When I am waiting for the train at the metro station I don't stand near the edge because I am afraid someone might push me in. I bring that fear to work with me every day. It does impact my ability to concentrate and do my best work."
> —male employee at a not-for-profit research organization

> "I was at work and got a call from my child at school. He was terrified because the kids were telling him that he was going to be deported. I felt a need to leave and go and get him. My boss understood."
> —Latina employee at a large service organization

"Our company sent out a statement after the Pulse Night Club shooting[21] but said nothing about the killings of unarmed black men. Why does one group deserve acknowledgment and sympathy and our group [African Americans] does not?"
—*African American employee at a large consulting firm*
(I heard similar statements from African Americans at several different companies.)

"I have not been affected by these events at all. I could not have imagined the impact that it is having on you. It is shocking to me that you are fearful based on who you are."
—*white senior leader in a not-for-profit research organization*

"I work from home. I am isolated. I don't know what the sentiment is at the company really. I just know that my ability to stay focused on work has been impacted. I did look for a message from leadership. I think it would have helped."
—*African American woman at a large consulting firm*

"One of my coworkers was literally gloating after Donald Trump won the presidential election. I don't mind showing happiness that your candidate won, but the tone was like, 'See, now you people will have to know your place again.'"
—*African American woman at a government agency*

"As a Muslim doctor, I have patients who ask for a different physician because they do not want to be seen by a Muslim. I have colleagues who are visiting nurses, who have doors shut in their faces when they arrive for home health care services because of the color of their skin. We have to talk about these issues in the workplace."
—*Muslim doctor at a large health-care organization*

"I am the only person of Middle Eastern descent on my team. I overhear conversations about terrorists, but they never discuss that with me. As a matter of fact, I think they purposefully avoid such conversations around me. It makes me feel isolated. I don't really feel like I am a part of the team."
—*Muslim engineer at a large technology company*

While over the past five years, our awareness of traumatizing events has increased, unreported incidences of unequal treatment that impact **historically marginalized groups** are certainly not new.

Fifteen years ago, I was conducting a diversity strategy session for a large insurance company in the Midwest. It was a three-day event comprised of senior leaders who were charged with developing the company's inclusion strategy. On the second day, one of the African American male participants arrived a few minutes late. He was visibly distracted. Later, I learned that he had been stopped by the police on his way to the session, which was held at a venue in a high-income part of town. No infraction had occurred. The police officer asked to see his license and wanted to know where he was going. He was asked where he lived, where he worked, and what brought him to that area.

This incident was extremely disturbing to this African American executive. He did not want to share the incident publicly with the rest of the group, even though it was a diversity session, because his organization, in his estimation, was not ready to really deal with such issues. He admitted to me that it was difficult for him to continue to engage in the session.

How many people are bringing similar stresses with them to work as a result of being targeted just because of what they look like? How many feel that they must suffer in silence?

Company Silence Translates Into "You Don't Care"

During The Winters Group's virtual learning sessions, we asked: "What is the impact when your manager and your company are silent about what is going on in the external world?" The most common response is "We don't think they care." Employees who are impacted, either directly or indirectly, by these events are looking for their companies to say something. Organizations do not operate in a bubble; what is happening in the external world has a direct impact on employees, and they are talking about it at work whether we like it or not.

CEO's Story Reveals Aha Moment

AT&T's CEO, Randall Stephenson, made a public statement at an employee meeting about Black Lives Matter. "Our communities are being destroyed by racial tension and we're too polite to talk about it," referring to shootings and protests in Charlotte, North Carolina; Ferguson, Missouri; Baton Rouge, Louisiana; and Dallas, Texas.[22]

Stephenson also shared a story of his struggles with understanding the US racial divide. One of Stephenson's longtime friends, who happens to be African American, provided an aha experience for him. Stephenson said that he learned that his friend's life as an African American male doctor is fraught with being called negative names, being mistaken for the server in restaurants, and needing to always carry his ID, even in his own neighborhood, because of experiences with law enforcement.

Stephenson told his employees that he was embarrassed that he had known this man for many years, had shared intimate moments, counted him as one of his best friends, and had no idea of his daily struggles as a black man in America. At the end of his speech, the employees cheered. In that moment, Stephenson made himself vulnerable and passionately articulated the compelling reason for having the courage to dialogue about our differences. The world now knows Stephenson's stance. The video has garnered over 160,000 YouTube views. In an increasingly competitive hiring market, I think this will boost efforts to attract diverse talent to AT&T.

Company's Proactive Approach Leads the Way

Sodexo is a company that is routinely heralded for its progressive inclusive practices. It has been number one on *DiversityInc*'s list of top 50 companies for diversity several times and has won a number of other awards for diversity and inclusion. It is also taking a proactive approach in supporting employees in navigating the current social and political environment. The company has issued several statements letting employees know that it cares and advising them on where they can seek support internally.

In addition, The Winters Group has designed several virtual learning labs for Sodexo's inclusion community, including HR and employee network group leaders, to provide tools and tips for engaging in bold conversations. The 90-minute learning sessions, entitled Affirming Inclusion: Meaningful Dialogue across Difference, explore strategies for maintaining inclusive environments after tragedies.

After the 2016 election, The Winters Group hosted a learning lab for Sodexo employees entitled Moving Forward: Reaffirming Our Commitment to Inclusion, with the goal of examining feelings after the results of the divisive 2016 presidential election and reaffirming what it means to be inclusive. The content was balanced, recognizing that their employees represent all political parties. We explored the complex reasons for political polarization, including the socio-economic divide, lingering effects of the 2008 recession, influence of social media, worsening race relations, and technological advances that are replacing human workers with automated solutions.

In addition to the virtual learning labs, Sodexo has a page on its diversity and inclusion site called Inclusion Amidst Turbulent Times—Fostering Understanding across Differences. It acknowledges the pain associated with the violence and terrorism and provides employees with several internal resources for different groups, including blacks/African Americans, immigrant employees, Muslims, and the LGBTQ community.

Sodexo's website is proactive in providing employees with tools to dialogue across difference. It believes that offering these resources will improve employees' overall sense of well-being and thus improve engagement. It is consistent with Sodexo's mission of "improving the quality of life for those they serve."

Virtual Learning Labs Provide Tools

A large trade association attended one of The Winters Group's public virtual sessions on race-based trauma. Following that, the organization hosted a series of what it calls Health Hints to continue to discuss the topic and provide employees with coping strategies and tips on how to be an ally. In conjunction with these efforts, they retained The Winters Group to offer a virtual learning opportunity to further enhance employees' capabilities in having culturally competent, constructive conversations around race and trauma. The session explored the current state of race relations and implications for the workplace and provided strategies for engaging in meaningful dialogue around race. The evaluations showed that employees who attended felt better equipped to manage the stressors and to engage in effective dialogue.

Engaging in Conversations Sends the Signal That an Organization Cares

There has been a consensus among participants that just allowing the opportunity for the dialogue is cathartic and sends a message that the organization is sensitive to the impact of these types of events. Most say that they just wanted to be able to share their feelings and hear how others may be coping. However, progressive companies recognize that this initial sharing session is not enough. People may feel better for the moment, but despite heightened awareness, there are no solutions. In order for effective dialogue to continue, employees need the skills necessary to go deeper in fostering mutual understanding. Skill building takes time, which is why Sodexo conducts ongoing skill-building training for its employees.

You may not be able to precisely account for the loss of productivity caused by the emotional toll of tragic events or immediately gauge the enhanced engagement that may come from employers' acknowledging the impact, but it can be significant. Taking a proactive approach demonstrates to employees that the company cares and wants to be supportive. It is critical to develop ways to have meaningful conversations across difference. In the end, it will help to create an environment that allows every employee to feel like they belong.

Tips for Talking About It!

- Recognize that whether we think it is right or not, employees are talking about topics like race, religion, politics, and other polarizing topics in the workplace.
- Because workplaces are increasingly diverse with different racial/ethnic groups, religions, sexual orientations, and so on, you will need to pay attention to the needs of different groups if you want to engage all employees.
- Realize that the tragic events that are occurring in our world impact different groups in different ways and can negatively influence productivity, engagement, and employees' sense of safety.
- Recognize that employees bring their fears and other emotions into the workplace.
- Promote inclusion and provide resources to support employees in addressing their concerns.
- Provide tools and resources to develop skills to effectively talk about polarizing topics.
- Create the space for bold dialogues to occur. This reduces anxiety and increases workers' sense of well-being, which, in turn, enhances productivity, engagement, and inclusion.

Notes

1   George Kohlrieser, "Leading at the edge," *Orchestrating Winning Performance* (2008): 193–197, http://www.georgekohlrieser.com/user files/file/articles/1.GK_LeadingAtTheEdge.pdf.

2   Race Forward Center for Racial Justice Innovation, "Race Reporting Guide: A Race Forward Media Reference," *Race Forward* (2015), New York, https://www.raceforward.org/sites/default/files/Race%20Reporting%20Guide%20by%20Race%20Forward_V1.1.pdf (Date Accessed: 1/25/2017).

3   Radio One, Inc., "Black, White & Blue: A Spotlight on Race in America" (2016), Silver Spring, http://blackwhiteblue.newsone.com/ (Date Accessed: 1/25/2017).

4   The Winters Group, Inc., "Race & Workplace Trauma During the Age of #BlackLivesMatter" (2016), http://www.wintersgroup.com/whitepapers-and-reports/.

5   Lisa McKenzie, "Brexit is the only way the working class can change anything," *Guardian* (2016), https://www.theguardian.com/commentisfree/2016/jun/15/brexit-working-class-sick-racist-eu-referendum.

6   Zack Beauchamp, "Brexit, explained in one chart," *Vox* (2016), http://www.vox.com/2016/6/23/12012962/brexit-eu-referendum-time-polls-close-chart (Date accessed: 1/31/2017).

7   Robert P. Jones, Daniel Cox, Betsy Cooper, and Rachel Lienesch, "Anxiety, Nostalgia, and Mistrust: Findings from the 2015 American Values Survey," *PRRI* (2015), http://www.prri.org/research/survey-anxiety-nostalgia-and-mistrust-findings-from-the-2015-american-values-survey/ (Date Accessed: 1/31/2017).

8   Hannah Fingerhut, "In both parties, men and women differ over whether women still face obstacles to progress," *PewResearchCenter* (2016), http://www.pewresearch.org/fact-tank/2016/08/16/in-both-parties-men-and-women-differ-over-whether-women-still-face-obstacles-to-progress/ (Date Accessed: 1/31/2017).

9   Unilever, "Unilever urges world leaders to unstereotype the workplace," *Unilever News* (2017), https://www.unilever.com/news/news-and-features/2017/Unilever-urges-world-leaders-to-unstereotype-the-workplace.html (Date Accessed: 1/31/2017).

10 Pew Research Center, "A Wider Ideological Gap between More and Less Educated Adults," *Pew Research Center U.S. Politics & Policy* (2016), http://www.people-press.org/2016/04/26/a-wider-ideological-gap-between-more-and-less-educated-adults/ (Date Accessed: 1/31/2017).

11 Perry Stein, Steve Hendrix, and Abigail Hauslohner, "Women's marches: More than one million protesters vow to resist President Trump," *Washington Post* (2017), https://www.washingtonpost.com/local/womens-march-on-washington-a-sea-of-pink-hatted-protesters-vow-to-resist-donald-trump/2017/01/21/ae4def62-dfdf-11e6-acdf-14da832ae861_story.html?utm_term=.7c56797d7399 (Date Accessed: 1/31/2017).

12 Rick Glazier, "18 Questions, 18 Answers: The Real Facts behind House Bill 2," *North Carolina Justice Center* (2016), http://www.ncjustice.org/?q=18-questions-18-answers-real-facts-behind-house-bill-2 (Date Accessed: 1/31/2017).

13 Tate Walker, "3 Things You Need to Know about Indigenous Efforts against the Dakota Access Pipeline," *Everyday Feminism* (2016), http://everydayfeminism.com/2016/09/dakota-access-pipeline/ (Date Accessed: 1/31/2017).

14 Jesse A. Steinfeldt, Lisa Rey Thomas, and Mattie R. White, "Legislative efforts to eliminate native-themed mascots, nicknames, and logos: Slow but steady progress post-APA resolution," *American Psychological Association* (2010), http://www.apa.org/pi/oema/resources/communique/2010/08/native-themed-mascots.aspx (Date Accessed: 1/27/2017).

15 Brian Montopoli, "DREAM Act Dies in the Senate," *CBS* (2010), http://www.cbsnews.com/news/dream-act-dies-in-the-senate-18-12-2010/ (Date Accessed: 1/31/2017).

16 Hardeep Aiden and Andrea McCarthy, "Current attitudes towards disabled people," *Scope about disability* (2014), http://www.scope.org.uk/Scope/media/Images/Publication%20 Directory/Current-attitudes-towards-disabled-people.pdf (Date Accessed: 1/25/2017).

17 Author's interview of Kate Vernon (January 2017).

18 Gallup, Inc., "State of the American Workplace: Employee Engagement Insights for U.S. Business Leaders," *GALLUP* (2013).

19 Jeanine Prime and Elizabeth R. Salib, "The Secret to Inclusion in Australian Workplaces: Psychological Safety," Catalyst website (August 25, 2015).

20 Jessica McBride, "Philando Castile: 5 Fast Facts You Need to Know," *Heavy* (2016), http:// heavy.com/news/2016/07/philando-castile-falcon-heights-minnesota-police-shooting-face-book-live-video-watch-uncensored-you-tube-police-shooting-man-shot-lavish-reynolds/ (Date Accessed: 1/27/2017).

21 Ariel Zambelich, "3 Hours in Orlando: Piecing Together an Attack and Its Aftermath," *NPR* (2016), http://www.npr.org/2016/06/16/482322488/orlando-shooting-what-happened-update (Date Accessed: 1/31/2017).

22 Shawn Shinneman, "'Tolerance is for cowards' ... AT&T CEO Randall Stephenson speaks on racial tension and Black Lives Matter," *BizJournals* (2016), http://www.bizjournals.com/dallas/ blog/techflash/2016/10/tolerance-is-for-cowards-at-t-ceo-randall.html (Date Accessed: 1/31/2017).

The Nonverbal Context

Terrence L. Warburton and Jaime S. Warburton

What is said is not always what matters and what matters is not always what is said. In effect, the unsaid is often a more important and influential factor in communication than might appear to be the case. In this chapter, we will look at nonverbal communication, the process of transmitting messages through codes not based on words.

We are probably all familiar with the classic adage, "Actions speak louder than words." In effect, what we do or don't do is more important and influential than what we say or don't say—and most people would agree. Watzlawick, Bavelas, and Jackson (*Pragmatics of Human Communication*) stated in their first tentative axiom of communication that "You Cannot Not Communicate," and that statement is premised largely on the significance of nonverbal communication. As they explained, so long as we are in a communicative context—a situation where someone else can attribute meaning to our behavior—whatever we do (or don't do) can have meaning attributed to it. In other words, behavior can be perceived by others to have meaning, and we are unable to *not* behave. Even doing nothing is behavior and meaning can be attributed to our doing nothing. Hence, you cannot not communicate.

Think of a situation where you are asked a question that might have an "awkward" response you would prefer to avoid, such as "Does this new outfit really look good on me?" or "Are you sure you don't mind not going out with your friends tonight and going out with mine instead?" When faced with a potentially problematic question like that you can give a truthful answer and risk upsetting the other person. You can lie and give an untruthful answer to avoid hurting the other's feelings, but at your own expense. Or you can remain silent and not say anything to avoid saying the wrong thing. However, according to the axiom of "you cannot not communicate," silence can have as much meaning as any verbal response you might give. In some cases, silence may have even more meaning because of the implications perceived by the other.

That is not to say that whatever meaning someone attributes to our behavior (or lack of same) is a correct or even an intentional meaning—remember the point from the first chapter that meaning perceived is not always meaning intended. We may engage in a behavior absent-mindedly or we may behave in a way that means one thing to us but something else to the person perceiving it.

Content and Relationship

As Watzlawick, Bavelas, and Jackson explain, although we may examine each separately, verbal and nonverbal communication are often part of the same overall process. They describe the association between the two in terms of what they call the content and relationship dimensions of communication. Content consists primarily of the verbal elements and the relationship is expressed more in the nonverbal elements. One way of applying this two-dimensional approach is to consider the content as the basic information within the message and the relationship component as the peripheral information about what to do with that information or how to interpret it. Saying "It's a beautiful day" with a certain tone of voice could convey the opposite meaning of what the words by themselves would mean. Telling someone that they sang beautifully at the concert you just attended while nudging your friend with your elbow might convey two different meanings—a compliment to the singer and sarcasm to the friend with the opposite meaning of what the words by themselves might suggest. And in some cases, the relationship dimension might be misperceived by the receiver and the overall meaning of the message misinterpreted. This is a good illustration of what was mentioned above—that verbal and nonverbal communication can operate in concert with each other.

High and Low Context

Hall talked about differences in cultures and settings on the basis of what he identified as high and low context. He did not consider these terms to be seen as mutually exclusive categories—all one or the other—but rather he envisioned them as the two extremes of a continuum, so that cultures tended toward one or the other.

High-context cultures employ communication in a way that depends on what was not explicitly said to provide much of the meaning. The implicit—what is understood or taken for granted because of the familiarity with the situation—conveys much more of what is understood. The statements themselves are not as important as the setting, the expectations, and the relationship between those communicating. The words themselves do not contribute to the meaning as much as the context of the communication. In high-context settings, the relationship dimension is the predominant determinant of meaning.

In low-context cultures, the opposite is true. The meaning is expressed in what is said; what is not said is not part of the meaning intended. Messages are explicit, with little to none of the meaning implied. In the words of the comedian Flip Wilson, "What you see is what you get." There is no need to consider peripheral cues because the content dimension is dominant.

Any number of communication contexts can be viewed from this perspective. Think about different families and individuals you know whose communication styles can be better understood in terms of high-and low-context. Organizations and even departments or offices within organizations can differ this way as well. Sometimes what is said is far less important that what is expected to be understood, and sometimes what is said is all that matters. Understanding the framework whereby the communication of others—and ourselves, for that matter—can be effectively interpreted is important in any setting.

Nonverbal Channels

One way of analyzing nonverbal communication is to consider the various channels through which meaning can be conveyed. We will look at each of them separately, but they often function in conjunction with each other and, as mentioned before, with verbal communication as well. We should also recognize that nonverbal communication is not always the same across various settings. The meaning and even the appropriateness of nonverbal communication may be dependent on where it occurs, especially when considered in terms of cultural and sub-cultural contexts.

Kinesics

The category of kinesics focuses on nonverbal messages sent by or related to the body. Posture, movement, and gestures can all communicate, intentionally or not. Sometimes this category is called body language, but many scholars of nonverbal communication tend to avoid this terminology because of certain misleading or inaccurate implications associated with the popular version of the body-language approach. It tends to overlook or minimize the number and variety of factors that contribute to accurate interpretation, implying a degree of constancy and universality that is potentially misleading if not downright incorrect. *Constancy* is implied by suggesting every time a certain behavior is demonstrated by someone it means the same thing, and *universality* is implied by suggesting every person who demonstrates a certain behavior means the same thing. As Freud purportedly once observed, "Sometimes a cigar is just cigar," and sometimes touching your nose means nothing more than touching your nose. That touch is often cited as a sign of deception, but qualifiers are seldom provided—touching your nose may signal deception but not all the time and not for everyone.

The important consideration is that interpreting nonverbal communication has to be done in reference to baseline behavior. A *baseline* is an initial state or set of observations used as a point of comparison, so we need to exercise caution when drawing conclusions about someone's nonverbal communication. It needs to be observed and interpreted according to the baseline behavior of that person, and that baseline is likely to be different for each person. As a result, behavior that is appropriately interpreted one way for one person might be appropriately interpreted very differently for another. We need to avoid overgeneralization.

Some specific examples of kinesics are:

Illustrators

Illustrators are gestures or movements that tend to be directly associated with verbal communication by accompanying our narration. They may reinforce, demonstrate or even contradict, thereby assisting in the transmission of information. When we tell a story about the size of the fish we caught on vacation, our hands may spread apart to demonstrate (or exaggerate) how big it was. When we talk about how "fed up" we are with class assignments, we might raise our hand to cover our head. When we describe how we ran after the bus to catch it for our early class, we might move our arms to simulate our sprinting. Information is conveyed verbally but supplemented nonverbally.

Emblems

Some nonverbal gestures, called *emblems*, have a direct verbal equivalent and are readily recognized as such. The peace sign, the "OK" sign, or even the sign you might use when you are cut off in traffic by an inconsiderate motorist are all examples of emblems. They are recognized and their verbal equivalent is understood by others. However, emblems are relatively context specific in that a sign in one culture or country might not be recognized in another—or it might be recognized but have a different meaning.

Affect Displays

Affect displays are nonverbal expressions of emotion. One of the differences Watzlawick, Bavelas, and Jackson point out between verbal and nonverbal communication is that verbal communication can have fairly precise meanings but is often inadequate to express emotions. We can look up a word in a dictionary to get exact definitions, but think about how many times we have thought or said "I don't know what to say" or "Words fail me" when we are dealing with an emotional situation. On the other hand, nonverbal communication does not have a precise meaning, but it can be very powerful in expressing emotions. There is no dictionary for gestures, so meaning is approximate at best, but hugging a friend when they are dealing with powerful emotions, as with death or other great loss, can communicate much more effectively than words.

Regulators

Human interaction can be complicated, especially when more than one person wishes to speak at the same time. To maintain some order, we often use *regulators*, or gestures that influence the nature and flow of interaction. For example, we look toward one person and away from another to demonstrate our primary audience. When we ask a question we turn toward the person we want to answer us. If we want to respond to someone's statement, we might sit up or lean forward rather than remain in our relaxed position. If we want to contribute to a discussion in class, we might raise our hand to be recognized. These are all examples of regulators that show how interaction can follow certain signals. Much like a traffic like at a busy intersection, regulators signal and influence interactional turn taking.

Adaptors

Adaptors tend to have a more unconscious or psychological foundation. They are gestures that are habitually demonstrated, often when stress or anxiety is experienced. Tapping a pencil or fingers on a desk would be examples of adaptors. Usually their meaning is taken more generally—someone is nervous or distracted, for example—instead of specifically, because adaptors do not have the same degree of intentionality that other gestures might have. They may even be more noticeable to the observer than to the person demonstrating the adaptor. They are not always conscious behaviors, but remnants of behavior from the past.

Proxemics

Proxemics deals with how people use and define space as well as the influence that space may have upon us. In his research Hall noticed that space is both an influence on and a reflection of interactional patterns.

Personal Space

Your comfort can be affected by the amount of personal space we perceive ourselves to have, and that comfort can vary based on the amount of space and the perceived external factors related to that. For example, if you had a picnic in the early spring and someone set up their picnic right next to you when not many others were in the park and there was a lot of open space available, you would probably feel as if your territory were being invaded. Even though the park is public territory and open to others, you would consider the space immediately around you to be personal space, if only temporarily. You would also expect others to respect that space. There may be no formal rule, but it is one of those "taken-for-granteds" when talking about culture. And if you already knew the people, you might expect them to join you rather than go elsewhere.

If the picnic were on Labor Day, however, you would expect the park to be much more densely populated, with discretionary vacancies much less available. In this case, you would expect less personal space, with picnics all around you, perhaps even with overlapping space. This illustrates that the environment and the relationship can affect the perception of territory including appropriate size and even the extent to which we would protect it from invasion.

We expect the shared use of space to be congruent with perceived relationships. Hall identified four different interactional spacing zones that were related to the perceived relationship between or among those sharing those zones:

- Intimate space: Ranging from touching to 18 inches, this zone is reserved for those with whom we share an intimate or very close relationship.
- Personal space: Family and friends occupy this zone, which extends from 1.5 to 4 feet.
- Social space: Appropriate for acquaintances, colleagues and associates, this zone extends from 4 to 12 feet.

- Public space: This is used for presentations or speaking to groups that are perceived as audiences rather than colleagues, at least for the duration of the presenting. This zone ranges from 12 to 25 feet for the close component and more than 25 feet for the extended component.

These spacing patterns are based on mid-American culture and will vary from one culture to another, which Hall distinguishes on the basis of what he calls high-contact culture, which would demonstrate greater closeness in spacing, and low-contact cultures, which would have greater distancing behavior. Violations of these patterns, based on cultural "taken-for-granteds" and perceived relationships, are experienced as social improprieties and causes of discomfort.

Territoriality

Territoriality is similar to personal space except it relates more to the physical surroundings than to one person. For example, your apartment or office rather than your personal being would be subject to your sense of territoriality. We stake out our territoriality by our markers so that others can see that it is occupied or otherwise used by someone. If you are at the library and want to leave your study carrel for a break but plan to return later to finish your assignment in business and professional communication, you might leave a backpack or several books on the carrel as markers. The expectation is that anyone who comes upon the carrel will see that it "belongs" to someone else and go elsewhere to work.

A carrel in the library is temporary territory, but your apartment is more permanent as would be your office or cubicle at work. In these instances, you are still protective of your territory, but perhaps not in such an exclusionary way. Here you are more apt to share, but since it is private rather than public territory, permissions are likely to be involved. Again, the perceived relationship is an important variable related to the nature and extent of the permission. The closer the relationship, the less permission is needed and the less is likely to be sought. If your friend found your apartment door open and you not there, you would probably not be upset to come back to find him or her sitting in the living room watching television. You might even be upset if they did not come in and wait for you. If you came back and found someone who took a class with you last semester and you had not seen since sitting in your living room, you would probably consider that to be a violation of your territory. Someone like that should seek and obtain permission before entering your territory, even if temporarily.

Status and status differential are also variables that affect permissions. A boss can enter a subordinate's office without permission, but a subordinate has to seek and obtain permission if the situation is reversed. In many cases, the permission process is formalized and official—you have to make an appointment, so the permission is granted only for a specific time and expires at the end of the appointment period. Degrees of permission may vary, from the appointment at one extreme to showing up at the office door and waiting for the occupant to say "Come in" at the other end. Even the format can differ, from the need or expectation of explicit permission, as with an appointment with a supervisor, to the assumption of implicit permission, as with a friend or sibling entering your unlocked apartment in your absence. The important consideration is that the method and extent of entering someone's territory is consistent with the mutual perceptions of the relationship that exists between the persons involved.

Chronemics

Chronemics deals with how people use and define time. Hall identifies two different approaches to time—what he termed monochronic and polychronic perspectives. The *monochronic* perspective sees time as a linear commodity where everything is done in sequence, one point in time followed by the next, which is followed by the next, and so on. The appointment with the supervisor referenced above was probably entered in an office calendar based on that approach, with certain times blocked off for certain obligations, with one following another throughout the day and across the week. One task is scheduled, and then the next task, progressing in a linear fashion. On the other hand, the *polychronic* approach sees time as a more wholistic entity, where multiple tasks are addressed with no preconceived or necessary sequence other than the order in which they become available. If Hall were still around, he would probably have termed the polychronic approach multitasking! Individuals, organizations, and whole cultures can vary in how they perceive and treat time, and the differences between the monochronic and polychronic approaches can lead to confusion, frustration and conflict is not recognized and addressed.

Vocalics

Sometimes called paralanguage or paralinguistics, *vocalics* refers to all vocalization with the exception of the words themselves. This includes vocal characteristics such as accent, volume, and articulation. It would also include intensity and rapidity of speaking. We may have certain preconceptions associated with vocalics that influence our perceptions, but those preconceptions may not always be accurate or factual. For example, we might consider someone speaking with a French accent to be more credible as an oenophile (a wine expert) than someone who sounded as if they came from Brooklyn. But a person from Brooklyn may know far more than someone from Paris; the knowledge of wine has nothing to do with someone's place of origin, and accent does not necessitate a certain place of origin in the first place.

People from different regions of the same country can demonstrate significantly different vocalics in terms of accent, speaking rate, and even word choice. Ask someone what they call a carbonated, non-alcoholic beverage and they might say "pop," "soda," or even "tonic" because of where they live. A sandwich on an elongated roll with lettuce, tomato, cheese, and some sandwich meat might be called a "hero," "grinder," "hoagie," "poor boy," or "sub," depending on where you order it.

The important consideration with vocalics is to be sensitive to potential stereotypes that lead to faulty

Haptics

Haptics refers to the study of touch. Important variables here include who is touching whom, where the touching occurs, under what circumstances, for how long, and for what apparent purpose. In the business and professional setting, touch would tend to be either functional or accidental, since touching outside of these categories might well be perceived as inappropriate.

Related Readings

Hall, Edward T. *The Silent Language* (Doubleday, 1959).

----. *The Hidden Dimension* (Doubleday, 1966).

----. *Beyond Culture* (Anchor, 1989).

Watzlawick, Paul, Janet Beavin Bavelas, and Don D. Jackson. *Pragmatics of Human Communication: A Study of Interactional Patterns, Pathologies and Paradoxes* (WW Norton & Company, 2011).

Cultural Competence

Geraldine Hynes

This chapter describes our second cornerstone, *cultural competence* (Figure 3.4.1). Diversity brings with it different cultural norms, leadership styles, and communication patterns, so you can see the critical link between cultural competence and your success as a manager. If you know how to navigate among cultural differences, you will be equipped to develop positive relationships with your employees, leading to productivity, profits, and organizational success.

What Is Cultural Competence?

Corporate response to the increasing diversity of the workforce varies widely, but cultural competence is generally valued. Cultural competence is defined as being "comfortable working with colleagues and customers from diverse cultural backgrounds."[1] Cultural competence is known as the "third wave" of diversity thinking—after affirmative action and inclusion. Indeed, today's employers consider intercultural skills as a top consideration when hiring. In a recent survey of 318 executives from both private sector and nonprofit organizations, 96 percent agreed that it's mandatory for their new hires to be culturally competent.

REACTIONS TO DIVERSITY IN BUSINESS:

1. Affirmative action
2. Inclusion
3. Cultural competence

| Diversity Appreciation | Cultural Competence |

FIGURE 3.4.1   Cornerstones of the Sequence for Success

Briefly, a culturally competent manager understands that culture profoundly affects workplace behavior and attitudes. Furthermore, a culturally competent manager knows how to navigate relevant cultural differences in order to maximize workers' loyalty, satisfaction, productivity, and ultimately the bottom line. The Economist Intelligence Unit recently surveyed 572 executives in multinational organizations around the globe. The business leaders overwhelmingly agreed that cultural competence improves revenues (89 percent), profits (89 percent), and market share (85 percent). The executives widely agreed that managerial communication skills are essential for workforce productivity.[2]

Why Culture Matters

Let's take a closer look at the notion of culture so we can see why it's such an important factor in managerial success. Culture is what we grow up in. Beginning in childhood, we learn acceptable behaviors, customs, and habits. We also adopt the beliefs, values, and moral attitudes of the society in which we mature. A body of common understanding develops. We know what to expect, and we know what is expected of us.[3]

Culture is what we grow up in.

Defined in such a way, culture includes the religious system to which we are exposed, the educational system, the economic system, the political system, the legal system, morals, recreational outlets, mores governing dress and grooming, standards of etiquette, food and how it is prepared and served, gift-giving customs, quality and quantity of communication among the people, greeting practices, rituals, modes of travel available, as well as the many other aspects of our lives.

There is some evidence that culture can even affect our personalities. For instance, a series of studies of people who spoke both Spanish and English showed that switching languages significantly affected personality variables such as extraversion (or assertiveness), agreeableness (superficial friendliness), and conscientiousness (achievement).[4] Bilingualism is becoming more common in the United States, especially among the younger generation. According to the U.S. Census Bureau, Millennials are the most diverse generation in history, with one in four speaking a non-English language at home.

Furthermore, culture can influence the way we see the world. If you show pictures of a monkey, a panda, and a banana to someone from Japan and ask which two go together, chances are that

FIGURE 3.4.2   What Do You See in This Picture?

the Japanese will pick the monkey and the banana, because the former eats the latter. Show the same pictures to someone from Great Britain and she or he will select the panda and the monkey, because they are both mammals. Westerners typically see classifications where Asians see relationships.

There is strong evidence that these differences in worldviews begin in childhood. In another study, Japanese and American children were asked to look at a tank of large fish, small fish, and some aquarium plants and rocks. When they were asked what they saw, the Japanese kids described the groups of fish and the environmental elements. The Americans talked about the big fish.[5] The researchers concluded that the collectivist Japanese culture encourages youngsters to focus on groups, while the individualist U.S. kids learn early on to focus on standouts (Figure 3.4.2).

Malcolm Gladwell explored the importance of culture in his best-seller, *Outliers: The Story of Success.* He concluded, "cultural legacies are powerful forces. They have deep roots and long lives. They persist, generation after generation, virtually intact ... and we cannot make sense of our world without them."[6]

A Closer Look at Cultural Differences

What are the "deep roots" of cultural differences that Gladwell was referring to? One of the most extensive studies of cultural differences was conducted at IBM Corporation by a Dutch management thinker, Geert Hofstede. He surveyed more than 116,000 IBM employees in 40 countries. A massive statistical analysis of his findings revealed six dimensions of national culture as shown in Figure 3.4.3: power distance, uncertainty avoidance, individualism/collectivism, masculinity/femininity, high and low context, and monochronic/polychronic time.[7] Examining Hofstede's framework can help you anticipate and then solve possible problems caused by misunderstandings between employees from different cultures.

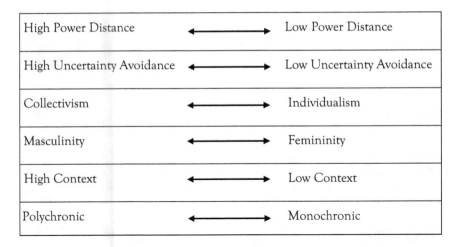

FIGURE 3.4.3   Hofstede's Dimensions of Cultural Differences

Power distance indicates the extent to which a society accepts the fact that power is distributed unequally. It is reflected in the values of both the more powerful and less powerful members of the society. The Philippines, Venezuela, and Mexico are countries with high power distances; and Denmark, New Zealand, the United States, and Israel are a few of the countries with low power distances.

> **High/low power distance: The extent to which society accepts the unequal distribution of power.**

A manager in a culture with high power distance is seen as having dramatically more power than a subordinate would have. This manager, who usually is addressed respectfully by title and surname, might favor a controlling strategy and behave like an autocrat. For instance, within the British Houses of Parliament, lawmakers can move to the head of the line at restaurants, restrooms, and elevators, while clerks, aides, and secretaries who work in Parliament must stand and wait. In a culture with a lower power distance, however, a manager is seen as having little more power than a subordinate, is often addressed by first name, takes her place in line, and manages by using an equalitarian communication strategy.

Uncertainty avoidance relates to the degree to which a society feels threatened by uncertainty and by ambiguous situations. People within such a society try to avoid these uncertainties and ambiguous situations by providing greater career stability, establishing and following formal rules, not allowing odd ideas and behaviors, and believing in absolute truths and the attainment of expertise. Greece, Germany, England, and Japan have strong uncertainty avoidance, while Hong Kong, Denmark, the United States, and Sweden have weak uncertainty avoidance.

> **High/low uncertainty avoidance: The extent to which society feels threatened by ambiguity.**

If you are managing subordinates whose culture values uncertainty avoidance, you will have difficulty getting them to embrace change. Most likely, they will prefer the status quo. To reduce resistance, try to get your people involved in the new strategy and highlight the benefits of change.

On the *individualism/collectivism* dimension, *individualism* suggests a loosely knit social framework in which people are expected to take care of themselves and their immediate families only. *Collectivism*, on the other hand, is a tight social framework in which people distinguish between in-groups and out-groups. They expect their in-group (relatives, clan, organization) to take care of them; and because of that, they believe they owe absolute loyalty to their in-group. The United States, Australia, and Great Britain are the most highly individualistic countries on Hofstede's scale, while Pakistan, Colombia, Nigeria, and Venezuela are more collectivist countries.

Individualism/collectivism: The extent to which society prefers loyalty to the group over loyalty to the individual.

If you are a manager from an individualistic culture and you are participating in negotiations with business professionals from a collectivist culture, you will be frustrated when they resist making decisions. They must first collaborate to reach consensus. You may ask to talk to a "decision maker," but there won't be one. Try to be patient while the other group spends so much time in conference.

Masculinity/femininity is the fourth Hofstede dimension. Masculinity includes assertiveness, the acquisition of money and things, and not caring about the quality of life. These values are labeled masculine because, within nearly all societies, men scored higher in these values than women. Japan, Austria, and Mexico were among the most masculine societies. Feminine cultures, by contrast, value family, children, and quality of life. Denmark, Sweden, and Norway are considered feminine cultures.

Masculinity/femininity: The extent to which society values quality of life.

Consider the following example. In the United States, people are judged at least partly on their ability to make a good salary. Frequently, this judgment precludes traditional U.S. feminine values of caring for children. Despite the passage of the Family Leave Act in 1993, the majority of U.S. working men and women do not take the full time they are eligible for when dealing with family and medical problems.

The fifth cultural difference in Hofstede's model is *context*. In a *high-context* culture, much information is gathered from the physical context or environment or the person's behavior. People look for meaning in what is not said—in the nonverbal communication or body language; in the silences, the facial expressions, and the gestures. Japan and Saudi Arabia are high-context countries, as are Chinese- and Spanish-speaking countries.

High/low context: The extent to which society gathers information from the environment.

In a *low-context* culture, the most information comes from the language. In such a culture, communicators emphasize sending and receiving accurate messages directly, usually by being highly articulate. Canada and the United States are low-context cultures. As you might suspect, negotiations between low-context and high-context cultures can be tricky. The value of contracts and documents used in business-to-business transactions will vary by culture. In high-context countries, agreements are sealed with handshakes between those with strong personal relationships.

The sixth dimension of cultural differences, according to Hofstede, is *monochronic versus polychronic time*. In a monochronic culture, such as Germany, the United States, and most westernized nations, we talk about saving time, wasting time, making time, and spending time. We measure time by the clock, often in nanoseconds. In hyper-punctual countries such as Japan, pedestrians walk fast and bank clocks are accurate. In Western businesses we read quarterly returns and define "long-term" projections as those going out 3 to 5 years into the future. Time is linear.

Monochronic/polychronic: The way a society perceives time.

In polychronic cultures, such as Spain, Latin America, and most Asian countries, time just *is*. These cultures trace their roots back thousands of years. Time is measured by events, not the clock. Thus, promptness diminishes in value, and being "late" is a sign of status. In Ecuador, for instance, politicians, military officers, and business people are less punctual than blue-collar workers are.

People in polychronic cultures are more patient, less interested in time management or measurement, and more willing to wait for their rewards than those in monochronic cultures. And the fact that polychronic cultures typically are less economically successful than monochronic cultures is not a compelling reason for change.

Developing Cultural Competence

All of us can benefit from increasing our understanding of cultural differences. Now that we have explored the deep roots of some of these differences, as described in Hofstede's model, you can see that culture has a profound effect on each of us. As a culturally competent manager, you will recognize that culture determines why your employees

- Prefer authoritarian or democratic leadership
- Need more or less personal space and privacy
- Perceive punctuality as important or not
- Are future-oriented or look to the past
- Are factual or intuitive in decision making
- Value individual achievement or loyalty to the group
- Focus only on the words or on everything except the words

When observing employee conflicts, other managers may not notice that the underlying issue could be cultural. They might think, "What's wrong with you? You shouldn't be so upset." But culturally competent managers will recognize that cultural background strongly influences the way employees respond to any situation.

Once you recognize how pervasive a person's culture is and how different it may be from yours, you can then begin to appreciate the complexity of good management. If you want to succeed in our highly competitive global marketplace, you will need to see and accept things as others see and accept them.

Cultural differences can affect work relationships in domestic as well as multinational corporations. Subcultures in the United States, primarily labeled by geographic region, may affect workers' behavior, communication style, and values just as much as national cultures do. My personal story as a Yankee who works in Texas provides an example of domestic cultural differences, as I described in the Preface of this book.

Understanding your workforce includes recognizing and respecting the cultural roots of their attributes, whether international or domestic, and trying to adapt to their culturally based values and behaviors. As a culturally competent manager, you will take better advantage of this type of diversity and see it as an asset to be valued, not a liability to be dealt with.

Barriers to Cultural Competence

The biggest roadblock to cultural competence is our own cultural values. From an early age, we are taught that our way of doing things is the right way, and everyone who is different is wrong. This bias against difference is natural and normal, not pathological, and mostly subconscious. But every day our biases determine what we see and how we judge those around us. We have biases about almost every dimension of human identity.

> **Bias is a normal psychological reaction to difference.**

We are attracted to and tend to like people who are similar to us, not different from us. The perceived similarities may or may not be real. When people think they're similar, they expect to have positive future interactions. Therefore, the discovery of similarities and differences is crucial in developing relationships. Here's how it works:

Think about a time you had to interview a job candidate. When the candidate walked in and greeted you, you immediately noticed her gender, race, dress, appearance, speech patterns, handshake, and even body size. And you immediately formed judgments based on those outward factors. If you perceived those factors to be similar to yours, you probably formed a positive impression of the candidate. If you perceived those factors to be different from yours, you probably formed a negative impression. As the interview went along and you gained more information about her background, experiences, and skills, you probably paid most attention to the information that confirmed your first impressions and disregarded the information that conflicted with them. That normal mental process can lead to bias and discrimination. It can also lead to costly hiring mistakes.

Overcoming the Barriers

How can you avoid scenarios like the one above? Howard Ross, the founder of Cook Ross, an international diversity consulting company and author of *Everyday Bias* and *Reinventing Diversity*, suggests four strategies for developing cultural competence:

1. *Recognize and accept that you have biases.* Bias is a normal psychological phenomenon. Rather than feel guilty about your biases, take responsibility for them. Once you accept them, you can begin to limit their impact.
2. *Practice "constructive uncertainty."* Slow down decision making, especially when it affects other people.
3. *Try to interact regularly with and learn about people you feel biased against.* Exposing yourself to positive role models will reduce the risk of discrimination.
4. *Look at how you make decisions.* Consider the impact of environmental factors, time of day, and your physical and emotional state in order to identify barriers to perception.[8]

> **STRATEGIES FOR DEVELOPING CULTURAL COMPETENCE:**
>
> 1. Recognize and accept that you have biases.
> 2. Practice constructive uncertainty.
> 3. Learn about people that you feel biased against.
> 4. Look at how you make decisions.

Let's apply Ross's four strategies to the job interview scenario described earlier. If your first impression of the candidate is negative because you perceived her outward characteristics (age, appearance, race, gender, voice, handshake) to be different from yours, what should you do? The first step is to recognize your bias and the possibility of premature judgment. Next, deliberately decide that you won't jump to conclusions. Ask questions and listen closely to her responses. Try to penetrate well below the surface so you can exchange information more accurately. Bring in another interviewer whose opinions you respect and then compare impressions afterward.

It's true that similarities make it easier to build relationships at work. It's also true that most work groups develop their own subculture over time; members adapt their values, behaviors, attitudes, and even appearance so they fit into the workgroup and gain a sense of belonging. However, different traits and outlooks will give your team balance, opportunities for growth, and possibilities for learning new ways of thinking. Becoming aware of your mental processes will help you to become culturally competent so you can make better decisions, whether it's about hiring or anything else.

Three Cases of Corporate Cultural Competence

After examining the roots of cultural differences and what's involved in becoming culturally competent, let's look more closely at how three very high-profile corporations respond to their multicultural environments.

Our first case is Walmart, the largest retailer in the United States, Canada, and Mexico, and the second largest in Britain. Worldwide, more than seven billion people shop at a Walmart each year. But Walmart stores failed in Germany. Why? For one thing, many Germans found the idea of a smiling greeter at the entrance to be off-putting. In fact, many male shoppers interpreted it as flirting. For another thing, German labor unions objected to Walmart's non-union hiring practices.

Walmart also has been insensitive to cultural values in Brazil and Mexico, where the company's stores focused sales campaigns on items the people in those countries don't use—golf clubs and ice skates. Cultural competence was in short supply in Korea, too, where Walmart built stores with shelves so tall that customers had to use ladders to reach the products.[9] These examples of failed management and sales tactics at Walmart demonstrate what can go wrong when decision makers lack cultural competence.

Our second case is Honda Motor Company, one of the most successful multinational companies in the world, employing 140,000 people globally. Astonishingly, Honda has been profitable every year since its inception in 1949. The Honda business model, known as lean manufacturing, is built on Eastern principles that emphasize

- Simplicity over complexity
- Minimalism over waste
- A flat organization over a complex hierarchy
- Perpetual change

Staying true to this cultural framework is the secret of the company's excellent performance. Just how does Honda do it? Jeffrey Rothfeder spent 5 years researching the company and describes in his book, *Driving Honda*, how the organization's processes align with their bedrock principles. Take one of these principles, for example—"respect individualism." Given the Japanese culture's emphasis on teamwork, this principle is surprising. Most companies encourage workers to team up toward a common goal. But Honda views collaboration from the vantage point of the individual, not the team. Honda sees the individual's capabilities, decision making, knowledge, and creativity as the source of the group's performance. In short, Honda practices cultural competence.

This quote from the founder, Soichiro Honda, captures the profound respect for individualism:

> "In the ocean you see a bunch of fish and they're going every which way. And something happens, a stimulus happens where one lines up, then another, and another, until they all line up and they go together in the same direction, perfectly. Later, they separate again to find their own way and nourishment. That's also how successful teams and businesses work."[10]

This emphasis on individualism and creativity translates into physical aspects of the workplace. Honda factories are flat environments. The offices are open bullpens with desks; there are no private dining rooms—just a cafeteria, and no reserved parking spaces. Employees have no job descriptions. The result, according to Rothfeder, is enthusiastic, efficient, productive workplaces with high morale and frequent communication.

Our third case study of cultural competence is Zappos, the largest online retailer of shoes, clothing, and accessories. Amazon bought the company for $1.2 billion in 2011. Similar to the Honda work environment, Zappos's corporate headquarters in Las Vegas has no offices, although there's a nap room. CEO Tony Hsieh eliminated job titles, instead creating a flat organizational chart.

Zappos requires its managers to spend significant time listening to employees. In his bestseller, *Delivering Happiness*, Hsieh wrote that he required his managers to spend 20 percent of their time away from their desks. The upshot is more opportunities for people to enjoy their work and to be self-reliant and responsible. Hsieh estimates that because of Zappos's flat and lenient culture, workers are 20 to 100 percent more productive.[11]

Hsieh recognizes that a workforce with different likes and dislikes, personalities, and ways of interpreting the world is the best source of improvements. As in Honda's culture, with its emphasis on respect for the individual, Zappos capitalizes on employees' cultural differences. The principle of individualism is tied to salaries and all other business activities. It's not just window dressing.

These three cases, Walmart, Honda, and Zappos, demonstrate what can go right when a company aligns and recalibrates its strategic goals with the company's basic principles, and what can go wrong when it doesn't. The takeaway is that maintaining a consistent corporate culture and being sensitive to the cultural environment are fundamental aspects of doing business.

Culture and Communication Style

At this point you may be thinking, "All this sounds true enough; it goes along with what I've seen in my own career. But the concept of cultural competence is pretty abstract. My job description doesn't cover establishing and maintaining the company's culture. What are some concrete actions I can take to enhance my cultural competence and help the company to succeed?"

The answer is that cultural competence is reflected in your communication style. Every day, when you interact with coworkers, subordinates, customers, suppliers, and other stakeholders, everyone's culture acts as a lens through which your messages are filtered. Similarly, their messages to you are filtered through your own cultural lens. Being sensitive to unintended distortions of the messages' meanings equals cultural competency.

Cultural competence is reflected in communication style.

Cultural Sources of Misunderstanding

Various cultures view feedback differently. For example, managers in the United States and Europe typically prefer direct communication; they deliver feedback that is explicit, honest, and authentic. In Asian cultures, communication is expected to be more vague and indirect, and managerial feedback is more likely to be nuanced because bluntness might injure the employees' self-esteem. Furthermore, Asian cultures value silence. Silence, like talk, communicates.[12]

CULTURAL SOURCES OF MISUNDERSTANDING IN CONVERSATIONS:

- Degree of directness
- Silence
- Loudness and pitch
- Appropriate topics
- Touch
- Eye contact

Here is an example of communication style differences that are culturally based. It is part of a conversation between a Chinese police officer in Hong Kong and his supervisor:

Chinese police officer:	My mother is not well, sir.
English supervisor:	So?
Chinese police officer:	She has to go into hospital.
English supervisor:	Well?
Chinese police officer:	On Thursday, sir.

The meaning of this exchange is clouded by cultural differences in communication style. The Chinese officer is hoping that his boss will realize what he wants and offer this before he has to ask for it. In British English, however, it is more typical to start with the request and then give reasons if required. So, the English version of this conversation would be something like this:

Chinese police officer:	Could I take a day off please?
English supervisor:	Why?
Chinese police officer:	My mother is not well and must go to the hospital.[13]

Typical British English speech patterns are similar to U.S. patterns in their degree of directness. When people from Asian cultures are more indirect, Westerners may view them as evasive. A Westerner lacking cultural competence might impatiently prod the speaker to "get to the point." On the other hand, a culturally competent Westerner would understand that the Asian roundabout pattern is used to avoid the risk of hurt feelings and is therefore often a more relationship-sensitive communication style.

Naoki Kameda, a prominent Japanese business communication researcher, explains that the indirect communication style represents important values, based on the "3Hs":

- Humanity—warm consideration for others
- Harmony—efforts not to hurt the feelings of others
- Humility—modesty[14]

By comparison, a direct style seems pretty self-centered, doesn't it?

Communication Style and Empathy

It's easier to communicate with others when you understand and agree with the cultural values behind their communication style preferences. Furthermore, if you can empathize with the other person, share his feelings, and relate to his intentions, then you might even adopt his communication style during the interaction. All you have to do is ask yourself, "If I were on the receiving end, how would I react to this message?" Then adjust your communication style so the receiver's understanding is closer to what you intended. Effective business communication leads to stronger relationships and feelings of empathy and trust. These emotional conditions, in turn, lead to improved performance, productivity, and organizational success.

> **"Successful business communication is about 10 percent business and 90 percent human relations."**
>
> —A. Wilson, 1975

Summary

Along with diversity appreciation, cultural competence is a cornerstone for getting along, getting it done, and getting ahead at work. Culturally competent managers understand that culture profoundly affects workplace behavior and attitudes, and they know how to navigate relevant cultural differences in order to maximize workers' loyalty, satisfaction, productivity, and the bottom line.

While bias against difference is natural and normal, it can restrict thinking and prevent the development of workplace relationships, empathy, and trust. Culturally competent managers recognize that culture is a lens that filters messages. They develop flexible communication styles to overcome barriers and increase shared meaning.

Notes

1. Hart Research Associates (2013). *It Takes More Than a Major: Employer Priorities for College Learning and Student Success* (Washington, DC: Association of American Colleges and Universities).
2. D. Bolchover (2012). "Competing Across Borders: How Cultural and Communication Barriers Affect Business" (The Economist Intelligence Unit Ltd. Report), p. 11.
3. N. Sigband, A. Bell (1986). *Communicating for Management and Business*, 4th ed. (Glenview, IL: Scott Foresman), pp. 69–70.
4. N. Ramirez-Esparza, S.D. Gosling, V. Benet-Martinez, J.P. Potter, J.W. Pennebaker (2006). "Do Bilinguals Have Two Personalities? A Special Case of Cultural Frame Switching," *Journal of Research in Personality* 40, pp. 99–120.

5   R. Nisbett (2004). *The Geography of Thought: How Asians and Westerners Think Differently... and Why* (New York, NY: Free Press).

6   M. Gladwell (2008). *Outliers: The Story of Success* (New York, NY: Little, Brown and Company), p. 175.

7   G. Hofstede (1980). "Motivation, Leadership and Organization: Do American Theories Apply Abroad?" *Organizational Dynamics* Summer, pp. 42–63.

8   H.J. Ross (2014, August 3). "An Appeal to Our Inner Judge," *New York Times*, p. D3.

9   J.W. Neuliep (2012). *Intercultural Communication: A Contextual Approach*, 5th ed. (Thousand Oaks, CA: Sage Publications), pp. 374–5.

10 J. Rothfelder (2014). *Driving Honda: Inside the World's Most Innovative Car Company* (New York: Portfolio/Penguin), p. 134.

11 T. Hsieh (2013). *Delivering Happiness: A Path to Profits, Passion, and Purpose* (New York, NY: Grand Central Publishing).

12 W.B. Gudykunst (1998). *Bridging Differences: Effective Intergroup Communication*, 3rd ed. (Thousand Oaks, CA: Sage Publications).

13 This example is from A. Kirkpatrick (2009). *World Englishes: Implications for International Communication and English Language Teaching* (Cambridge, England: Cambridge University Press) as reported in N. Kameda (2014). "Japanese Business Discourse of Oneness: A Personal Perspective," *International Journal of Business Communication* 51, no. 1, pp. 93–113.

14 N. Kameda (2014). "Japanese Business Discourse of Oneness: A Personal Perspective," *International Journal of Business Communication* 51, no. 1, p. 102.

SECTION FOUR

COMMUNICATING ACROSS RACE AND GENDER DIFFERENCES

Intersecting with all of the categories discussed in section 3, race and gender operate as dominant factors that influence workplace relationships and communication. Understanding how race and gender influence workplace and professional relationships will allow students to promote diversity, avoid problematic situations, and think deeper about privilege. Allen begins this section with a critical look at how race functions as the central feature that acts as a conduit for power relations in both liberatory and oppressive roles. After a brief review of history and the 1964 Civil Rights Act, Allen argues that through communication, the workplace can operate as a site where interaction can reinforce or challenge dominant social power relations, especially in terms of racial harassment. Joyce takes up a critical lens on gender to draw attention to the everyday experiences of women in the workplace as they navigate gendered norms and expectations. Joyce explores the interconnections between gender, communication, and leadership in professional settings and everyday experiences. Understanding how workplace conversations can operate in the service of discriminatory gender relations is essential to uncovering those aspects of communication that shape the power dynamic between speakers.

Consider the following questions when reading this section:

1. According to the authors, why is the workplace an important site for investigating race and gender relations?
2. What does it mean that racism has been a social construction throughout American history?

3. Can you explain the difference between conscious and unconscious racism?
4. What is the difference between "whiteness" and "racism"?
5. How is power "talked" into existence? Or, how do we "talk power"?
6. What does Joyce mean by "women's language"?
7. How do gender, communication, and leadership converge in the workplace?

Key Terms and Concepts

- Race
- Racism
- EEOC
- E-RACE
- Hostile environment
- Racial harassment
- Critical race theory (CRT)
- Whiteness studies
- Critical communication pedagogy
- Gender
- Agency
- Power
- Discourse
- Language

Racial Harassment in the Workplace

Brenda J. Allen; ed. Pamela Lutgen-Sandvik and Beverly Davenport Sypher

Former clerk gets $44,000 racial bias settlement with Los Gatos clinic:
   Supervisor used offensive code words

Corrections officer's suit alleges racial harassment

Racial slurs alleged in suit; CdA Paving tolerated harassing behavior,
   lawsuit claims

Firm's owner used racial remarks: Newark animal-waste processor shut down

Target Corp. to Pay $775,000 for Racial Harassment

Sara Lee settles race-harassment case

Nooses, Symbols of Race Hatred, at Center of Workplace Lawsuits

As these recent headlines imply, race-based conflict continues to occur in the workplace, despite significant progress toward racial equality in the United States. Large corporations such as Coca-Cola, Eastman Kodak, Texaco, FedEx, and Sara Lee Foods have faced class action lawsuits due to formal complaints of racial discrimination, resulting in payouts of billions of dollars. In 2006, the U.S. Equal Employment Opportunity Commission (EEOC, 2006b) received over 27,000 charges of racial discrimination, maintaining the longstanding record of race as the most-alleged claim filed with the agency. During that year, the EEOC resolved 25,992 race charges, and recovered $61.4 million in monetary benefits for charging parties and other aggrieved individuals (not counting litigation payouts).

These formal charges reflect only the tip of the iceberg, as research and anecdotal data suggest that countless other racially-charged incidents in the workplace go unreported (see, e.g., Haefner, & Ramsay 2007). Employees may remain silent about their concerns due to fear of retaliation, apprehension about losing their job, a sense of futility, perceived or actual lack of structures for filing complaints, and worries that others will think they are hypersensitive. The problem is so serious that the EEOC launched an outreach, education, and enforcement campaign known as "E-RACE" (Eradicating Racism and Colorism from Employment) "to advance the statutory right to a workplace free of race and color discrimination" (EEOC, 2007, para. 1). E-RACE focuses on new and emerging race and color issues in the 21st century workplace.

This chapter explores destructive workplace communication by focusing on racial harassment. First, I discuss the importance of the workplace as a critical context for addressing racial discrimination and harassment. Second, I offer a brief historical overview of race and racism because we need to understand these constructs in order to develop strategies for combating them and for creating social justice. Third, I summarize Title VII of the Civil Rights Act of 1964, which concentrates on race and color discrimination in the workplace. I also present examples of racial harassment cases filed with the EEOC and highlight communicative aspects of those cases. Fourth, I discuss consequences of racial harassment at work and provide ideas for organizing in more constructive ways around this issue. I conclude with implications for research and practice. My primary goal is to illuminate the potential of communication to both perpetuate and counteract racial harassment in the workplace.

The Critical Context of Work

The workplace comprises a critical context for addressing racial discrimination. After all, the workplace is not only where most of us spend the bulk of our waking hours, it also is "the single most significant site of regular interaction among adult citizens of different racial and ethnic identities" (Estlund, 2000, p. 21). At work, people increasingly must interact with racially different others, due to rising percentages of racial minorities and decreasing numbers of white persons in the United States. According to a report by the U.S. Department of Labor (DOL, 1999), by 2050, the U.S. population will increase by 50%, and minority groups will make up nearly half of the population.

The workplace is also a political site where members "enact, reinforce, or challenge various power relations endemic to society at large" (Allen, 2004, p. 82). For instance, many organizations are implementing programs to manage or value racial diversity. These programs are based on a belief, and research supporting this belief, that diverse workforces can improve profits, increase creativity, and deflect lawsuits (Richard, 2000). Thus, organizations often require employees to engage in diversity training and other related activities. Furthermore, although persons of color continue to disproportionately occupy lower levels of organizational hierarchies (due mainly to the legacy of racism), many of them have attained or are seeking roles of authority that whites traditionally have filled. Minority employees' efforts to advance often are supported by initiatives such as affirmative action programs and laws that offer recourse to perceived racial discrimination.

This situation can aggravate ongoing racial power dynamics, resulting for example, in backlash by some white workers who fear that affirmative action or diversity programs will hinder their own employment opportunities, or tendencies among some persons of color to pull "the race card" whenever they perceive conflict. In addition, although many whites view racism as a thing of the past, often invoking colorblindness, many persons of color believe that racism is still alive and well (Allen, 2007; Pierce, 2003). As a result, the workplace can become a breeding ground for racial strife. However, the workplace also is a promising setting for racial harmony. Through proactive, persistent, and informed efforts, organizations can help employees to value racial differences, counteract racism, and facilitate anti-racism.

An important common denominator in workplace scenarios of racial strife and racial harmony is communication. As employees use communication to produce, interpret, and share meaning with one another, they usually rely (consciously and non-consciously) on dominant societal discourses about race. For example, they often enact and enforce formal and informal policies based on racial stereotypes and attributions and Euro-centric norms during both personnel procedures (e.g., recruiting, hiring, evaluating, and promoting employees) and day-to-day interactions (Allen, 2004). The headlines at the beginning of the chapter implicate various aspects of communication and racial harassment, including language ("slurs," "offensive code words"), interaction ("racial remarks"), and symbols (nooses). They also demonstrate the potential for communication to effect positive change. Thus, communication serves both oppressive and liberatory roles in the quest for racial equality and harmony, in society in general, and the workplace in particular.

What Is Race?

Race is an enduring construct conceptualized in the eighteenth century as a fixed, physical aspect of identity based primarily on skin color. During that time, European scholars (e.g., French naturalist George-Louis Leclerc, botanist Carl Linnaeus, German physical anthropologist Friedrich Blumenbach) developed an arbitrary hierarchical classification of human races. Describing this typology in 1795, Blumenbach proclaimed, "I have allotted the first place to the Caucasian ... which makes me esteem it the primeval one" (Orbe & Harris, 2001, p. 27). This typology generated a white supremacist ideology or belief system that helped to rationalize, legitimize, and maintain the idea that the white race was (and is) superior to others. In the United States, this ideology helped to justify oppression of native people and the institution of slavery, as well as mistreatment of various non-white immigrant groups. White supremacy attained its fullest ideological and institutional development in the southern United States between the 1890s and the 1950s.

Across that time span, the United States developed differing designations of racial categories. For instance, the first census (in 1790) distinguished white persons from black slaves; the 1900 form asked census takers to designate individuals as white, black, Chinese, Japanese, or Indian (American Indian). At one point, Jewish identity was listed as a racial category. Currently, the Office of Management and Budget (OMB), which is responsible for the census, cites five racial categories: American Indian or Alaska Native, Asian, Black or African American, Native Hawaiian or Other Pacific Islander, and White, and one ethnicity category, Hispanic or Latino. These categories relate race primarily with physical characteristics like skin color and hair texture and base ethnicity on cultural phenomena such as place of origin, language, and traditions.

The OMB maintains, however, that all of these categories are "sociopolitical constructs ... and should not be interpreted as being genetic, biological, or anthropological in nature" (U.S. Census Bureau, 2000, p. 153). Their definition designates race as *a social construction*, similar to the current stance of numerous disciplines (Omi & Winant, 1994; Orbe & Harris, 2001; Smedley & Smedley, 2005). Regarding racial categories, sociologist Howard Winant (2005, p. 1988) explains, "Although they refer to corporeal characteristics like skin color, hair texture, and eye shape, these categories acquired their significance for sociohistorical reasons, not because they have any 'natural' importance." As such, race is an artificial social construction that dominant groups have used to reinforce and perpetuate a racial hierarchy based on white supremacist ideology. As in other settings, this ideology facilitates racism and racial harassment in the workplace.

What Is Racism?

Similar to race, racism as a social construction has undergone varying connotations and denotations. Although varying types of racism exist around the world, the most prevalent and pernicious form has historically been European racism against non-European peoples (Cashmore, 2003). Early versions of this brand of racism referred to "any theory or belief that a person's inherited physical characteristics, such as skin color, hair texture or facial features, determine human intellectual capacity and personality traits" (Cashmore, p. 352). This ideology assumes genetic differences between population groups, a related hierarchy of race categories, and a sense that the presumed superior race deserves privileged treatment while the presumed inferior races deserve mistreatment.

History of Racism in the United States

This type of racism was especially evident in the United States in the 1880s, when southern states and municipalities developed "Jim Crow" statutes to legalize segregation between blacks and whites. In 1896, the Supreme Court ruled in the *Plessy* v. *Ferguson* case that separate facilities for whites and blacks were constitutional. This landmark ruling precipitated discriminatory laws that segregated almost all public contexts and designated separate, generally inferior, institutions for blacks. By World War I, places of employment also were segregated. Throughout this timeframe, laws, policies, and practices targeted various racial groups in order to reinforce white supremacist ideology. Government legislation often was based on preference of white to non-white people, and skin color prevailed as a determinant. For instance, the Naturalization Law of 1790 reserved citizenship only for "free white immigrants."

After World War II, groups of citizens (people of color and whites) began a civil rights movement to challenge Jim Crow. Activism against this belief system included lawsuits, boycotts, marches, and sit-ins. These efforts led to historic governmental interventions, such as the 1954 Brown v. Board of Education case, in which the U.S. Supreme Court ruled unanimously against state-mandated segregation in pubic schools. Legislation such as the Civil Rights Act of 1964, the Voting Rights Act of 1965, and the Fair Housing Act of 1968 ended the legal sanctions of

Jim Crow Laws. Most important to this chapter, the Civil Rights Act sought to eliminate racial segregation and discrimination in the workplace. Title VII of the Civil Rights Act prohibits "employment discrimination based on race, color, religion, sex, national origin, or protected activity" (EEOC, 2006a, Section 15, pp. 15–16).

Due to the Civil Rights movement and ensuing legal victories in the 1950s and 1960s, the United States began to make progress in racial matters. Blatant acts of racism declined as interracial marriages and interracial contact in public settings such as schools and the workplace increased. Plus, equal opportunity in employment improved. However, despite these and other gains, significant gaps still persist between whites and persons of color in terms of socioeconomic status and related aspects of life (Oliver & Shapiro, 1997). In essence, "racial inequality remains a robust feature of American life by nearly any commonly accepted measure of well-being" (Moran, 2006, p. 900).

Recent research projects repeatedly demonstrate racially discriminatory responses to persons of color that signify the tenacity of white supremacist ideology (Deitch et al., 2003). In several studies where researchers kept all variables constant except race, participants tended to prefer persons whom they perceived to be white to those whom they assumed were persons of color (Moran, 2005). A study in California found that temporary agencies selected white applicants three to one over African-American applicants (Bussey & Trasvina, 2003). Another project in Chicago and Boston reported that resumes of persons with "white-sounding" names (e.g., Emily, Brendan) were 50% more likely to elicit interview invitations than were the exact same resumes, only with "black sounding" names (e.g., Lakisha, Jamal) (Bertrand & Mullainathan, 2004).

Due to changes such as rising numbers of interracial marriages and families, immigration, and racial-ethnic minorities in the workforce, the issue of race discrimination at work has become more multi-dimensional and complex than in earlier times. For example, the EEOC has received a growing number of race and color discrimination charges related to multiple or intersecting categories (e.g., religion, age, disability, gender, and national origin) (EEOC, 2006a). Moreover, although conscious, blatant, violent acts of racism appear to have decreased, a resurgence of racially symbolic acts, such as hanging a noose in a person of color's workspace, seems to be occurring. That is, racism has become more covert, politicized, and strategic.

Racism's Connotations and Denotations

This synopsis embeds a history of changing connotations and denotations of racism that have important implications for workplace interactions. Early notions of racism depicted a *racial animus* model of explicit, overt, often violent acts that white individuals or groups perpetuated against people of color, especially blacks, to assert white superiority and black inferiority. This version of racism helped to inculcate *internalized racism*, a belief in white supremacy among persons of color that can lead to self-fulfilling prophecy as well as intra-racial discrimination. Initial civil rights reform efforts concentrated on the racial animus model and tended to target actions of individuals.

The Civil Rights movement also helped to implicate insidious, systemic racial issues that became known as *institutional racism*. In the late 1960s, black nationalist Stokely Carmichael coined this term to refer to collective patterns and practices that help to entrench racial inequality. Institutional (i.e., structural) racism draws attention to

> the endemic character of racial injustice and inequality. As a social structure, racism is understood to be a product of the systematic allocation of resources, privileges, and rights differentially by race: It is distributed across the whole range of social institutions both historically and in the present, and it does not require intention or agency to be perpetuated. (Winant, 2005, p. 1988)

To elaborate, "Institutional racism results from the social caste system that sustained, and was sustained by, slavery and racial segregation. Although the laws that enforced this caste system are no longer in place, its basic structure still stands to this day" (Head, 2007, p. 2).

Therefore, the history of white supremacist ideology and racial hierarchy influences and maintains institutional patterns and practices that reproduce inequalities. Institutions engage in this type of racism through overt behaviors, such as specifically excluding people of color, or in covert ways, such as adopting policies that are not specifically designed to bar people of color but can, nonetheless, result in exclusion. For instance, a policy of "seniority rules," which tends to apply to jobs that white persons historically have held, makes it difficult for more recently appointed persons of color to advance or to retain their jobs because of this "last in, first out" policy. Another example of institutional racism is the prevalence of standardized academic tests or criteria unrelated to job requirements or success that typically measure the cultural and educational norms of middle-class white males. Furthermore, informal corporate policies and procedures that interfere with minority hiring and promotion can lead to racist employment patterns. Indeed, the recurring class action lawsuits cited earlier imply an institutional bias perspective.

Conscious and Unconscious Racism

Subtle versions of racism encompass a complex, multifaceted, interlocking system that pervades many levels and contexts of society, involving individuals as well as institutions. As Moran (2006, p. 911) observes, "Both individual cognition and social structures remain tainted by the legacy of racism." Thus, racism emerges from individuals' behaviors, as well as from institutional or corporate policies. Both can be conscious or unconscious. For instance, individuals who realize that they may face sanctions may consciously veil discriminatory behaviors, or they may unconsciously enact biases based on how they have been socialized about race. On the other hand, perpetrators may genuinely be oblivious to the racist nature of their behaviors, and they will protest that they are not racist. Yet, "even people who are strongly motivated not to be racist are subject to automatic cognitive activation of stereotypes that can unconsciously influence behavior" (Deitch et al., 2003, p. 1317).

Psychological research, particularly studies using the Implicit Association Test (IAT),[1] provides convincing proof of the unconscious impact of living in the United States, "where we are surrounded every day by cultural messages linking white with good" (Gladwell, 2005, p. 85). Regardless of conscious beliefs, over 80% of persons taking the IAT had pro-white associations—even "people who explicitly disavow prejudice" (Greenwald & Banaji, 1995, p. 4). Such beliefs can have profound consequences: A study of physicians found a positive relationship between physicians' pro-white implicit bias and their likelihood of treating white patients and not treating black patients with acute coronary syndromes (Green et al., 2007). On the other hand, when persons were exposed to social texts about admired blacks (e.g., articles or films of Martin Luther King, Nelson Mandela, Denzel Washington) such exposure "significantly weakened automatic pro-white attitudes" (Dasgupta & Greenwald, 2001, p. 800).

The historical view of racism—blatant acts of individuals who believe explicitly in white superiority—allows many persons to deem racism as a thing of the past that occasionally rears its ugly head through atrocious behaviors of dysfunctional individuals. The before-mentioned IAT research refutes this notion. Indeed, an African-American participant in a qualitative study about physicians explained, "We have as a society figured out ways to systematically deny that racism exists. And that structure is in the medical institutions that train us. There is no way to have a discussion about it because it has been decided that it doesn't exist" (Nunez-Smith et al., 2007, p. 49).

Most people connote the label "racist" with someone who is forthrightly prejudiced against people of color and who believes unequivocally that whites are superior. Blatant expressions of racism are less socially acceptable today, and, as such, few persons will state such sentiments publicly (Deitch et al., 2003). Rather, some persons are enacting newer, covert forms of racism, including "modern racism" (McConahay, 1986), "aversive racism" (Dovidio & Gaertner, 2000), and "ambivalent racism" (Deitch et al., 2003).

These forms of racism encompass less conscious and more subtle forms of racial prejudice than in earlier times. They basically refer to attitudes of white people who disdain racism, profess egalitarian values toward race, and characterize themselves as non-prejudiced. However, these persons also harbor negative attitudes towards persons of color. Although they will tend not to engage in direct acts of racial prejudice such as uttering racial slurs, they may indirectly enact racial biases in a way that maintains their sense of being non-racist. And, they will protect that image by rationalizing behaviors that others might construe as racist. For instance, an employer might invoke the premise that homogenous workgroups will work more harmoniously than racially mixed groups to justify hiring only white sales representatives (Brief, Dietz, Cohen, Pugh, & Vaslow, 2000).

These types of contemporary racism may help to explain persistent racial disparities in society as well as findings of research such as the project on "white sounding" versus "black sounding" names. In fact, research concludes that modern racist views can predict discriminatory behavior (Deitch et al., 2003). Thus, it is important to distinguish personal/individual racism (and its variations) from institutional/structural racism, while also recognizing potential threats and promises of both.

Title VII of the Civil Rights Act of 1964

The perspective of "multi-racisms" also reveals important complexities of racism and racial discrimination in the workplace. Notably, Title VII of the Civil Rights Act of 1964 acknowledged and allowed for most of these complexities by implicating individuals and institutions, by invoking past and present notions of race, and by encompassing conscious and unconscious behaviors. Consequently, Title VII offers a viable framework for understanding racism and racial discrimination in contemporary workplaces. In addition, examples of Title VII cases illustrate or indicate ways that communication processes facilitate racial harassment in the workplace. Therefore, this section details elements of Title VII regarding race discrimination.

Race and Color

Title VII "prohibits employer actions that discriminate, by motivation or impact, against persons because of race." Interestingly, Title VII does not define "race," although the EEOC Compliance Manual refers to the OMB's categories of race and ethnicity and its perspective that these are socio-political constructs (EEOC, 2006a). Race discrimination, as distinct from many other forms of discrimination, operates on a group basis; it works on perceived attributes and deficiencies of groups, not individualized characteristics. Discrimination occurs when groups are denied opportunities or rewards for reasons unrelated to their capabilities, industry, and general merit. They are judged solely on their membership in an identifiable racial group.

In addition to race discrimination, Title VII prohibits employment discrimination because of "color" as a separate item. Although the Compliance Manual does not define "color," it explains that "the courts and the [EEO] Commission read 'color' to have its commonly understood meaning—pigmentation, complexion, or skin shade or tone" (EEOC, 2006a, pp. 15–16). The manual elaborates that color discrimination applies to acts "based on the lightness, darkness, or other color characteristics of an individual" (pp. 15–16). All of the issues related to racial discrimination apply equally to color discrimination. Title VII prohibits race and color discrimination "in every aspect of employment, including recruitment, hiring, promotion, wages, benefits, work assignments, performance evaluations, training, transfer, leave, discipline, layoffs, discharge, and any other term, condition, or privilege of employment" (pp. 15–16).

Intention, Liability, and Protected Class

Title VII prohibits intentional discrimination (based on the racial animus model), as well as job policies that appear to be neutral, yet disproportionately affect persons of a certain race or color, that are unrelated to the job and the needs of the business. Moreover, Title VII allows for liability of *any* parties in the workplace, not just those in positions of power, including supervisors, coworkers, and non-employees such as customers or business partners over whom employers have authority. Title VII's prohibitions apply to members of *all* racial or multi-racial groups. Prohibitions also apply to issues such as ancestry, physical characteristics, race-linked illness, reverse discrimination, and so forth.

Generally, race and color discrimination comprises three categories: (a) evaluating employment decisions; (b) equal access to jobs (recruiting, hiring and promotion, diversity, and affirmative action); and (c) equal opportunity for job success (racial harassment, racial bias in other employment terms and conditions, and retaliation). The following discussion centers on the third category, particularly racial harassment, because it is most germane to this chapter.

Hostile Environments and Racial Harassment

Title VII defines racial harassment as "unwelcome conduct that unreasonably interferes with an individual's work performance or creates an intimidating, hostile, or offensive work environment" (pp. 15–35). A hostile environment encompasses various types of conduct, including "offensive jokes, slurs, epithets or name-calling, physical assaults or threats, intimidation, ridicule or mockery, insults or put-downs, offensive objects or pictures, and interference with work performance" (pp. 15–35).

These types of conduct implicate various elements of communication, including nonverbal cues (e.g., use of voice, gestures), semantics, symbols, style, speech acts (e.g., assertions or threats), and so forth (Cashmore, 2003). These and other aspects of communication are evident in the following examples of allegations of racial harassment in the workplace[2]—uses of communication to enact various connotations of racism and thus reinforce and recreate the ideology of white supremacy.

In some workplaces, employees used symbols historically associated with racial violence, such as nooses, swastikas, and KKK garb, graffiti, and symbols. In addition, employees sometimes made remarks related to violence. One employee commented that it should not be against the law to shoot Mexican men, women, and children or to shoot African Americans and Chinese people. This employee also allegedly stated, "If I had my way I'd gas them [referring to black employees] like Hitler did the Jews."

Some cases also replicate racist beliefs that people of color are subhuman. In one worksite, someone posted a picture of a gorilla with an African-American employee's name written on it, while in another office, someone pasted a picture of an ape over an African-American's child's photograph. In yet another case, white postal workers threw bananas and made racist comments to 17 black postal workers who worked in a metal enclosure.

Reported acts of hostility include physical assault. An African-American male employed as a used-vehicle salesman said that his white manager grabbed him by the collar and dragged him through the dealership. He also reported that his manager berated him in front of coworkers and customers. Employees often report uses of racial slurs and epithets, such as calling an employee the "N" word. In one case, several employees, including supervisors, routinely used egregious ethnic slurs for African Americans, Hispanics, and Asians. In another situation, a middle-management Japanese American's white employer frequently used anti-Japanese slurs and racist slogans.

Racial harassment also emphasized dominant belief systems about language usage and race. An Asian employee said his supervisor ridiculed him for how he pronounced a word. In another lawsuit, the plaintiffs contended that the facility's managers prohibited Haitian workers from speaking in their native Creole even though they allowed other non-English speaking groups (of European descent) to converse in their native languages.

Some alleged behaviors referred to racial stereotypes and caricatures. A technician of Chinese and Italian ancestry was subjected to repeated racial and sexual harassment including mimicking martial arts movements and mockingly calling him "Bruce Lee." In another workplace, coworkers pulled their eyes back with their fingers to mock Asian appearance.

Internalized racism, which occurs when members of racial minority groups consciously or unconsciously accept tenets of white supremacist ideology, seems to function through harassment related to skin color based on an ascending order of dark to light (i.e., white) pigmentation. Members of racial groups that comprise a range of skin hues often socialize one another to value light skin over dark, thereby indoctrinating one another to white superiority. Thus, color bias is primarily an intra-racial phenomenon, and cases usually involve remarks based on skin color (Findley, Garrott, & Wheatley, 2004). A lighter-skinned black woman reported that her supervisor, a darker-skinned black female, made statements such as "you need some sun"; and "why don't you go back to where you belong?"(p. 33). In another case, "a dark-skinned black waiter alleged that his light-skinned black supervisor ... called him a 'tar baby,' 'black monkey,' and 'jig-a-boo,' and directed him to bleach his skin" (p. 36).

Another example of intra-racial harassment involved a group of white employees who reported a hostile work environment due to their white coworkers' harassing behaviors towards some of their black coworkers. A final example of intra-racial harassment implied the "model minority" stereotype. In this case, a Korean supervisor with stereotypical beliefs about the superiority of Korean workers held the Korean plaintiff to higher standards than other employees, required him to work harder for longer hours, and subjected him to verbal and physical abuse when he did not meet those expectations.

Silencing Dissent: Minimizing, Stigmatizing, and Retaliating

Power plays often ensue when employees attempt to voice their concerns about perceived racial harassment. In many cases, supervisors minimize or ignore complaints and concerns. Employees who feel victimized report that when they inform their supervisors of incidents, the supervisors take no steps to resolve or prevent the hostile conditions. Sometimes supervisors dismiss employees' concerns, asserting that alleged perpetrators "were just joking." For instance, coworkers of an African-American employee "joked" that they were going to burn a cross in that person's yard, and they thought the person should laugh about their "joke" (Eng, 2007). In San Francisco, a swastika was placed near the desks of Asian-American and African-American inspectors in the newly integrated fire department. Officials explained that someone had presented the swastika to the battalion chief as a "joke" gift, several years earlier, and that it was unclear why or how it ended up at the work stations of the minority employees.

Persons of authority and coworkers often dismiss concerns by stigmatizing accusers and labeling them as hypersensitive or politically correct. Another stigmatizing reaction is simply to blame the victim (Wooten & James, 2004). Persons of authority also may retaliate by impeding promotion opportunities or even firing employees for speaking out against racial harassment on the job. In one case of retaliation, a Mexican American filed a lawsuit claiming that his coworkers called him names like "Taco Bob" and "Burrito Bob." Subsequently, the harassment increased, with the union local's blessing, because the claimant had violated their "no ratting" policy by complaining to plant management. The employee said that someone wrote "Ratserio" and other epithets on the men's room wall in three-foot letters. In addition, the union local purchased 200 "No Rat" stickers for his coworkers to wear. In another case, the owner of a company attempted to force employees to withdraw their EEOC charges by making harassing telephone calls to one of the claimant's family members.

The preceding examples offer a glimpse of types of behaviors and attitudes that motivate employees to report feelings of racial harassment and stigmatizing responses to such reports. Employees who perceive that others are harassing them because of race often face a lose-lose dilemma: If they report the incident(s), others may retaliate by additional harassment; if they do not report, they may face additional harassment (Meares, Oetzel, Derkacs, & Ginossar, 2004). Due to contemporary ideas about racism based on traditional views of racial animus, they may not report perceived race discrimination for fear of being labeled hypersensitive (e.g., Nunez-Smith et al., 2007). In fact, research suggests that increased perceptions of racial discrimination are unrelated to increases in formal grievances (Ensher, Grant-Vallone, & Donaldson, 2001). As such, targeted workers may suffer in silence and endure a number of negative consequences.

Consequences of Racial Harassment

Actual and perceived racial harassment in the workplace can induce costly consequences for individuals, organizations, and society at large. People of color in workplaces where they routinely feel harassed report feelings of hopelessness and lowered organizational commitment and job satisfaction (Deitch et al., 2003). They also experience health problems, depression, and racial fatigue (i.e., feeling drained and weary due to permanent anxiety about racial strife at work) (Meares et al., 2004; Nunez-Smith et al., 2007; Pierce, 2003).

These workers can suffer from internalized racism, which can lead to self-fulfilling prophecy and feeling resigned to remain in lower levels of organizational hierarchies. Based on the stigma of racial prejudice and discrimination, they may segregate themselves and withdraw from their work duties, doing only the bare minimum. In workgroups, they may fail to contribute fully to accomplishing team goals. Indeed, for racially and ethnically-diverse workers, "perceived discrimination [can] have an effect on organizational commitment, job satisfaction, and organizational citizenship behavior" (Ensher et al., 2001, p. 53). In addition, some persons may lash out through physical violence against their perpetrators.

They also may feel shame. Beejey Enriquez, a Filipino worker who filed a complaint in the EEOC's San Francisco District Office, recounted how he was targeted for dismissal by his employer due to his race and ethnicity—despite his qualifications and special recognition by his company. He said, "Now I was just a checkbox to eliminate ... I was almost embarrassed to be who I was." He explained further, "I don't want anyone else to be ashamed of who they are, or who their parents and grandparents are" (EEOC, 2007).

White employees who are targets of racial discrimination from persons of color can experience similar consequences. In addition, if they witness other whites engaging in racial discrimination, they may experience various stressors of hostile work environments, including fear of retaliation and bystander guilt.

Organizations too can pay dearly for race and color discrimination through monetary costs (e.g., attorney fees, compensatory damages, punitive damages); negative public relations; reduced productivity; divided teams; low employee morale; decreased profit due to boycotts; higher turnover; and increased health care spending due to worker stress-related absences and illnesses (Meares et al., 2004). Hostile work environments also send negative signals about organizations to their current (and potential) workforce.

Finally, society at large endures incalculable costs associated with consequences of racial harassment in the workplace. If all members of the workforce do not feel empowered to reach their full potential, or to contribute to their greatest capacity, the United States will never meet its potential as a productive force in all areas of global and local commerce. Moreover, persistent racial strife at work reinforces and perpetuates racial disharmony and segregation across other contexts of society. To alleviate these and other costs, and to begin to reap benefits of multiracial, diverse workforces (see, Cox & Blake, 1991), organizations can strive to develop and maintain contexts that value racial differences. The discipline of communication can play a pivotal role in those efforts.

Communication Matters: Constructive Ways of Organizing

The preceding discussions about race, racism, and racial harassment illuminate a clear, though challenging, set of implications for research and practice that can move organizational communication in more constructive directions regarding race. Research on communication and racial harassment in the workplace must take a critical, discursive stance on how racialized power dynamics exist and occur through institutional practices and policies, as well as through individual communication processes. Research also should study recursive relationships between macro-level discourses about race and organizational micropractices, for instance by exploring ways that members of organizations reinforce or resist white supremacist ideology during everyday interactions (see, Ashcraft & Allen, 2003).

Research also must investigate varying connotations of racism, differing perspectives (between and among racial groups) about racism, and blatant-versus-subtle as well as conscious-versus-unconscious acts of racial harassment. We also should analyze diverse communicative experiences of members of all racial groups while acknowledging the salience of other intersecting identity categories (e.g., gender, age, class, sexuality, national origin, ability, religion, etc.). Two strands of scholarship provide preliminary starting points for such studies.

First, whiteness studies embody a relatively recent focus on the sociohistorical construction of whiteness and its implications. Whiteness studies extend scholarship about race and racism beyond foci on persons of color and oppressive aspects of race to encompass how race affects white persons. Scholars from various disciplines render "whiteness visible as a central aspect of racial inequality" (Pierce, 2003, p. 55). They contend that members of white power structures created race and a racial hierarchy to justify discrimination against persons who are not white. They believe that exposing systems of racial power will facilitate attaining equality in American society. Advocates of whiteness studies strive to help white people understand their own racial identity, rather than view race as relevant only to persons of color.

For instance, sociologist Peggy McIntosh (1995) developed the concept of "white privilege" to illuminate ways that white persons routinely receive unearned advantages based solely on their race that persons of color do not receive. She hopes that edifying whites about their invisible privileges will motivate them toward anti-racist attitudes and behaviors. Communication scholars are among those engaged in this burgeoning area of study (e.g., Cooks, 2003; Mayer, 2005; Nakayama & Martin, 1999; Warren, 2001). Organizational communication researchers can refer to this work as they investigate whiteness in the workplace (see, Allen, 2007; Grimes, 2002).

Second, critical race theory (CRT) explicitly concentrates on key issues of institutional racism. CRT regards race as an ongoing site of struggle and asserts that racism is prevalent in U.S. culture. CRT scholarship seeks to eliminate racial oppression by unmasking everyday structures and practices that perpetuate race-based subordination. Thus, this perspective challenges dominant discourse about equal opportunity as well as "larger cultural discourse of liberal individualism" (Pierce, 2003, p. 68) by stressing the realities of race and racist structures that reinforce racial oppression (Hasian & Delgado, 1998; Matsuda, Lawrence, Delgado, & Crenshaw, 1983). CRT also advocates situating current racial dynamics in light of the history of race in the United States, and it disputes dominant perspectives on race of neutrality, objectivity, and color blindness. Along with whiteness studies, CRT shows strong promise for informing endeavors to eradicate racism in the workplace.

Although ridding the workplace of racism is admittedly a daunting proposition, many organizations are being proactive. Some of them require and provide diversity training for employees with race as the primary topic. Although diversity programs are not a cure-all, they can be effective:

> Diversity programs certainly cannot ameliorate the pervasive plight of racism in our society, but they can help make the workplace a less hostile, more accommodating, and healthier setting for all its members. Even where cooperation remains at the instrumental or superficial level, it has the proven potential to reduce stereotyping and bias, and to foster greater familiarity, greater empathy, and fairer judgments. The law has a limited capacity to prohibit, punish, or even detect the unconscious or well hidden biases and stereotypes that often infect judgments about and relations among individuals and groups. But the law can help—and has helped—to create social environments in which these destructive attitudes gradually wane. (Estlund, 2003, p. 83)

Based on projects about implicit bias such as the ones cited above, diversity training programs often include exercises to reveal participants' hidden prejudices (Babcock, 2006; Pendry, Driscoll, & Field, 2007). Trainers have begun to employ tools such as the Implicit Association Test and white privilege scales in hopes that participants will become more self-aware and thus receptive to diversity training. Although these approaches can be effective, they also can elicit a variety of responses from participants, including confusion, anger, sadness, and guilt (Pendry et al., 2007). Thus, trainers must be prepared to deal with complex reactions from participants, or their efforts may backfire. Effective uses of the IAT in diversity training represents a promising area of research for organizational communication scholars.

Other diversity training strategies aimed at individuals include social identity exercises that invite participants to list and rank social groups to which they belong, and to discuss their lists with one another. This type of technique has proven effective in diversity training because it can increase the salience of coworkers' common social identity (e.g., as a member of a team or organizational unit), leading to improved cooperation in work-groups (Pendry et al., 2007). These and other diversity training techniques can sensitize individual members of organizations to racial issues, and provide strategies to enhance interracial interactions.

However, as this chapter implies, we cannot optimize the potential for transformation in the workplace if we do not also critique and change institutional practices, processes, norms, expectations, and policies (formal and informal). For starters, the EEOC encourages employers to clearly communicate to their employees that they will enforce policies on racial harassment, to adopt effective means for addressing complaints, and to train managers on how to recognize and respond immediately to racial harassment (EEOC, 2006b). The EEOC also enjoins employers to adopt "best practices" to reduce the likelihood of discrimination and to address impediments to equal employment opportunity (e.g., Thomas & Ely, 2001). Organizational communication scholars can conduct research and practice related to these issues.

We also need to explicitly name and frame racism as a persistent problem and to help organizational decision-makers understand and adapt to changing notions of racism and racial discrimination. Basically, we must help organizations to assess and address institutional and cultural issues while also enlightening and empowering individual employees.

A promising means for accomplishing these goals is the racial justice approach (Rogers, 2001). In contrast to diversity training programs, which tend to focus on individuals, the racial justice approach depicts racism as "a set of societal, cultural, and institutional beliefs and practices— regardless of intention—that subordinate and oppress one race for the benefit of another" (p. 12). This perspective advocates analyzing ways that organizational systems, along with individual attitudes and behaviors, perpetuate racism. Furthermore, the racial justice approach attends to differences in how persons of color and whites tend to experience race. It educates whites on privilege, new forms of racism, and alliance building, while helping persons of color to understand internalized racism and its impacts. Basically, "a racial justice approach requires an organizational transformation of power relations" (p. 13) that delves into racism and establishes "a basis for understanding systemic inequality and oppression based on other identities such as classism, sexism, heterosexism, and ableism" (p. 13).

Conclusion

In conclusion, I urge organizational communication scholars to consider whiteness studies, critical race theory, and the social justice approach as they develop and implement research and practice about racism and racial harassment in the workplace. I also invite them to identify other sources that might prove useful. Furthermore, I encourage all of us to engage these issues in our primary institutional setting—the academy (e.g., Artz, 1998). In particular, I endorse critical communication pedagogy as a framework for teaching students about issues raised in this chapter and this volume.

Critical communication pedagogy directly attends to assumptions about context, power, communication, and identity in educational settings and processes (e.g., Cooks, 2003; Fassett & Warren, 2007). This perspective advocates a dialogic, reflexive approach to teaching and learning where all actors collaborate with one another to critique educational practices and to generate ideas for social change while being mindful of the constitutive role of communication.

Although we might struggle to locate external organizations that might allow us (as researchers or consultants) to apply the social justice approach outlined above, most of us are empowered in our classrooms to create a learning context based on tenets of critical communication pedagogy (Ashcraft & Allen, 2009). In doing so, we can prepare students to enter the workplace with knowledge and skills to minimize racial harassment and other types of dysfunctional communication in the workplace. Moreover, we can incorporate our classroom experiences into our research and practice. Thus, we can help our discipline to make major headway towards eradicating racism in the workplace.

Notes

1 Available online: http://implicit.harvard.edu/implicit/.
2 Unless otherwise noted, these are taken from the EEOC Compliance Manual and the EEOC website.

References

Allen, B. J. (2004). *Difference matters: Communicating social identity.* Long Grove, IL: Waveland Press.

Allen, B. J. (2007). Theorizing communication and race. *Communication Monographs, 74*(2), 259–264.

Artz, L. (1998). African Americans and higher education: An exigence in need of applied communication. *Journal of Applied Communication Research, 26*(2), 210–231.

Ashcraft, K. L., & Allen, B. J. (2003). The racial foundation of organizational communication. *Communication Theory, 13*(1), 5–38.

Ashcraft, K. L., & Allen, B. J. (2009). Politics closer to home: Teaching and learning critical organization in our own work/place. *Management Learning, 40*(1), 11–30

Babcock, P. (2006). Detecting hidden bias. *HR Magazine, 51.* Retrieved 1–30–08 from http://www.shrm.org/hrmagazine/articles/0206/0206cover.asp.

Bertrand, M., & Mullainathan, S. (2004). Are Emily and Brendan more employable than Lakisha and Jamal? A field experiment on labor market discrimination *The American Economic Review, 94*(4), 991–1013.

Brief, A. P., Dietz, J., Cohen, R. R., Pugh, S. D., & Vaslow, J. B. (2000). Just doing business: Modern racism and obedience to authority as explanations for employment discrimination. *Organizational Behavior and Human Decision Processes, 81*(1), 72–97.

Bussey, J., & Trasvina, J. (2003). Racial preferences: The treatment of White and African-American job applicants by temporary job agencies in California. Retrieved August 17, 2007, from http://www.impactfund.organization.

Cashmore, E. (2003). *Encyclopedia of race and ethnic studies*. New York: Routledge.

Cooks, L. (2003). Pedagogy, performance, and positionality: Teaching about whiteness in interracial communication. *Communication Education, 52*(2), 245–257.

Cox, T. H., & Blake, S. (1991). Managing cultural diversity: Implications for organizational effectiveness. *Academy of Management Executive, 5*(3), 45–56.

Dasgupta, N., & Greenwald, A. G. (2001). On the malleability of automatic attitudes: Combating automatic prejudice with images of admired and disliked individuals. *Journal of Personality & Social Psychology, 81*(5), 800–814.

Deitch, E. A., Barsky, A., Butz, R. M., Chan, S., Brief, A. P., & Bradley, J. C. (2003). Subtle yet significant: The existence and impact of everyday racial discrimination in the workplace. *Human Relations, 56*(11), 1299–1324.

United States, Department of Labor (DOL) (1999). Futurework: Trends and challenges for work in the 21st century. *United States Department of Labor.* Retrieved August 19, 2007, from http://www.dol.gov/oasam/programs/history/herman/reports/futurework/report.htm.

Dovidio, J. F., & Gaertner, S. L. (2000). Aversive racism and selection decisions: 1989 and 1999. *Psycholgical Science, 11*(4), 315–319.

United States Equal Employment Opportunity Commission (EEOC) (2006a). Equal Employment Opportunity Commission Compliance Manual. *United States Equal Employment Opportunity Commission.* Retrieved July 15, 2006, from http://www.eeoc.gov/policy/docs/retal.html.

United States Equal Employment Opportunity Commission (EEOC) (2006b). Questions and answers about race and color discrimination in employment. *United States Equal Employment Opportunity Commission.* Retrieved August 17, 2007, from http://www.eeoc.gov/policy/docs/qanda_race_color.html.

United States Equal Employment Opportunity Commission (EEOC) (2007). EEOC takes new approach to fighting racism and colorism in the 21st century workplace. *United States Equal Employment Opportunity Commission.* Retrieved December 31, 2007, from http://eeoc.gov/press/2-28-07.

Eng, D. (2007). Success should breed willingness to lend a hand. *Television Week, 26*(10), 10–12.

Ensher, E. A., Grant-Vallone, E. J., & Donaldson, S. I. (2001). Effects of perceived discrimination on job satisfaction, organizational commitment, organizational citizenship behavior, and grievances. *Human Resource Development Quarterly, 12*(1), 53–72.

Estlund, C. L. (2000). Working together: The workplace, civil society, and the law. *Georgetown Law Journal, 89*(1), 1–91.

Estlund, C. L. (2003). *Working together: How workplace bonds strengthen a diverse democracy.* Oxford: Oxford University Press.

Fassett, D., & Warren, J. (2007). *Critical communication pedagogy.* Thousand Oaks, CA: Sage.

Findley, H., Garrott, S. C., & Wheatley, R. (2004). Color discrimination: Differentiate at your peril. *Journal of Individual Employment Rights, 11*(1), 31–38.

Gladwell, M. (2005). *Blink: The power of thinking without thinking.* New York: Little, Brown.

Green, A. R., Carney, D. R., Pallin, D. J., Ngo, L. H., Raymond, K. L., Lezzoni, L. I., et al. (2007). Implicit bias among physicians and its prediction of thrombolysis decisions for Black and White Patients. *Journal of General Internal Medicine, 22*(9), 1231–1238.

Greenwald, A. G., & Banaji, M. R. (1995). Implicit social cognition: attitudes, self-esteem, and stereotypes. *Psycholgical Review, 102*(1), 4–27.

Grimes, D. (2002). Challenging the status quo? Whiteness of the diversity management literature. *Management Communication Quarterly, 15*(3), 381–409.

Haefner, R., & Ramsey, N. (2007, 9/24). Discrimination on the American job. Retrieved August 17, 2007, from http://www.careerbuilder.com/JobSeeker/careerbytes/CBArticle.

Hasian, M., & Delgado, F. (1998). The trials and tribulations of racialized critical rhetorical theory: Understanding the rhetorical ambiguities of Proposition 187. *Communication Theory, 8*(3), 245–270.

Head, T. (2007). Institutional racism. Retrieved September 5, 2007, from http://civilliberty.about.com/od/raceequalopportunity/g/inst_racism.htm.

Matsuda, M. J., Lawrence, C. R., Delgado, R., & Crenshaw, K. W. (Eds.). (1983). *Words that wound: Critical race theory, assaultive speech, and the First Amendment.* San Francisco: Westview Press.

Mayer, V. (2005). Research beyond the pale: Whiteness in audience studies and media ethnography. *Communication Theory, 15*(1), 148–167.

McConahay, J. B. (1986). Modern racism, ambivalence, and the Modern Racism Scale. In J. F. Dovidio & S. L. Gaertner (Eds.), *Prejudice, discrimination, and racism* (pp. 91–125). Orlando, FL: Academic Press.

McIntosh, P. (1995). White privilege and male privilege: A personal account of coming to see correspondences through work in women's studies. In M. L. Anderson & P. H. Collins (Eds.), *Race, class, and gender: An anthology* (pp. 76–87). Belmont, CA: Wadsworth Publishing Company.

Meares, M. M., Oetzel, J. G., Derkacs, D., & Ginossar, T. (2004). Employee mistreatment and muted voices in the culturally diverse workforce. *Journal of Applied Communication Research, 32*(1), 4–27.

Moran, R. F. (2005). Whatever happened to racism? *St. John's Law Review, 79*(9), 899–927.

Nakayama, T., & Martin, J. (1999). *Whiteness: The communication of social identity.* Thousand Oaks, CA: Sage.

Nunez-Smith, M., Curry, L. A., Bigby, J., Berg, D., Krumholz, H. M., & Bradley, E. H. (2007). Impact of race on the professional lives of physicians of African descent. *Annals of Internal Medicine, 146*(1), 45–51.

Oliver, M. L., & Shapiro, T. M. (1997). *Black wealth, white wealth: A new perspective on racial inequality.* New York: Routledge.

Omi, M., & Winant, H. (1994). *Racial formation in the United States: From the 1960s to the 1980s.* New York: Routledge & Kegan Paul.

Orbe, M., & Harris, T. (2001). *Interracial communication: Theory into practice.* Belmont, CA: Wadsworth.

Pendry, L. F., Driscoll, D. M., & Field, S. C. (2007). Diversity training: Putting theory into practice. *Journal of Occupational and Organizational Psychology, 80*(1), 27–50.

Pierce, J. L. (2003). 'Racing for innocence': Whiteness, corporate culture, and the backlash against affirmative action. *Qualitative Sociology, 26*(1), 53–75.

Richard, O. C. (2000). Racial diversity, business strategy, and firm performance: A resource-based view. *The Academy of Management Journal, 43*(2), 164–177.

Rogers, D. (2001). Good for business but insufficient for social change. *Western Studies Center News* (Winter), 12–13.

Smedley, A., & Smedley, B. D. (2005). Race as biology is fiction, racism as a social problem is real: Anthropological and historical perspectives on the social construction of race. *American Psychologist, 60*(1), 16–26.

Thomas, D. A., & Ely, R. J. (2001). Cultural diversity at work: The effects of diversity perspectives on work group processes and outcomes. *Administrative Science Quarterly, 46*(2), 229–273.

U.S. Census Bureau. (2000). 2000 Census of Population, Public Law 94–171. Retrieved February 22, 2007, from http://quickfacts.census.gov/qfd/meta/long_68184.htm.

Warren, J. T. (2001). Doing whiteness: On the performative dimensions of race in the classroom. *Communication Education, 50*(1), 91–108.

Winant, H. (2005). Race and racism: Overview. In M. Horowitz (Ed.), *New dictionary of the history of ideas* (pp. 1987–1989). Detroit: Charles Scribner's Sons.

Wooten, L., & James, E. H. (2004). When firms fail to learn: The perpetuation of discrimination in the workplace. *Journal of Management Inquiry, 13*(1), 23–33.

Talking Power

Women's Experiences of Workplace Conversations

Anne Murphy

This chapter explores women's experiences of power and influence in workplace conversation. Gendered norms are woven into the patterns of mundane everyday workplace interaction; they shape people's choices about what is appropriate, and they influence the ways in which power and authority are expressed. Therefore, to explore the connections between gender, communication, and the leadership gap, the chapter examines the relationship between women's leadership and the conversational detail of how power is "talked" into place in everyday interactions. Working with data gathered during a series of short, women-only development programs dealing explicitly with the expression of power in corporate settings, the chapter's aim is to contribute to understandings of women's experience of agency in professional settings and to explore ways in which theoretical insights can be translated into leadership development practices. This chapter combines organization studies and discourse studies perspectives to reveal how patterns of spoken interaction in the workplace produce and reproduce gendered-power relations. This dual perspective frames two interconnected research questions:

1. How do women experience power, influence, and inclusion in workplace conversations?
2. Which discourse features shape the dynamics of power in spoken interaction in these settings?

The chapter focuses on the meanings women give to these concerns in their professional worlds and the ways in which they are expressed in terms of the dynamics of power in workplace conversations. I draw on feminist organizational theory to reveal dialectic tensions in the ways participants interpret and articulate their experiences, and on discourse analysis to examine some example features of spoken interaction, which mediate their experiences of power, inclusion, and agency.

Gender, Leadership, Language, and Power

A growing number of multi-national corporations have introduced learning and development initiatives aimed at increasing the numbers of female managers in their executive teams. Under the banner of "diversity and inclusion," or "gender balance," these initiatives aim to bring about a significant increase in the numbers of women in senior roles (see, for example, Mercer, 2016). However, despite a more relational discourse of leadership (Fairhurst & Uhl-Bien, 2012) that potentially allows women to express authority in ways beyond those traditionally associated with leadership (Cameron, 2000), very significant challenges continue to face women in positions of authority. This constraint on women's behavior highlights a conflict between the attributes stereotypically associated with femininity and those traditionally associated with leadership (Baxter, 2010; Litosseliti, 2006). This classic "double bind" for women in positions of authority is widely recognized by gender and organizational scholars (Lewis & Simpson, 2012; Mavin & Grandy, 2012; Stead & Elliott, 2009) as well as by scholars working in the field of language, gender, and workplace discourse (Angouri & Marra, 2011; Cameron, 2003; Eckert & McConnell-Ginet, 2003; Holmes, 2006; Litosseliti, 2013.)

Scholars with their homes in different disciplinary traditions examine different constellations of gender, leadership, language, and power. Before applying them together, it is useful to examine them separately.

Gender and Leadership

In mainstream management literature as in organizational life, women's lives and experiences are largely invisible. Leadership theory has been "developed for men on male samples based on men's experience of leadership" (S. Madsen, personal communication, May 25, 2016). Feminist scholars whose work is informed by post-structuralism focus on the hidden processes that (re)produce the underlying structures of power, keeping this privileged norm hidden from view (Simpson & Lewis, 2005, 2007). These processes are not held in place by particular people in certain positions of power, but are diffuse and hidden. One hidden area is the way language is used in interaction. Workplace conversations often follow predictable and stable patterns, which conceal the norms and values within them. Such norms can override our surface awareness of fairness and inclusivity precisely because we take such conversational patterns for granted, and because of this, the exclusionary processes and effects remain invisible.

In discussing this phenomenon in relation to visibility, invisibility, and power in organizations, Lewis and Simpson (2012) have noted that while "judgments about normality are based on visibility and surveillance, the power of normalization lies in its *invisibility*" (p. 146, emphasis in original). Drawing on Lewis and Simpson's (2010) concept of the "(In)visbility Vortex" (p. 9) which represents processes of revealing, exposure, and disappearance around the strong pull of an invisible norm, these authors theorize that standing out on the periphery brings the threat of exposure and erasure, a backdrop against which some women sometimes "seek to enter" what Lewis and Simpson (2010) call "the invisible norm" (p. 5) to avoid being marked as women. For example, some female business leaders choose to distance themselves from stereotypically feminine behaviors and enact a version of leadership that draws principally on the stereotypically masculine. Gendered advantage and disadvantage thus remain hidden in normative, gendered expectations to which both men and women hold women accountable (Mavin & Grandy, 2012). Language is one such expectation. Women who express their power in traditional masculine ways—in fact, women who want power at all—violate social norms by disrupting the gender and structural hierarchies that protect the invisible norm (Mavin, Gandy, & Williams, 2014). Thus, gender conformity and structural invisibility combine to naturalize the rules of who gets to gain and use power. To resist these rules, women have to be the same and different—to fit in and stand out. To theorize how this might work, feminist organizational scholars explore ways of going beyond limiting oppositional binaries by questioning the over-simplified dualisms of mainstream management and leadership literature and by examining mutually (and simultaneously) reproductive dialects such as control/resistance, dissent/consent, and men/women (Collinson, 2005; Fairhurst, 2001; Mumby, 2005; Mumby & Stohl, 1991; Putnam, 2015). Dialectics of (in)visibility, [not] speaking, and powerful[less]ness shape women's experiences of leadership.

Gender and Language

A close study of situated language use can provide a window into the way such experiences are shaped. Feminist linguistics is interested in "identifying, demystifying, and resisting the ways in which language is used to create and sustain gender inequalities" (Litosseliti, 2013, p. 24). In what ways, for example, do people draw on discourses of gender difference, and what are the consequences of these differences; what linguistic practices are seen as appropriate for particular workplace interactions, and what is the social meaning of these on a large scale; how do specific linguistic choices made by women and men in everyday interactions shape views about gender differences that ultimately serve to reinforce female disadvantage (Litosseliti, 2013). Although some feminist language scholars have commented that expectations of leaders have been influenced by a relational discourse of leadership that holds the potential to license women to express authority in ways that are not limited to acceptable feminine (motherly) leadership models (Baxter, 2008; Cameron, 2000), expectations of appropriate behavior for women in the workplace continue to be associated with normatively consistent ways of doing femininity (Baxter, 2010; Holmes, 2006; Litosseliti, 2006). In fact, despite growing evidence that challenges stereotypical expectations about the conversational behavior of women and men at work, traditional expectations endure and lead to the negative evaluation of anyone who does not conform (Litosseliti, 2013). Constraints such as this shape and are shaped in discourse (Eckert & McConnell-Ginet, 2003; Litosseliti & Sunderland, 2002; Mullany, 2007; Sunderland, 2004). Such gendered discourses offer common-sense knowledge about the ways in which women and men "should" behave at work, including the way they behave, or are perceived to behave, in conversation. To consider this further is to examine language and power.

Language and Power

Discourse, language, and power are inextricably linked. Discourses, or ways of understanding and experiencing the world, reflect and constitute a web of explanations that create practical knowledge about the world that shape and are shaped by social processes. The role of discourse in creating and maintaining such power relations has long been the focus of study for critical linguists (Fairclough, 1989, 1992, 2003).

This chapter draws on two separate but connected conceptualizations of power because power is at the core of approaches to analyzing talk in institutional settings. The first conceptualization of power comes from linguistically informed approaches to studying the detail of situated talk that assume power is made visible, and thus can be analyzed, in conversational moves (Thornborrow, 2002). Power, from this perspective, is a shared conversational resource that is dynamically and collaboratively constructed (Holmes & Stubbe, 2003). In this approach, the direction of analyses mostly moves from the detail of talk in situ, to its socially constituting effects. For example, the specific linguistic feature of interruption, when analyzed in the context of a culturally diverse business meeting, may reveal not only different social and cultural assumptions and expectations about when one is able to speak, but also the asymmetrical patterns of legitimate access to power which then reinforce social and cultural inequalities.

The second understanding of power, favored by feminist organizational studies and organizational communication researchers—which is connected but stands on different theoretical ground—is influenced by Foucauldian notions of power. A constantly shifting set of relations emerges from social interaction, which is "everywhere, not because it embraces everything, but because it comes from everywhere" (Foucault, 1990, p. 93). In this approach, the direction of analyses mostly moves from social practices toward their manifestation in the Foucauldian sense of discourse as historically and culturally specific sets of ideas and their expression in social interaction through language. For example, who gets to speak in an ordinary management meeting is largely shaped not by particular ways of using language, but by deeper, structural inequalities. By combining the two perspectives, my research aims to understand the dynamics of power from the participants' point of view, and at the same time I bring the magnifying glass closer to the linguistic activity, allowing the hidden to come into view.

The Research Project

The analysis was carried out on excerpts drawn from a larger project aimed at understanding the meanings professional women attach to transacting power in workplace conversations. Methodologically, the project was informed by linguistic ethnography (Blommaert & Rampton, 2016; Rampton, 2007; Rampton, Maybin, & Roberts, 2015), which combines an ethnographically informed, field-based approach to investigating and comprehending understandings of participants' perspectives and activities, with linguistic and discourse analytical tools and empirical procedures. The research was situated in sites of leadership learning and development directed at professional women. In order to engage with research participants in reflective conversations about experiences of power in corporate settings, a community of interest was built so as to afford opportunities for inquiry and for gathering data relevant to answering the research questions. The project researches and, at the same time, builds a community of professional women with management and leadership roles, sympathetic to the research, and prepared to engage in sharing and reflecting on their experiences of power. This "English and Power" project was a short (stand-alone) individual and small-group learning event aimed at raising awareness of the relationship between conversational behavior and power in workplace conversations in corporate settings. The event, which was repeated on several occasions in five different European cities during 2014 and 2015, was held jointly with members of the European Professional Women's Network (PWN), an international network of professional women that offers opportunities for training, mentoring, and networking. The learning event, which comprised guided reflection, one-to-one coaching, and a group workshop, was designed to serve both as a method of data collection and as a learning intervention in its own right. The participants, all PWN members or their guests, represented a range of levels of seniority, professional roles, nationalities, native languages, businesses, and sectors.

The data set comprises 60 individual written reflections about power and influence completed as pre-work, field notes taken during preparatory telephone coaching conversations with each participant, and 14 total recorded hours of the same women talking in their (geographically) different small groups about their experiences of influence and power in corporate conversations. In their written accounts and in the workshops, participants described their experience of the conversational balance of power and drew attention to features of spoken interaction such as interruption, politeness, turn taking, and topic management. Thus, these data offer access to firsthand accounts of the stories, meanings, and linguistic or pragmatic features that were important to the women themselves.

The data were analyzed inductively by adopting a grounded approach, identifying unresolved tensions and their potential meanings within the specific encounters the women describe (Charmaz, 2006). After close reading and comparative analysis of codes, emerging categories of the experience of power and influence were identified. Informed by feminist post-structural discourse analysis (Baxter, 2003), the next step was a more detailed analysis of the texts, focusing on specific features of spoken interaction, which, according to the women's accounts, played an important role in shaping their experiences. By articulating conversational dynamics, the women's accounts offer a metalinguistic commentary on their experiences of influence.

Aspects of power and powerlessness interact in complex ways in the women's accounts, shaping and shaped by their experiences of inclusion and exclusion. Oppositional binaries and dialectic tensions evident in their reflections—being present (or not), heard (or not), powerful (or not)—revealed an opaque and uneasy relationship with power. It was clear from the accounts that for these (women) leaders and managers, specific conversations, and specific conversational behaviors, constitute important sites for the experience of power asymmetries. These experiences were described by the participants in terms of their distinctive linguistic features. Three related areas of interest were identified from the data, discussed in relation to theory, and analyzed from a discourse perspective: First, *what* are the women saying about their experience of power, and how this is reflected in conversational behavior? Second, *where* does this take place? Where do they experience this absence and presence most keenly? What are these sites of inclusion and exclusion? And third, *how* does this happen? What are some of the specific discourse features through which these elements of experience are realized?

Experiences of Power

I draw attention to two main categories to discuss what the women said about their experiences of power in everyday, mundane workplace conversations. The first category is the tension in the women's descriptions of how power is exercised and experienced. The second category is how this experience is framed by the sense of being either present or absent in a conversational space. In both categories, the women described their experiences in binary terms—for example, being seen (and/or overlooked), being heard (and/or ignored or silenced), being powerful (and/or powerless). The categories intersect with each other and also with meanings the women assigned to being included or excluded in interactions where power is was exercised, brokered, and/or withheld. The names used are not the women's real names.

A Sense of Powerful(less)ness

Given that the group is comprised of successful, professional (and relatively powerful) managers, powerlessness is omnipresent. Ana, a senior human resource (HR) director in a global manufacturing company, said,

> It is difficult to be seen as senior as I am. How do I get the attention of others without having to show my business card with "director" on it? Are there clues to status and presence in the tone of voice or the words you use? I want to know how to feel more powerful, and more comfortable with that feeling.

Ana's reflections on her experience of power are a testament to an important unresolved tension. She holds a senior-level role but does not feel powerful, or at least she does not feel comfortable with her authority. She wants her authority to be heard and interpreted differently. She went on to say: "I feel judged. Men are always judging what women say. They just give their opinions; they are not afraid to fail and be judged while we women, (or at least me), are."

Being unmarked and unseen can indeed be a powerless position to occupy, or it can be part of a strategy to take up power, as Yolanda explained: "I want to possess and convey power (a new thing for me), so I need to strengthen my message and learn how to translate it into this entrepreneurial tough business talk—a language they will understand." Gendered power is often assumed, and "fitting in" presents itself as the best strategy to avoid the discomfort (and powerlessness) of standing out from the norm. Powerlessness, however, is always present in that it is part of judging the experience of being powerful. The (In)visibility Vortex (Lewis & Simpson, 2012) manifests in spoken interaction as a powerful pull towards a conversational norm.

Being There (or Not)

Being present and being absent are central to the experience of power, which is mainly about being seen and being heard and is often expressed through dualistic interpretations of conversational behavior. For example, some cast blame upon themselves for what they experience as unwanted behaviors (aspects such as not speaking in meetings), while at the same time they aspire to occupy more of the conversational floor. However, the women were very clear about *wanting* to be seen and heard, and they provided rich detail of the conversational constraints, which account for their "failure" to speak out. Juana, manager of a 70-strong international customer experience team in financial services, reflected on her experience of influence:

> When there is a meeting or conference call where I am not leading the meeting but would like to give my opinion to add value to the conversation, I normally struggle to be heard as I am not sure when I can start talking, and I often lose the moment to talk, so then it is too late and the topic has already been discussed.

This is not about shyness. Francesca, a senior partner in a professional services firm, the only woman at her level in her country, explained what prevents her from being fully present:

> My lack of a strong command of English stops me from more proactive participation. My colleagues are much more proud of their capability in general and take a much more proactive word-turn in the discussion. This lack of confidence in my English prevents me from taking advantage from the conversation with top managers when they visit my country. This is a mix between the opportunity for certain comments and the way to express them in English. Due to this under-confident feeling, I usually prefer to shut up and pass to a second line.

In terms of linguistic disadvantage, Francesca is not alone in making sense of her experience of the tension between standing out or standing back. For older (now senior) women whose first language is not English, there was a particularly strong sense of frustration at being somehow prevented, or preventing themselves, from "being there."

Unexamined dualisms were evident in many of the women's accounts and present "good" conversational behavior (assertive, powerful, masculine) against "bad" (passive, powerless, feminine). Donna, a brilliant young engineer, began her career with confidence and assertiveness but was warned by her line manager that her colleagues felt threatened, that she should hold back. Now she's gone too far the other way: "My fear is that because I speak less now, they might think I am not so aggressive as the others and therefore not so good at my job."

Frequent comparisons were made to the behavior of other people the women perceive as powerful (e.g., senior men, native speakers of English, northwestern Europeans), which they contrasted with their own experience of feeling unseen and powerless. For example, one participant reflected, "I can't process my thoughts quickly enough. It makes me withdraw, choose to stay silent—and be unhappy." The problem of simply *being there* presented itself in personal terms. Power was experienced as personal, finite, and something to be gained or lost. It is difficult to see—or people are unaccustomed to looking for (or it is simply hidden from view)—how one "side" of the experience of power simultaneously serves to construct the other. When personalized in this way, dichotomous values may reinforce passivity because assuming personal responsibility for this "failure" could also lead to self-exclusion. Becoming more comfortable with visibility and power promised a different experience as Cristina, a senior consultant in an international professional services firm explained: "I want to come out of the place of hiding (behind the numbers); come out and be seen. I know if you're not seen, you're not promoted, and I want to get some space for myself."

Conversational Sites

Where does the negotiation of power take place, and where did these women experience absence and presence most keenly? What were their sites of inclusion and exclusion? I distinguish here between internal and external conversations in order to explore two related sites where a sense of inclusion and exclusion seemed to play an important role. These are a reflective site, which is mainly focused on "being me," and an interactive site where the women explore "being different."

The Reflective Site

The first site is reflective. These were inward-looking places where the participants pondered about power in their accounts of themselves in flux. Moments of individual and organizational transition heightened the experiences of power as well as many cases of powerlessness and exclusion. Individual transitions (taking up a new position, returning from maternity leave, being promoted, and so on) brought with them what seemed like a perpetual need to position and present oneself in an unfamiliar and often hostile conversational setting. For Monica, for example, promotion brought a new and difficult boss. She reflected:

> I am feeling completely powerless—judged and undermined and criticized—feeling under attack. I am 48, but in this situation I'm like a baby, ... The thing is we keep going, keep trying to solve the problem because we think if we ask for help we will show ourselves to be weak, and we know can't do that.

For Emilia, who has a senior role in a technology consulting firm recently taken over by another "foreign" firm, proving herself was becoming exhausting:

> My new interlocutors don't know me personally, and most of our interactions take place on the phone. I have to demonstrate my professional value in this diverse environment, fully populated by men, without being myself. I'm just fighting, trying to demonstrate my worth again and again.

Accounts like this are a testament to the women's consideration of the importance of their own conversational performances, trying as they present themselves as professionals who matter, to make sense of themselves as people. The reflections were infused with a strong sense of the importance of "being me," of designing themselves, celebrating who they are, defining what they will and will not tolerate as part of their professional identities. Melody, a foreigner in a northern European country, explained:

> I need to make my presence here felt but not in the local, overbearing way. I can't fake it. I want to be genuine. I want to make things work better but without being very uncomfortable and not being myself.

The participants reflected on how they used language to achieve their goals: which words to choose, when to speak and when to stay quiet, and how to defend their sense of self-worth. The reflective space was where the participants reflected out loud about the ways language is used both in snippets of remembered conversation and in imagined talk, but where no *actual* interaction takes place.

The Interactive Site

This site involves interactive contexts, such as formal meetings in both face-to-face and virtual settings. Of these, virtual settings stand out as being particularly problematic. In their accounts, the women repeatedly cited conference calls as a primary site of exclusion, raising concerns about the effect of imbalanced participation, ineffective chairing practices, and reified, exclusionary patterns of talk (Murphy, 2015). Participants talk about their frustration with the apparent lack of awareness of their interlocutors. For many, the conversations were unproductive, unstructured, and alienating. Frequently, the participants with the most organizational power would take control. Susana, a communications manager in the banking sector explained:

> There is a weekly conference call with all the Comm & Marketing Heads in EMEA. Normally the Heads of the "strongest" countries lead the conversation (Netherlands, Germany, and Nordics), so there are not many opportunities to make comments or to interrupt. They talk a lot, no matter if they are monopolizing the conversation.

It was so difficult to be part of the discussion that some of the women opted out altogether. Belinda, marketing manager in the automobile industry remarked:

> On international conference calls, I often want to make a comment but cannot because either suddenly everyone is talking at the same time or I am not able at all, no chance. Therefore, in the last meetings I tend not to talk unless being asked. I don't think is the best behavior but it is very tiring to try to speak without success.

In this virtual context, the most openly (and viscerally) cited mechanism of exclusion is what the participants call "native speaker power" (i.e., the power native speakers hold because they are native speakers of English). Again and again the women pointed out that their most keenly felt daily disadvantage is being one step behind the native speakers who, even if they are less expert, are able to influence more because they control the language better. Disadvantage here came from *being different* from what is accepted in many corporate contexts as the linguistic norm. Experiences of power for these women were across and between a complex discriminatory intersectionality of gender, culture, and native language. Georgina, HR manager in a global professional services firm, explained:

> Non-native speakers have less credibility than they deserve. Because we are sometimes uncertain about our language, they perceive us as insecure. They just take up all the space. And because you can't compete in the conversation, you lose ground and power with native speakers; you feel you are being put on a different level.

She concluded:

> The best English speakers get their action plans approved. It takes my energy away and makes me feel like not trying. It's not just that the native speakers take over. We give up. We sit back and think—so let them get on with it.

Contexts, places, and occasions like these, where the negotiation of power in conversation is particularly salient, point to specific discourse features, and can benefit from closer examination.

Discourse Features

Finally, how does all this happen? What are some of the specific discourse features through which these elements of experience are realized? Here I examine two broad areas related to dynamics of power in workplace conversations. These are as follows:

1. Opportunities to access the conversational floor (Thornborrow, 2002).
2. Politeness and power, and how the former is often in tension with people's perception of the latter (Angouri & Marra, 2011; Holmes & Stubbe, 2003).

The Conversational Floor

The accounts disclose internal commentaries that associate (dis)engagement with the negotiation and control of turns and topics, a perspective that equates influence with domination of the conversational floor. Thornborrow (2002) explains:

> This type of approach is based on what I can best describe as a "territorial" model of power in interaction, where the more turns you can take (or stop other people from taking) and the greater your occupation of the floor, the more power you have as a participant in the talk. (p. 27)

The participants appeared to prefer this conceptualization of power in interaction. Being unable to hold on to one's turn, find the right time to interject, or simply speak out, were the most cited features of spoken interaction in the women's accounts.

While this understanding reveals significant patterns on the surface of the interaction, it also conceals the ways in which this finite manifestation of power in conversation is normalized and reproduced. By drawing attention only to conversational power as a finite resource that can be shared either equally or unequally, this interpretation does not account for possible alternative meanings and positions. Establishing and defending speaking rights, reducing or maintaining social distance, and building solidarity are equally important discursive strategies to assert or subvert power relationships (Holmes & Stubbe, 2003). We can get a glimpse of this in Amelia's analysis of the reified nature of turn-taking patterns:

> If the situation is with a well-established team, they have established patterns of interaction. They know each other well, and they interact in a way that doesn't invite participation. They are mostly men, and they have certain patterns of talk. It seems as if they have an informal agreement on how to proceed—they know the rules. If you raise your hand to speak everyone looks at you as if to say, it's not your place to speak.

This, and accounts like it, bring the relational nature of doing power (Grint, 2005) into much sharper focus. To reveal more of how inclusion and exclusion are collaboratively produced (or not), it is helpful to look beyond trading power in interaction as a finite resource and pay attention to the ways speakers, discourse, and contexts interact, a perspective explored in the section that follows.

Politeness and Power

Influenced by unfounded but persistent popular accounts of "women's language," the participants described an uneasy relationship with power in which confusion over speaking styles, deference and powerlessness, directness and appropriateness, and politeness and weakness combined to keep them silent. They did not want to be "too strong or too direct," or to be seen to be either rude or weak. This was not courtesy; it was the process of delicately negotiating power. They do not know how to take up the power their position *should* hold for fear of causing offence or of appearing incompetent in a language which is not their own.

Monica, regional HR manager in a global construction firm, explained: "You don't want to use words that may sound impolite or too strong, but you don't want to be too soft either. Between one and the other, I would chose being soft, and that's what makes me fail." Directness was experienced as gendered. It was not that women or men were more or less direct in their interaction because they are women or men, or have been socialized this way or that—there is ample linguistic evidence to the contrary (Cameron, 2007)—rather, the persistence of gendered stereotypes of feminine and masculine behavior provides scripts for ways of speaking, as Monica pointed out: "Maybe I speak too directly and could be softer and more smiley. If I smile, the president likes it. He likes women to be more girly."

The main issue, though, is accomplishing appropriateness: how to interrupt or change the subject, clarify a point, or introduce a different perspective without sounding rude, and this is highly contextual. Contextual variables include considerations of who else is in the conversation, how much power each person has, the nature of the joint task. The variables combine to constrain what is and is not appropriate. Power and politeness are both important here. Angelina, whose international risk and quality role brings her into frequent contact with people of different cultures, reflected:

> When there's a big power distance you daren't ask—you don't want to be rude or threaten face. So in order not to be impolite, you let it slide. It's like walking a tightrope. ... How do I interrupt without sounding too abrupt, and yet I don't want to sound too informal. My main problem is how to communicate and sound more senior.

This analysis has drawn upon two conceptualizations of power to illustrate, by means of examples of situated conversations, how these perspectives intertwine to frame experiences of power for this group of professional women. First, using categories and ideas drawn from discourse studies, specifically interactional sociolinguistics and conversation analysis, the chapter has examined conversational behavior that is visible on the surface of the talk. Here power, which is a collaboratively constructed resource, is quite literally talked into place in and through interaction (Holmes, 2006). This surface expression of power dynamics is visible and felt in experience. Threaded through every conversation, and deeply constitutive of the experience of power, are practices, norms, and values that are hidden from view. Informed by post-structuralist understandings of (in)visibility (Lewis & Simpson, 2010; Simpson & Lewis, 2005, 2007), this perspective, rooted in Foucauldian understandings of power, offers an analytical means of revealing deeper social and political asymmetries that are shaped and reinforced in everyday workplace interaction. These perspectives, combined with accounts of experience, reveal tensions and contradictions in everyday conversational practices that open potential new ground for women's leadership and leadership development.

Women's Leadership and Leadership Development

How can the insights from the "English and Power" project be translated into leadership development practice? Normative advice about how to behave or speak differently is superficial and short lived, yet it all too easily fits the dominant discourse of corporate learning and development programs. The sort of programs that are based on binary differences perpetuate gender stereotypes and conceal the power relations that protect the norm (Lewis & Simpson, 2012; Mavin & Grandy, 2012). To engage with critical feminist debates while also working effectively in multiple contexts is an important aspect of feminist praxis. This may involve making what is hidden more visible and, thus, available for shared reflection and discussion. Anchoring the debate in the realm of practice, Stead (2013) used the theoretical lens of (in)visibility to interpret how the lived experience of women leaders provides a context for learning that both reveals and conceals power relations. Similarly, awareness of interactional processes that shape the experience of power can also contribute to learning, which reveals such hidden dynamics and mechanisms (Murphy & Parkinson, 2016). To that end, it is important to create learning spaces where women can explore together some of the constraints and possibilities of their power and agency while, at the same time, developing insights into the relationship between language use and the sites of experience.

   In the final section of the chapter, three examples of linguistically informed approaches to leadership development are described. These approaches, which developed out of the research insights and with the research participants, function by changing conversational behavior on the visible surface of the interaction. These subtle shifts in power dynamics, connected as they are to the invisible values and norms that usually remain hidden, offer a developmental space where experiences of power can be reflected upon and shared, and where, returning once more to the surface, discursive changes that disturb the conversational and political norm—but also get the job done—can be realized.

Changing Conversations

This section describes three of the conversation tools that have been tested with the research community. By tools I mean physical artifacts that externalize aspects or patterns of conversations in order to render the relationship between interaction and power more visible, and, therefore, more readily available for scrutiny and discussion. The principle learning objective for the women participating in the research was to improve their understanding of and skill in navigating the conversational power dynamics of their everyday interactions. All had significant managerial responsibilities (with differing degrees of positional power) and all wanted to be able to change their conversations in some way. Irrespective of their formal power, the majority of participants expressed frustration and confusion about how to break through or challenge established communication patterns. Externalizing the normally hidden patterns of power in interaction furnished the participants with choices about their conversational behavior. Choosing to be hyper-polite, for example, was thus no longer only associated with normatively defined "feminine" and powerless conversational behavior (Lakoff, 2004), but also with flexible and powerful discursive strategies that could be calibrated according to the context, the task, the power others bring, the power each participant wants to exercise in that moment, and so on. Small and seemingly inconsequential conversational moves (whose turn it is to speak, or who can, and who cannot ask questions) are thus recast as opportunities for change.

Three key discourse features identified through the research and described in this chapter are turn, topic, and directness. To conclude the chapter, I briefly describe the three "conversation tools" with which research participants worked and which can be easily replicated in discussions and meetings.

By using markers such as counters, coins, or children's building bricks to visualize the interaction process, it becomes possible to see how different choices are available to change the course of a conversation. For example, to visualize the power asymmetries of imbalanced turn-taking and to enable participants to recalibrate their contributions, put a pile of counters or small bricks in the center of the table and ask everyone, every time they speak, to take one and leave it in front of them on the table. Some people may have a great many, where others have none. By seeing this power dynamic unfold, and perhaps even noticing their own role in enacting it, participants can choose to change their behavior by staying quiet, by inviting an opinion, or by asking a question of someone who has not found the space to speak out.

The bricks can also be a useful tool to make visible the subtle moves around the topic of conversation. The individual who defines the agenda often gets to define the action, so maneuverings around topic are an important conversational power dynamic. To visualize this, have each person take two bricks that, this time, represent a new topic. Whenever someone changes the subject or introduces a new theme, a brick should be played. But there are only two chances. Once an individual has played both, he or she can participate in the conversation, but he or she cannot change the subject or introduce any new ideas—*unless* one of the other participants freely chooses to give them one of their bricks—for which *in return* he or she is allowed to take two from the pile in the center. This exercise reverses the usual dynamic of excluding a colleague or her ideas in order to win more conversational power and topic territory.

Finally, confusion and doubt about how to be direct enough—but not be impolite—can, as we have seen, put severe limitations on a person's ability to grasp leadership opportunities. In this exercise, everyone has three bricks, which represent legitimate turns at speaking out to raise important issues. When a person chooses to speak out to say, "I have a question," "I'd like to challenge that," or "I have some thoughts about that" in the right time, everyone else stops to listen so that appropriateness can be seen and collaboratively achieved. Speakers must play a brick when they speak out so that everyone can see this legitimacy and give way. Speakers must use all three of their bricks during the course of the meeting. This constrains some and challenges others in the name of rebalancing the micro-dynamics of power.

By providing a visual means of illustrating some of the dynamics of difference that conceal the conversational norm, the tools create a more nuanced awareness of the way certain patterns of interaction produce and reproduce gendered power relations. The tools enhance linguistic awareness and illustrate the discursive choices about changing power dynamics in practice.

Conclusion

The research reported here reveals how patterns of spoken interaction in the workplace produce and reproduce gendered power relations. Overall, the analysis adds linguistic detail to understandings of power dynamics in workplace conversations and the ways in which these contribute to women's experiences of agency in professional settings. There is evidence in the accounts of the ways women police their own conversation styles and habits in line with traditionally masculine norms of leadership behavior. At the same time, the analysis revealed parallel inner commentaries that referred superficially to a sense of passivity but which, by examining the dialectic tension of experiences of power in conversation, were also testament to a powerful sense of agency.

The ultimate aim in praxis of the research program is to illuminate the way patterns of spoken interaction constrain (and enable) getting work done and how they shape (gendered) asymmetries of power. These are important issues for scholars and practitioners who share a commitment to creating discursive spaces in which women are able to formulate oppositional interpretations of their experiences in corporate life.

References

Angouri, J., & Marra, M. (Eds.). (2011). *Constructing identities at work*. Basingstoke, England: Palgrave Macmillan.

Baxter, J. (2003). *Positioning gender in discourse: A feminist methodology*. Basingstoke, England: Palgrave Macmillan.

Baxter, J. (2008). Is it all tough talking at the top? A post-structuralist analysis of the construction of gendered speaker identities of British business leaders within interview narratives. *Gender and Language, 2*(2), 197–222.

Baxter, J. (2010). *The language of female leadership*. Basingstoke, England: Palgrave Macmillan.

Blommaert, J., & Rampton, B. (2016). Language and superdiversity. In K. Arnaut, J. Blommaert, B. Rampton, & M. Spotti (Eds.), *Language and superdiversity* (pp. 21–48). New York, NY: Routledge.

Cameron, D. (2000). *Good to talk? Living and working in a communication culture.* London, England: SAGE.

Cameron, D. (2003). *Gender and language ideologies.* In J. Holmes, & M. Mayerhoff, (Eds.), *The handbook of language and gender* (pp. 447–467). Malden, MA: Blackwell.

Cameron, D. (2007). *The myth of Mars and Venus: Do men and women really speak different languages?* Oxford, England: Oxford University Press.

Charmaz, K. (2006). *Constructing grounded theory: A practical guide through qualitative analysis.* Thousand Oaks, CA: SAGE.

Collinson, D. (2005). Dialectics of leadership. *Human Relations, 58*(11), 1419–1442. doi: 10.1177/0018726705060902

Eckert, P., & McConnell-Ginet, S. (2003). *Language and gender.* Cambridge, England: Cambridge University Press.

Fairclough, N. (1989). *Language and power.* New York, NY: Longman.

Fairclough, N. (1992). *Discourse and social change.* Cambridge, England: Polity.

Fairclough, N. (2003). *Analysing discourse: Textual analysis for social research.* London, England: Routledge.

Fairhurst, G. T. (2001). Dualisms in leadership research. In F. M. Jablin & L. L. Putnam (Eds.), *The new handbook of organization communication: Advances in theory, research, and methods* (pp. 379–439). Thousand Oaks, CA: SAGE.

Fairhurst, G. T., & Uhl-Bien, M. (2012). Organization discourse analysis (ODA): Examining leadership as a relational process. *The Leadership Quarterly, 23*(6), 1043–1062.

Foucault, M. (1990). *The history of sexuality, volume I: An introduction* (R. Hurley, Trans.). New York, NY: Vintage.

Grint, K. (2005). Problems, problems, problems: The social construction of "leadership." *Human Relations, 58*(11), 1467–1494. doi:10.1177/0018726705061314

Holmes, J. (2006). *Gendered talk at work: Constructing gender identity through workplace discourse.* Malden, MA: Blackwell.

Holmes, J., & Stubbe, M. (2003). *Power and politeness in the workplace: A sociolinguistic analysis of talk at work.* London, England: Longman.

Lakoff R. T. (2004). *Language and woman's place: Text and commentaries.* New York, NY: Oxford University Press. [Ed. Bucholtz M. Rev. and expanded edn.]

Lewis, P., & Simpson, R. (2010). Introduction: Theoretical insights into the practices of revealing and concealing gender within organizations. In P. Lewis & R. Simpson (Eds.), *Revealing and concealing gender: Issues of visibility in organizations* (pp. 1–22). Basingstoke, England: Palgrave Macmillan.

Lewis, P., & Simpson, R. (2012). Kanter revisited: Gender, power, and (in)visibility. *International Journal of Management Reviews, 14*(2), 141–158. doi:10.111/j.1468-2370.2011.00327.x

Litosseliti, L ([2006] 2013). *Gender and language: Theory and practice.* New York, NY: Routledge.

Litosseliti, L., & Sunderland, J. (Eds.) (2002). *Gender identity and discourse analysis.* Philadelphia, PA: John Benjamins.

Mavin, S., & Grandy, G. (2012). Doing gender well and differently in management. *Gender in Management, 27*(4), 218–231.

Mavin, S., Grandy, G., & Williams, J. (2014). Experiences of women elite leaders doing gender: Intra-gender micro-violence between women. *British Journal of Management, 25*(3), 439–455. doi:10.1111/1467-8551.12057

Mercer. (2016). When women thrive, businesses thrive. Retrieved from http://www.mercer.com/our-thinking/when-women-thrive.html

Mullany, L. (2007). *Gendered discourse in the professional workplace.* Basingstoke, England: Palgrave Macmillan.

Mumby, D. K. (2005). Theorizing resistance in organization studies: A dialectical approach. *Management Communication Quarterly, 19*(1), 19–44.

Mumby, D. K., & Stohl, C. (1991). Power and discourse in organizational studies: Absence and the dialectic of control. *Discourse and Society, 2*(3), 313–332.

Murphy, A. (2015, October). So have we heard from everybody? A pragmatic analysis of exclusion and inclusion in international conference calls. Paper presented at the International Communication Association regional conference, Copenhagen, Denmark.

Murphy, A., & Parkinson, C. (2016, December). Women's experiences of power in everyday workplace conversations: Discourse features of power-in-interaction. Paper presented at the International Studying Leadership Conference, Edinburgh, Scotland.

Putnam, L. L. (2015). Unpacking the dialectic: Alternative views on the discourse–materiality relationship. *Journal of Management Studies, 52*(5), 706–716. doi:10.1111/joms.12115

Rampton, B. (2007). Neo-Hymesian linguistic ethnography in the United Kingdom. *Journal of Sociolinguistics, 11*(5), 584–607.

Rampton, B., Maybin, J., & Roberts, C. (2015). Theory and method in linguistic ethnography. In J. Snell, S. Shaw, & F. Copland (Eds.), *Linguistic ethnography: Interdisciplinary explorations.* Palgrave Advances Series (pp. 14–50). Basingstoke, England: Palgrave MacMillan.

Simpson, R., & Lewis, P. (2005). An investigation of silence and a scrutiny of transparency: Re-examining gender in organization literature through the concepts of voice and visibility. *Human Relations, 58*(10), 1253–1275. doi:10.1177/0018726705059840

Simpson, R., & Lewis, P. (2007). *Voice, visibility and the gendering of organizations.* Basingstoke, England: Palgrave Macmillan.

Stead, V. (2013). Learning to deploy (in)visibility: An examination of women leaders' lived experiences. *Management Learning, 44*(1), 63–79.

Stead, V., & Elliott, C. (2009). *Women's leadership.* Basingstoke, England: Palgrave Macmillan.

Sunderland, J. (2004). *Gendered discourses.* London, England: Palgrave Macmillan.

Thornborrow, J. (2002). *Power talk: Language and interaction in institutional discourse.* Harlow, England: Pearson.

SECTION FIVE

LIFE AND THE WORKPLACE

Existing in a workplace is so much more than paperwork, client meetings, and sales quotas. We are *human beings* relating to one another. Our everyday communicative interactions represent who we are as people. We make decisions about what elements of our lives we communicate in the workplace on a conscious level. However, many authors in this volume argue that those unconscious aspects require greater attention. Fleming offers a few very necessary contributions to our understanding of business and professional communication. In the first article, Fleming offers tips for navigating those everyday experiences that involve eating, drinking, and basic socialization. The scenario-based discussions present accessible context for students based on real-life interactions. What are the "rules" for eating and drinking? How do we (or should we) interact in a small social gathering at work or other professional setting? Fleming's second article delves into the more conversational aspects of communication, or "small talk." Small talk involves one aspect of living as a social being in workplace and professional environments. Fleming argues for the concept of small talk as a potential bridge across difference. Noting that humans generally construct Us/Them dichotomies, engaging in even a banal verbal exchange with someone of a different race, age, culture, or religion can work to break down the barriers we socially construct to divide us. This is an important discussion for the workplace, given its primacy as a site and vehicle of relationship influencers. Fleming also highlights gossip as a common example of how we communicate those differences and barriers. Medved explores the role of human resource managers in administering benefits, as well as helping to maintain a supportive work environment. Rarely do we think about the people in charge of assisting employees as work and family issues converge, but they play a vital role in maintaining an inclusive and productive workplace.

Consider the following questions when reading this section:

1. What are the roles of small talk in maintaining and managing workplace relationships?
2. What are some of the key sites in your target future industry that might lend themselves to small talk? Where might small talk be required?
3. In what ways might small talk be able to bridge difference?
4. How might social anxiety and introversion affect small talk?
5. What do you think are the most common mistakes someone might make in a workplace social situation, such as sharing a meal?
6. What role does gossip play in mediating workplace relationships? What do you consider to be "gossip"?
7. Which of the three communication roles inhabited by human resource managers would you find most challenging?
8. What types of issues might cross the work-life divide?

Key Terms and Concepts

- Small talk
- Us/Them dichotomies
- Discrimination
- Human resource management (HRM)
- Work-life balance
- Work-life communication
- Coach
- Strategist

Eating, Drinking, and Walking Around

Carol Fleming

How to Circulate and Not Spill

I just barely noticed you last night at the company cocktail party, slithering through the doorway and heading for the nearest dark corner. You stood out of the light until you spotted the food table. Then you left the corner for the croissants, the shadow for the salmon, and the dark for the drinks. It was clear you had not eaten dinner before you came, as you piled the chicken wings and quiche on your paper plate. I did get a glimpse of you standing in apparent confusion with plate in one hand and drink in the other, wondering how in the world you were going to eat with both hands occupied. I entertained the vision of someone approaching you to shake hands while you were so encumbered. But no, you had made a dash for your dark corner where you could deal with your meal. The next time I looked, you were gone. In my mind, I asked you, "Why did you come to the cocktail party? For the chicken wings?"

You actually came because you thought you "should" be socializing and meeting new people.

Now we're going to reimagine this scene so it ends successfully: You circulate and meet new people (it's called a "mixer," get it?), and you will get free food—but maybe more conversation than quiche this time.

Here's a step-by-step rundown of how you get there:

Before You Leave Home:

1. Consider your appearance for appropriateness and attractiveness so you can be more confident.
2. Select an interesting accessory, making approaching you easier for others.

3. Eat something so that meeting people, not hunger, directs your path.

When You Get There:

1. Pause momentarily just inside the room to catch your breath.
2. Notice how people's facial expressions of energy and goodwill make them attractive.
3. Manage your own face. Be in the moment with positive expectations.
4. SOFTEN: Smile. Open posture. Forward lean. Touch. Eye contact. Nod.
5. Turn on your politeness radar.
6. Turn off your cell phone and put it away.
7. Think "There you are!"
8. Scan the room for familiar faces, ready to light up in recognition.
9. Is there a host or hostess you should greet? If so, let them know you're there. Say something nice about the event or the party. Be brief.

   Your house looks lovely.
   It smells so good in here.
   Gorgeous flowers.
   What a great turnout.
   You look terrific.

10. Do not tie up your host's time and attention, even if they are the only people you know. Hosts are busy; they need to be free to greet and introduce other people, open wine bottles, take coats, and put out that small fire that has started in the kitchen. If this is a private party, your host will probably find someone to introduce you to; that's their job. Cooperate with this procedure. They'll introduce you to someone and hopefully be able to identify an area of mutual interest between you. They will get you started in a conversation, then they'll disappear and now you just go with the flow.
11. Perambulate, have pleasant exchanges with various people, nibble some hors d'oeuvres, and contribute to the general air of goodwill and conviviality (that's your job as a guest).
12. Be available for meeting new people. If you came with a friend, it's a very good idea to separate. Now, I know you shy folks would just as soon hunker down with your buddy and sit out the event, but no, you are going to split up and circulate so you're available and open to other people. You can touch bases with your buddy from time to time, but you will really cut down on your opportunities to meet others if you stay glued to each other.

Suppose There Are Two People

So you're at the party and you've just finished a conversation with a new acquaintance and you see two people talking together. Perhaps you sort of know one of them. That should be an easy group to join. Sure, but first read their body language to see if they're approachable.

You don't want to interrupt an intense or personal conversation, so observe the people. Are they squared off facing each other? Do they have direct eye contact? If so, they're involved. Don't barge in.

Try standing at the edge of a group that is engaged in a lively conversation—they've got what you're looking for! But don't feel bad if you're ignored. They may not be ready to stop their topic and introduce a new person. It's okay! Shake it off and move on, and don't take it personally. You, too, would have closed ranks if you'd got that group conversation really spinning with something you care about. The next time you find yourself in this particular situation, see if you can figure out what is keeping you paralyzed in silence. You'll probably find that you don't know how to excuse yourself because you haven't even been socially recognized yet. Shrug it off and get on with it; nobody will even notice.

When people are ready to respond to others, you will see them open their positions so they're not facing each other so directly. Their eye contact will not be quite so unwavering. They may continue to talk to each other, but their body and eye lines are now open and oriented to the room. Now you can approach. Pay attention to these cues because the time will come when you will want to broadcast the signal that you're available for a new contact with this same nonverbal communication.

These are natural gestures that we all have in our repertoire. There is something weird about performing a gesture or expression on purpose that is already known at the subconscious level, but there it is. We have become estranged from some of these emotional signals. Perhaps we have become convinced that real communication is only something you consciously put into words, instead of trusting the unconscious nonverbal micro-gestures.

***

Examine just how you understand the attitude of another person. Is it in what they say? How they say it? Or how they look when they say it? Psychologist Albert Mehrabian alerted us to the importance of considering all three channels of communication when there is ambiguity in the expression of feelings and attitudes. Have you ever seen a scowling face and a low grumbly voice saying, "I love you"? Then you know what I mean. Then you know that when there is a mixed message, the nonverbal components—body and facial language and vocal tone (our primate heritage)—will be believed over verbal content.

Let's say you are one of the two people talking. Just as you are ready to roll out your carefully developed elevator pitch, your partner blurts out that his dog just died, or that her mother has just had a stroke—something clearly emotionally important to them. You forget the pitch. Now you must be empathetic and receptive, and you should pretty much just shut up and listen. But then you see somebody approaching you ready to offer a cheery hello and join your group. What do you do?

You choose empathy and deliberately give the new person the cold shoulder: you move your shoulder closer to the emotionally vulnerable person to form a psychological barrier. You slightly pivot away from the approaching person, but you take care of them, too. You make a small hand gesture to halt them, raise your eyebrows and subtly nod your head to communicate, "I see you and mean no rejection, but I must deal with this issue privately." They'll get it.

Now you let your friend have your full attention. This is what we must do for each other.

Here's another scenario: You are feeling monopolized or socially captured by a person who has embarked upon a long story. You graciously give them your eye contact. At the same time, you open your body positioning away from the closed, face-to-face position to be more observably open to the room and available for escape. Perhaps someone will rescue you, but if your hero does not arrive, follow the emergency escape steps.

And now back to the original setup.

***

You've joined two such people who've displayed this open position and you've practiced the conventional rituals of self-introduction. A conversation develops that really engages just two of you, and the third person is standing (uncomfortably) listening. This is the time for that third wheel to peel off and go seek somebody else. They take a step back and formalize their leave-taking with a phrase like "Nice talking with you," or maybe a little salute with their glass and a toasting gesture, and vamoose.

Are you asking, "Isn't that rude?" The answer is no, but I understand why you might think so. It's not rude because the exit, if noticed, makes everyone more comfortable. It also makes it possible for people to circulate the room and join and leave groups, which is appropriate at networking events or mixers where you are supposed to be meeting a lot of people. Being stuck with one person is not what you want to do here.

Observe the CEO at the Christmas party. She will engage briefly with someone, give full, radiant attention to that person, "throw a bouquet" (give a compliment or make some pleasant noises), and then move on:

> I'm so glad to have had a chance to say hello!
> It's been wonderful to meet your husband ... and you look fabulous!
> Good to see you, Susan! I'll look forward to hearing your report at the board meeting.
> You never disappoint!

Each contact has the full engagement of the CEO, who maintains eye contact and makes the recipient feel fully appreciated. Then the CEO must move on to acknowledge more people, and you, one of the people, must let that happen gracefully. Do not try to hog the CEO with some last-minute plan or idea. It is not the time or place. But you can say something like "I'll be making an appointment with you for next week; I think I've got an idea you will like." That's fine. Otherwise, as Archie Bunker used to say, "Stifle!"

The CEO needs to actually circulate the room, making as many contacts as is graciously possible, and then exit. She probably has three more events at which to make an appearance—which she does because showing up at office celebrations is a thing that everybody does, from the stock boy to the CEO. If you happen to be that young stock boy, you may not have the social confidence and fluency of your practiced seniors, but you can observe them and try to take a step or two in that direction. Perhaps you approach your manager and say something like "I just wanted to say that I'm enjoying my work and really appreciate the advice you've given me." Then go away.

Eating, Drinking, and Not Spilling

Now you head for the drink or food table simply because that's where the people are. You'll always find refreshments at social gatherings because they facilitate socialization. When people eat and drink together the tension level is reduced (the same is true for most primates). If your anxiety is high, you may feel the need for more refreshments than is appropriate. That can get you in a rather awkward situation with an embarrassing outcome.

The first rule of social eating: Eat something before you go to a social function. Disasters await you if you try to balance a loaded plate of food at a crowded function. You could drop food, you could spill food, you could dribble cocktail sauce down your shirt and on some lady's white coat. Just how comfortable are you going to be when this happens? You may decide, as I sometimes do, that the perils of food handling outweigh the benefits and simply use the food as a conversation starter.

The same thing goes for alcohol. In formal or professional situations, consider your drink as something to sip, not to drink. You don't ever want to find yourself out of control. Social opportunities are too important to blemish with behaviors that you might regret. Carry your drink in your left hand so your right hand is free to shake hands and isn't wet or cold. With some practice, you can also carry a small plate in your left hand at the same time. (For advanced partygoers only: Carry your glass with your thumb and your index finger toward the bottom of the glass. Now you can support a small plate with your last two fingers underneath and the middle finger on top. Yes, it takes a little practice, but it does keep your right hand free for shaking. It avoids all that awkward fussing with finding a place to put things down, clunky food and drink shuffling, and, most of all, it avoids making you feel foolish.)

Don't Make a Dinner out of the Hors D'oeuvres

Hors d'oeuvres usually come in the form of an attractive finger food, are supposed to be for everybody, and are not meant to be a full meal unless it's specifically called dinner. It doesn't look good if you pile a lot of food on your plate.

Here is a horror story—a true one—to really nail the point. Come with me now to a luncheon party, in a private home, featuring a white rug in the living room. You can feel the tension, can't you? Buffet of Italian food. Mayor and board of supervisors types of politicos, all dressed up. Two men turn to each other and reach out to shake hands.

At this very moment, a woman tries to walk between them, carefully carrying a plate full of spaghetti and meatballs with red sauce. Well, folks, the timing couldn't have been better (worse?). The hands came up in the shake, right under the plate, sending it spinning up into the air, and landing at their feet, food side down. Imagine the following ten minutes (for the woman, the men, the hostess, and the rug). Though the rest of us all shook our heads in sympathy, it was vastly entertaining.

The second rule of social eating is to take really small bites. Don't put any more in your mouth than you can swallow quickly with just a chew or two. Have you ever been caught with a stuffed mouth when somebody starts talking to you? It's very awkward.

Don't let it slip your mind that you're there for the people contact, the social opportunities, and not the food and drink. But do use the food as a good anchoring topic to get a conversation started:

> *That quiche looks delicious, I wonder what's in it. Have you tried it?*
>
> *Wow, that's a spectacular cake. I hope it tastes half as good as it looks. Can you see what's on the inside?*
>
> *This is my first time here, I wasn't expecting this much food. Do they always provide an extensive buffet?*

You will, of course, be looking for ways to move off the topic of food and on to something of greater mutual interest. I'll have a lot more to say on the development of conversation later. Right now, let's just work the room.

What Is Small Talk For?

Carol Fleming

Do You Want New Friends? Start Here.

You say small talk is a waste of time or a necessary evil. I say small talk is a very good thing indeed.

Let's define small talk as a light, pleasant, and safe verbal exchange that allows people the time and association to get a sense of each other before developing a deeper sense of relationship. When meeting new people, it consists of introductions, exchanges of personal information and interests, and searching for topics of mutual interest. With people already known to you, it involves the sharing of feelings, opinions, gossip, jokes, and observations.

Small talk implies aimlessness, where what is said is less important than the fact that we are actually saying something (anything!) to a particular person. Small talk has an important social-emotional role in life; it is universal, ubiquitous, and fundamental for knitting a society together.

Small talk is the language of relationship and friendship.

And you love small talk. (Oh, yes, you do!)
Do you doubt me? Take the following test:
    Do you stop and chat as you pass a neighbor on the streets?
    Do you "shoot the breeze" with the guys at the filling station?
    Do you "dig the dirt" at the beauty parlor?
    Do you "schmooze" with your old friends?
    Do you "chew the fat" with your coworkers?

Do you "kill time" as you wait at the train station?
Do you "chill" with your buddies?

And you're going to tell me that you hate doing all of those things? No, you are not. You just have never thought of these exchanges as being small talk, the heart and soul of the social communication flow that keeps you in touch with people and your community.

Human beings have a tendency to form Us/Them dichotomies and to favor the former. These conversations are comfortable for you because you perceive these people as being your tribe, your Us. We chat easily with "our folks." We stiffen up with the "elsewhereians" whom we're not so sure about.

You can read Robert Sapolsky's book *Behave* for his thorough review of the research on this concept. In it he shows us how much "Us/Them-ing" is subconscious stuff with biological under-pinnings. For example, before you are even one year old, you are marking distinctions between sexes and races. You are also noticing if the language spoken to you sounds different from that of your mother tongue. Of course, the learned component is well known to us all:

> You've got to be taught to hate and fear
> You've got to be taught from year to year,
> It's got to be drummed in your dear little ear,
> You've got to be carefully taught.
> You've got to be taught to be afraid
> Of people whose eyes are oddly made
> And people whose skins are a different shade,
> You've got to be carefully taught.
>
> From *South Pacific* by Rodgers and Hammerstein

"Dear little ears" is the scary part here. Us/Them distinctions learned early are the hardest ones to overcome. And Sapolsky writes that we make these Us/Them decisions in a fraction of a second, decisions that dictate our attitude and behavior toward a new person. We're talking about the mechanism of discrimination, aren't we? By "discrimination" I mean simply that we can see a difference—but when does a difference make a difference? That's another question.

From time to time, I call a friend from high school who has lived in a small town in eastern Washington all her life. Since high school, our lives have taken on dramatically different dimensions, which were never more clear than with the 2016 US presidential election.

ME: So, how you doing, Ellie?
ELLIE: Now, that's a trick question! I ain't dead yet, how's that? Ya got your Trump sign on your lawn? (HAHAHA!)
ME: No, I don't, but I know you do.
ELLIE: You got any Trump signs on your block?
ME: Nooo, don't believe I do.
ELLIE: Yeah, but down there in San Francisco, you've got a lot of ... you've got a lot of them ...

ME: Are you asking about people of color, Ellie?
ELLIE: Yeah!
ME: The answer is, "Yes, we do."
ELLIE: ... and you ... you talk to them, do you!?
ME: Yes, Ellie, I do.

In her words, tone, and context, Ellie was showing how clearly she saw the distinction between Us and Them.

I'll quote now from the wonderful book by J. D. Vance, *Hillbilly Elegy*. The author, the hillbilly who made it to Yale, was back in his hometown of Middletown at a gas station.

> As I realized how different I was from my classmates at Yale, I grew to appreciate how similar I was to the people back home. Most important, I became acutely aware of the inner conflict born of my recent success. On one of my first visits home after classes began, I stopped at a gas station ... the woman at the nearest pump began a conversation, and I noticed that she wore a Yale T-shirt. "Did you go to Yale?" I asked. "No," she replied, "but my nephew does. Do you?" I wasn't sure what to say. It was stupid—her nephew went to school there, for Christ's sake—but I was still uncomfortable admitting that I'd become an Ivy Leaguer ...
>
> I had to choose: Was I a Yale Law student, or was I a Middletown kid with hillbilly grandparents? If the former, I could exchange pleasantries and talk about New Haven's beauty; if the latter, she occupied the other side of an invisible divide and could not be trusted.

***

If you believe that prejudice based on any personal distinction is pernicious, then might I interest you in a mechanism for bridging the social gap, a tool available to everyone? It's called small talk.

The small talker is on the front line of engaging with Thems. It makes Thems safe, it makes Thems welcomed. This can be fun for you—and there are also lots of reasons why it may be scary, like finding yourself on the tightrope, in front of a crowd, without a net, extending friendship to a person who has not yet qualified as an Us.

But these divisions are not immutable; they can be changed in the twinkling of the eye. A person once regarded as a Them can easily become an Us. I argue that this is truly the Serious Business of Small Talk.

This is what you want out of social conversation:
turning strangers into friends.

It is you and I with our friendly overtures to erstwhile strangers who can move the dial to greater circles of comfort and friendship. The talk may be small, but the impact is big. You negotiate the beginning of all relationships through appropriate small talk.

The Serious Business of Small Talk

The serious business of small talk is:

- To bring people together
- To facilitate understanding and trust
- To find or confirm friendships
- To avoid conflict
- To expose you to different points of view

Got the picture? Small talk is your social future.

Now, how can you say you "just hate" this? What I think you actually hate is that teensy-weensy small percentage of situations where you must negotiate a stone-cold start with a stranger.

You feel okay when a Them is selling something or giving directions. This shared purpose clarifies and comforts. And you can be with old friends and not have anything in particular to talk about and that feels okay too.

But to act overtly friendly with total strangers with nothing to talk about, possibly being witnessed by other people—that's what you hate. You hate that flood of anxiety, the feeling of foolishness, the fear of the phony, the awkwardness of making it all up on the spot. Your emotional centers are on high alert: "Watch out, there's a Them!"

All of this Us/Them tension usually goes unacknowledged, as is the cognitive/emotional war going on inside your head. Your emotional brain is yelling, "Stranger-danger!" while your cognitive brain is trying to comply with the social expectation that you act as if you were already friends. And the cherry on top is that there is always the possibility of rejection!

I think that's the small talk you hate, and who can blame you? It is painful!

These stressful situations call for a mechanism, a tool, an attitude for moving through the discomfort of bridging this social gap. The rituals and pleasantries of small talk are designed to deal with just these ambiguities. It starts with a smile, a hello, and an outstretched hand. If you can do this, we can get started with all the rest.

Small talk is a crucial social lubricant,
as valuable as wine or laughter.

Small talk takes many forms. Remember the tofu analogy from the introduction? Its goal is to be easily digestible, readily available, and utterly bland, taking on the flavor of whatever context you're in. At one extreme is the simple exchange of acknowledgment between people: one person knocks, the other opens the door. To not acknowledge the knock would be felt as an affront (but maybe that's exactly what you want to communicate). The polite thing to do is to offer and acknowledge these greetings as a matter of course. It costs you nothing and engenders goodwill on your behalf. It's just common courtesy to get something verbal going when you come into contact with someone—even if it is totally banal.

Small talk may not reveal your intellect,
but it does reveal your humanity.

Here's something very interesting about small talk in an elevator. As a new person gets on, she may make the slightest of accidental eye contact with someone, and she may say, "Good day." The recipient will then acknowledge the greeting with a minimal response: "Hello." And that's it until the elevator stops.

Now, observe: If there has been such an exchange, these two people will also say something as one of them exits the elevator, even if they are complete strangers to each other.

> *Have a good one.*
> *Take it easy.*
> *Enjoy the rest of your day.*

The door they knocked on ever so slightly was still open and needed closure. But if there hadn't been a "howdy" when one of them entered, there wouldn't have been a "so long!" when they exited. This is an example of the courtesies and rituals that characterize the first stages of chit-chat. It lays the foundation for further exchanges to ensue.

And this is why it is good practice to acknowledge people with some kind of greeting. A "hello" or "good day" will do. Even a nod and a grunt can register as an acceptable acknowledgment. Later on, you may find yourself nodding to each other going down the hall. You'll want that in your social pocket.

> *Oh yes! We ran into each other at the Fairmont, right? Allow me to*
> *introduce myself ...*

This could be the beginning of a relationship that can be useful to you.

Speaking of usefulness, people can have strong motives in initial conversational exchanges. We cannot characterize all of them as aimless, since there is an exploratory exchange going on. As an example, let's go to a commercial convention to observe some of the conversations going on.

On the convention floor:

> *Hello! I'm Joe Bailey with Lucky You! cosmetics. I've brought some product*
> *samples if you're interested. Perhaps you can visit our booth so I can get to*
> *know you better.*

Here, the greeting is the first face of networking, which is the social edge of marketing your business.

Now, at the bar:

> *Hey, baby! Can I buy you a drink? I'd like to get to know you better!*

Now Joe is chatting up a woman. His intention is clear, and it's not cosmetics. Again, it's the early negotiating phase of relationship building. If this phase of social conversation has you stymied, believe me, the Internet is full of advice for you, usually from young men who have all kinds of tricks up their sleeves to achieve success.

Both examples qualify as a subset of small talk but with the degree of intent as the variable. It's the invisible X factor behind the banalities in these early conversations—the sort-of hidden agenda—that supplies much of the discomfort and uncertainty.

The Serious Business of Gossip

MOM: Thumper, what did your father tell you?
THUMPER: "If you can't say something nice, don't say nothing at all."

Thumper's daddy probably also told him:

> Great minds discuss ideas.
> Average minds discuss events.
> Small minds discuss people.

Well, sorry, Thumper. Small-minded or not, we are all constantly talking about other people. And for good reason—what is more interesting than other people?

According to social psychologist Nicholas Emler of the London School of Economics, more than 80 percent of our small talk is about other specific and named individuals. In fact, evolutionary psychologist Robin Dunbar suggests that the evolution of human language was powerfully motivated by the need to gossip as a primary function. That is because gossip allows you to learn the lessons of your culture about what is acceptable and what is not, according to Daniel Menaker, the author of *A Good Talk: The Story and Skill of Conversation*. Gossip tells us:

> That neighbor is in need of some help.
> So-and-so is in line for a big promotion, but we're not supposed to know.
> That piano teacher was reeking of alcohol on his last home visit.

It's why most of this kind of small talk has to do with status change: Who's going up? Who's on the way down? And who's got a new Tesla?

Okay, so we understand its social regulation purpose, but why is gossip so delicious?

It's because the sharing of secrets gives you a taste of intimacy. It bestows a sense of "kindred souls," without which there is scant access to the inner thoughts and feelings that make our lives (and the lives of others) comprehensible, even to ourselves.

Gossip supplies facts that personal observation cannot. It is a form of small talk in that the process is more important than the substance. The sense of intimacy is paramount, and the shared information is incidental.

When you share a secret, you are making an effort to build a bridge to another person—a Them—so that they start feeling like an Us.

Gossip is respectable, universal, essential, and fun. It is the stuff of community.

**If you can't say something good about someone,
sit right here by me.**

Remind me to put that on a pillow.

Bibliography

Menaker, David. *A Good Talk: The Story and Skill of Conversation*. New York: Hachette Book Group, 2010.

Sapolsky, Robert M. *Behave: The Biology of Humans at Our Best and Worst*. New York: Penguin Press, 2017.

Vance, J. D. *Hillbilly Elegy: A Memoir of a Family and Culture in Crisis*. New York: HarperCollins, 2016.

Work-Life Issues

Caryn E. Medved; ed. Vernon D. Miller and Michael E. Gordon

Throughout the last four decades, work-life issues have attracted considerable media attention, corporate policy effort, and scholarly consideration. Many organizations have work-life policies and practices such as flextime, flex-place, part-time work, maternity and paternity leave, and eldercare or child care referral services. Still, impediments often exist to executive-level collaboration, managerial support, and implementation of work-life policies (Myers, Gaillaird, & Putnam, 2012; Ryan & Kossek, 2008). Different from most industrialized countries, minimal federal-level policy exists in the United States to aid individuals with caregiving responsibilities (Gornick & Myers, 2005). Thus, support with work-life conflicts in the United States primarily rests on employer accommodation and family or community assistance.

Human resource management (HRM) professionals must collaborate with executives, legal departments, management, employees, and, at times, unions to develop optimal solutions, even during difficult economic conditions (Galinsky & Bond, 2010). HRM departments are often responsible for developing work-life programs, gathering and sharing policy information, training or coaching employees, and managing related employee relations issues (Kossek, Bates, & Matthews, 2011). Although all these tasks require specific communication knowledge and skills, only a small but vital corpus of work-life communication research exists, little of which explicitly investigates the role of HRM in communicating effective work-life policies. The goal of this chapter is to bring research on work-life communication, as well as related communication theory and skills, together with the study and practice of HRM. To do so, relevant communication research is organized around three roles an HRM practitioner may play in relation to work-life policy issues: resource, coach, and strategist. In the following each role is explored by (a) detailing practitioner tasks and goals, (b) synthesizing existing communication research, and (c) identifying knowledge gaps critical to HRM research and practice. In closing, I propose a research agenda for scholars interested in further investigating the intersections among HRM, communication, and work-life policy, and I offer suggestions for HRM practice.

To achieve these goals, I weave three literatures together. The interdisciplinary work-life policy research is touched upon to situate the underlying HRM policy context (e.g., Kelly et al., 2008; Matos & Galinsky, 2012; Pitt-Catsouphes, Kossek, & Sweet, 2006). In addition, the small yet bourgeoning body of work-life communication research illustrates the centrality of messages, interaction, and language to successful work-life policy design and implementation (e.g., Hoffman & Cowan, 2008, 2010; Kirby & Krone, 2002; Medved, 2010; Miller, Jablin, Casey, Lamphear-Van Horn, & Ethington, 1996; Ryan & Kossek, 2008; Tracy & Rivera, 2010). Finally, HRM-related work-life communication research is extended and directions for future research forged through considering insights from previously unrelated studies of internal strategic communication planning (Welch & Jackson, 2005), information giving and seeking (Miller & Jablin, 1991; Rowan, 2003; Street, 2003), upward influence (e.g., Olufowote, Miller, & Wilson, 2005), and information richness (Daft & Lengel, 1984; Trevino, Daft, & Lengel, 1990), as well as gender and manager-employee negotiations (Babcock & Laschever, 2003; Meiners & Boster, 2012).

One additional prefatory remark is necessary. Conversations about communication and work-life issues must begin and end with issues of credibility. HRM must provide leadership that is honest, inspiring, and competent with respect to work-life issues (Kouzes & Posner, 2005; O'Keefe, 1990; Ulrich, 1998). To successfully create a supportive organizational work-life culture, HRM credibility must be established across relationships with various organizational stakeholders. Credibility with the C-suite gets HRM a seat at the decision-making table. HRM credibility also is important with midlevel managers, the gatekeepers of policy implementation (Peper, Den Dulk, & van Doorne-Huiskes, 2009). Finally, HRM must be perceived by employees as a credible source of information, advice, and conflict resolution regarding work-life issues. Balancing goodwill for employees' concerns with vital work unit and organizational outcomes is a difficult communicative dance (McCroskey & Teven, 1999). While few would argue with the value of credibility for the success of HRM work-life policies, research on how HRM professionals attain and maintain credibility is sorely needed.

Work-Life Policy: A (Very) Brief Introduction

In the 1980s, work-life initiatives (then labeled "work-family") emerged to attract and retain professional women in the workforce. These programs initially targeted high-performing women who were also mothers who struggled to manage both paid work and "second shift" family responsibilities (Hochschild, 1989). These initiatives over time broadened in scope, popularity, and inclusiveness. Men and women employees experience work-life conflict. Recently, men report increased rates of work-life conflict (Aumann, Galinsky & Matos, 2011; Williams, 2012).

HRM professionals must be knowledgeable about several pieces of legislation that affect both workers and employers in the United States. The Fair Labor Standards Act (1938) established the

40-hour workweek for nonexempt employees, guidelines for overtime pay, and federal minimum wage standards. The Pregnancy Discrimination Act (1978), an amendment to Title VII of the Civil Rights Act (1964), prohibits discrimination by mandating that employers provide pregnant women the same benefits offered other employees. Further, the Patient Protection and Affordable Care Act (2010) requires large employers to provide "appropriate breaks and locations so that working mothers covered by FLSA can pump breast milk" (Boushey, 2011, p. 171). The Family Medical Leave Act (FMLA, of 1993) is the only U.S. legislation designed explicitly to provide employee protection and employer guidance on family caregiving leave (see U.S. Department of Labor, 2013). HRM professionals in organizations employing 50 or more workers must be experts on the terms of the FMLA, including issues of employee eligibility, employer responsibility, documentation procedures, and state-level leave provisions.

Employer-sponsored work-life benefits take various forms. Some policies permit employees to vary work schedules and/or locations around caregiving duties (Galinsky, Sakai, & Wigton, 2011). Specific forms of workplace flexibility include the following: flextime (e.g., traditional flextime, daily flextime, compressed workweeks), reduced time (e.g., part-time work, part-year work), flex-leaves (time off during an individual day, illness time off, paid time off for child care, parental leave), flex-careers and flex-place (e.g., full-time telecommuting, hoteling; Friedman, 2002). Other work-life benefits include employment conditions (e.g., job design, terms of employment) along with organizational and professional cultures and norms (e.g., managerial support, face-time pressures; Kossek, 2005). Recently, benefits have been scrutinized in relation to being "single friendly"; i.e., attention now is being paid to the nonwork needs of employees without children (e.g., Casper, Weltman, & Swesiga, 2007).

Lastly, a strong business case exists for work-life programs and policies (e.g., A Better Balance, 2010; Council of Economic Advisors, 2010). Assisting employees with work-life balance is not only good for employees but also financially benefits the organization in terms of recruitment, retention, health care costs, and productivity. To illustrate, in a survey of 200 human resource managers, two-thirds of respondents identified family supportive policies as the single most important factor in attracting and retaining employees (Williams, 2000). Absenteeism attributed to family caregiving costs U.S. organizations more than $5 billion a year (MetLife, 2006), and 63% of workers using flexible work arrangements said they were absent less from work due to the availability of these policies (Flatley McGuire, Kenney, & Brashler, 2010). Further, work-life balance is the second best predictor, after economic security, of an employee's quality of health, frequency of sleep problems, and level of stress (Aumann & Galinsky, 2009). Finally, employees with access to flexible work schedules tend to have higher job satisfaction and appear to be more willing to work hard (Flatley McGuire et al., 2010).

HRM Work-Life and Communication

Work-life communication research may be organized around three communication roles HRM professionals play in the implementation of work-life policies: resource, coach, and strategist.

Resource

HRM professionals must serve as credible *sources of information* about a range of employment issues (e.g., benefits, compensation, recruitment, etc.). When HRM practitioners assume the work-life *resource* role, they must efficiently and effectively gather, monitor, and disseminate work-life policy information. At a basic level, serving as a resource involves creating awareness among stakeholder groups. HRM professionals as organizational resources must craft organization-wide messages regarding policy details, procedures, and vision. Indeed, credible HRM departments continuously gather and share information about the ever-changing external environment and employee needs (Ulrich, 1998).

Successful policy implementation includes "developing comprehensive and well-organized communication strategies with consistent messaging" (Boston College Center for Work & Family, 2008, p. 6). Effective communication about work-life programs is argued to "signal inclusion and employer caring by demonstrating that policies exist not merely as public relations vehicles" (Ryan & Kossek, 2008, p. 300). That is, the presence of work-life policies de facto has *symbolic value*. The empirical work of Casper and Harris (2008) found that the availability of work-life benefits influenced attachment of female employees to the organization *irrespective of actual policy use*. Conversely, ineffectively communicating about work-life programs limits employee awareness of policy availability and applicability (Christensen, 1999) and creates perceptions of exclusion (Ryan & Kossek, 2008).

Yet as evidenced by the scant organizational-level communication research, we know little about how HRM professionals strategically and effectively gather, monitor, and disseminate work-life information. Consequently, our attention now turns to knowledge gaps and connecting these openings to existing communication research. HRM professionals, for instance, often are charged with preparation of corporate messages for global employee populations or for various internal stakeholder groups (Welch & Jackson, 2007). Research does not exist exploring levels and/or forms of effective communication planning during policy implementation, although it is known that communication affects the acceptance of HRM and managerial innovation (Kossek, 1989). Fruitful investigation might explore the role of storytelling in creating work-life organizational change (Tucker, Yeow, & Viki, 2013) or ways that the media undermines or supports internal messaging about high-profile work-life issues. The recent media frenzy and fallout of Marissa Mayer's global "memo" sent to Yahoo employees about the elimination of all telecommuting only underscores the critical role that internal corporate communication plays in managing work-life initiatives (Kleinman, 2013).

Future research also might investigate questions such as, how should corporate messages be tailored to various employee groups in ways that facilitate uptake and inclusiveness (Welch & Jackson, 2007)? Or, how can communication about work-life programs strategically be used to externally shape corporate image (and, simultaneously, aid in employee recruitment) and internally create employee engagement (Cheney & Christensen, 2001; Saks, 2006)? Studies of communication during policy implementation could explore critical factors in success such as communication needs analysis, message timing, voice, and issue framing (Fairhurst, 2011).

After the announcements and kickoff events are over, HRM's role during the day-to-day management of work-life programs often is that of *informing* stakeholders about basic policy utilization rules and regulations. Informing is the provision of information that generally is not in dispute (Rowan, 2003). Effective explainers offer a variety of examples and counterexamples, encouraging learners to practice, and "communicate familiar but often misunderstood notions by explaining what these notions do not mean as well as what they do mean" (Rowan, 2003, p. 420). To date, investigations have yet to explore the information-giving skills of HRM professionals as well as the information needs of executives (as well as other stakeholders) faced with decisions about supporting work-life policy decisions (Tracy & Rivera, 2010). Existing studies on information giving, primarily conducted in the context of health communication research (e.g., Street, 2003), could be imported into the work-life policy context to provide directions for research to explore assessing the amount of information that executives want, gauging the amount of information that they already possess about work-life issues, and avoiding technical jargon that might alienate executives (Street, 2003). Researchers must also investigate policy implementation materials, including Web site FAQs and HRM handbook materials, in terms of effective information-giving strategies; information giving in the virtual and textual space also has important consequences for policy adoption (Cowan & Hoffman, 2008).

In addition to message content, HRM professionals also make decisions about ways of conveying information via communication technologies. When aiming to be a credible resource about work-life issues, HRM must consider the match between the nature of the information being conveyed and the richness of the communication channel (Daft & Lengel, 1984). Scant research explores Information Richness Theory in the context of new work-life policy adoption. Under what circumstances is lean media perhaps more or less effective during the implementation of a new work and family policy? Conversely, when is a rich media critical to new policy adoption by executives, managers, or employees? Thus, more extensive research on media preferences for communication about work-life policy also could help to inform media richness theory as well as HRM practice.

Coach

HRM professionals, at times, also *coach* managers on the front line of implementing flexibility programs. HRM coaching also assists employees with concerns about when and/or if to raise work-life conflict issues with supervisors (Liu & Buzzanell, 2004; Miller et al., 1996). Supervisory support from a psychological, rather than a communicative perspective often has been a focus of interdisciplinary work-life research (e.g., Thompson, Beauvais, & Lyness, 1999). We know that managerial support is critical to the success of work-family programs and/or policies. Supervisors and coworkers can either facilitate effective policy integration or become stumbling blocks to utilization (Fay & Kline, 2011; Kossek & Nichol, 1992).

A growing body of empirical research has begun to explore the role of communication in constructing managerial support across episodes of work-life conflict and leave negotiations (Buzzanell & Lui, 2007; Kirby, 2000; Kirby & Krone, 2002; Ter Hoeven, Miller, Den Dulk, & Peper, 2012), including the structuration of rules and resources embedded in employee requests for workplace accommodation (Hoffman & Cowan, 2010) and employee decision making about when to "speak up" in the workplace (Edmondson & Detert, 2005).

Kirby's (2000) study of the communication processes shaping work-life conflict and policy utilization at a governmental agency found that managerial support in practice is not simply an issue of management endorsement. Rather, subtle forms of contradictory and ambiguous communication, over and above individual managers' attitudes, shapes policy utilization, including coworker interaction (Fay & Kline, 2011; Kirby & Krone, 2002). Although complex, the central role of managerial communication still cannot be discounted. Peper and colleagues' (2009) case study of a Dutch bank reported, "It was managers who made the difference when it came to flexibility about the company's work-family" benefits (p. 123). Managers' decision making was, at times, perceived by some employees as arbitrary or contradictory.

Further, Ter Hoeven and colleagues (2012) identified four communication tensions inherent in work-life policy implementation, all of which touch on the manager-employee relationship: (a) policy exists but management discourages its use, (b) workplace culture supports policy implementation yet coworkers actively discourage use, (c) policy exists yet career and economic costs for employee negate uptake, and (d) managers want to facilitate use of policies yet workflow and productivity issues prevent their use. Extant research also shows that productivity pressures may discourage managerial approval for employee flexibility (Den Dulk & Ruijter, 2008). Managerial fears of losing control or lack of policy knowledge or resources also may create roadblocks (Boston College Center for Work & Family, 2008).

Workplace accommodation, as aptly noted by Hoffman and Cowan (2010), is not just a function of top-down HRM information dissemination but also immediately results from employee attempts at *upward influence*. Hoffman and Cowan found that employee appeals were made only after careful weighing of risk and were largely framed in terms of organizational, rather than personal, interests. Further, requests that centered on family-related conflicts, versus nonfamily issues, more often were made and supported. Edmondson and Detert (2005) support Hoffman and Cowan's work in their proposal that four conditions influence when an employee will decide to "speak up" or remain silent about work-life conflict: (a) feelings of psychological safety, (b) weighing the costs of anticipated gains, (c) motivations for speaking up, and (d) leadership behaviors.

In addition to identifying and interrogating manager-employee tensions and the nature of employee requests or reasons for speaking up, communication researchers have also *relationally* positioned policy implementation as "role negotiation" (Miller et al., 1996) and "conflict management" processes (Buzzanell & Liu, 2007). Miller and colleagues theorize maternity leave as a three-stage process of role negotiating. Their theoretical model posits antecedents, role negotiation attributes, and outcomes that comprise the role negotiation process. Buzzanell and Liu (2007) empirically explored maternity leave as a communicative process. In their exploration of interviews specifically with women who had been discouraged at the point of beginning their maternity leave, these authors identified three sets of discourses and practices that accounted for both the disparities between these women's expectations and experiences as well as related tensions. Overt, covert, and institutional discourses and practices all served to discourage the manager-employee negotiation process around maternity leave; in fact, many of these discouraged leave-takers expressed an inability or unwillingness to negotiate the details of their maternity leaves with their supervisors.

Future research should dig deeper into the range of successful to unsuccessful leave nego-tiations and the role of HRM in facilitating leave-taking conversations. In particular, what is the nature of paternity leave negotiations, reasons for lack of negotiations, and/or changing gendered assumptions affecting paternity leave requests? Further, although leader-member exchange (LMX) relationships and other structural and relational variables affect the nature of supervisor-employee negotiations (Meiners & Boster, 2012), no research exists about how LMX specifically affects maternity leave negotiation outcomes and/or satisfaction with outcomes. Finally, how might perceptions of gendered negotiation skills potentially influence outcomes (Babcock & Laschever, 2003)? We need to know more about how gender dynamics are operat-ing, and perhaps changing, in organizational communication about work-life accommodation.

High-intensity teleworkers typically enjoy flexible work arrangements, and this may contrib-ute to their greater satisfaction than office-based workers (Fronner & Roloff, 2010). We know little, however, about how HRM professionals effectively coach employees and managers to have effective conversations about performance in the context of telecommuting or job sharing (see Gordon & Miller, 2012), as well as how to facilitate meaningful and productive coworker interactions given that we know these relationships can be challenging (Fay & Kline, 2011).

Finally, studies could query under what circumstances HRM professionals serve as proactive coaches for managers and employees on work-life issues in comparison to situations in which they act as reactive conflict mediators. Knowing more about how HRM professionals fashion and carry out their work-life communication roles could help diagnose implementation chal-lenges and/or identify strengths (e.g., Pounsford, 2007). Wrench, McCroskey, Berletch, Powley, & Wehr (2008) suggest that organizational coaching is a form of instructional communication and propose to measure effective coaching with the perceived coaching scale. Do higher levels of perceived HRM coaching for either managers or employees relate to more effective work-life negotiations? What communication strategies do HRM professionals use, such as storytelling, in the context of work-life coaching interactions (Pounsford, 2007; Tucker et al., 2013)?

Strategist

The final role that HR professionals can play in the successful development and implementation of work-family policies and practices is to communicate at the strategic level. The *strategist* role allows HRM professionals to shift from a singular focus on specific HRM functions to assess how work-life issues integrate into larger organizational goals and plans. Being a strategist requires being invited to the executive decision-making table at the highest levels of the organization. Yet we know little about the communication aptitudes or skills of HRM professionals who are central to organizational decision making or how credibility is established by HRM at this level regarding work-life policy development.

The strategic level is often framed through the language of the "business case." This role for HRM professionals requires persuasively posing and answering the following question: *What critical business needs or problems can be addressed through work-life programs or initiatives?* To respond to this question, HRM professionals must be well versed in leadership goals and know how to frame work-life issues as solutions to key business problems (Fairhurst, 2011).

For instance, if turnover of highly talented women is a leadership concern, HRM can provide data and arguments about possible connections between these incidents of turnover and the availability (or, most likely, lack of availability) of work-life support. Thinking and communicating strategically demands engaging in four intersecting tasks across all organizational levels: assess, design, implement, and evaluate work-life policies (Boston College Center for Work & Family, 2008).

First, to work at the strategic level requires hard data. Assessment means gathering extensive information on various employee needs, communication climate, managerial relationships, performance, work design, technology, and industry best practice. Conducting a thorough work-life needs assessment is essential to policy design and to building support at the highest levels of the organization (Friedman & Galinsky, 1992). Research findings detailed in the previous sections can guide HRM professionals to broaden their scope of data collection to issues such as perceived coworker support (Fay & Kline, 2011), employee willingness to speak up about work-life conflict (Edmondson & Detert, 2005), and perception of current managerial attitudes toward requests (Hoffman & Cowan, 2010).

Second, even armed with high-quality data, strategic-level policy and program design is never easy. In addition to HRM outcomes such as retention and recruitment, design must also take into consideration the functionality of work-life programs vis-à-vis other business units' outcome measures such as those of operations, sales, and finance. Representatives from other business units must have a voice in work-life policy design, when appropriate. Little research exists about ways to effectively frame work-life policy initiatives across organizational units (Fairhurst, 2011). HRM professionals often must formulate internal communication plans for policy roll-outs and training as well as proactively address public relations issues. Limited communication research exists to provide HRM practitioners with assistance in the design phase and to connect to the literature on communication and organizational change (Deetz, Tracy, & Simpson, 1999).

Further research on designing communication aspects of new policy development might explore questions such as these: How do employees without children or significant eldercare responsibilities talk about their needs for personal accommodations (see Casper et al., 2007)? How do managers communicate in their workgroups about accommodations in ways that create a climate of perceived fairness? In addition, communication research also urges HRM professionals to question the very language of *flexibility*. Talking about work-life programs through the language of *adaptability* recently is argued to provide a more comprehensive approach to how "organizations and workers mutually adapt to each other's changing needs to benefit both the individuals and the institutions" (Myers, Gaillaird, & Putnam, 2012, p. 213).

After assessing and designing, execution of new strategic initiatives is the third stage the HRM work-life strategist faces. Four work-life policy attributes have been theorized to affect the success and inclusiveness of their implementation: supervisor support, universality, negotiability, and quality of communication (Ryan & Kossek, 2008). Existing communication research supports the criticality and tension-filled nature of supervisor support (Kirby, 2000; Ter Hoeven et al., 2012). Communication research is necessary to explore the attribute of negotiability: What is the nature of manager-employee negotiations and upward influence strategies during non-leave related work-life accommodations? What is the nature of employee information-seeking strategies in addition to direct supervisor requests (Miller & Jablin, 1991)?

Finally, measuring the impact of work-life programs is not easy, yet evaluation is essential to their ongoing realization and success. Evaluation of work-life policies and practices should be executed at the employee, managerial, workgroup, and organizational levels. To fully understand the impact of work-life programs as implied in the aforementioned research, it is essential to include evaluation metrics on the nature of and satisfaction with communication relationships, corporate messaging, and communication about flexibility programs. To date, no communication research focuses on developing metrics and assessment tools for program evaluation (e.g., Wrench et al., 2008). Scholars could make a contribution to practice by developing the tools and research to evaluate the communicative aspects of work-family programs.

An HRM Work-Life Communication Research Agenda

HRM professionals can play three critical communication roles in the design and implementation of work-life policies and programs: resource, coach, and strategist. Although in its infancy, the growing body of communication work-life research has much to offer the study and practice of HRM. Looking across the numerous and peripatetic threads of research initiated in the prior discussion, I close this chapter by prioritizing three future directions for communication scholarship related to HRM and work-life policy.

First, while communication scholars have begun to explore issues of maternity leave, managerial and coworker communication, work-family accommodation requests, and telecommuting, a wide range of work-life accommodation contexts and concepts remain unexplored. The full range of HRM related work-life communication issues sorely needs investigation, including, but not limited to, coworker communication in job-sharing relationships, performance appraisal conversations for telecommuting, coworker and managerial support for eldercare responsibilities, talk about domestic partnerships and gay/lesbian work-life conflicts, career counseling conversations around work-family issues, and workplace interactions between part-time and full-time employees. In short, only a handful of policy contexts comprising the communication HRM research agenda have been explored.

Second, most, if not all, of the communication research is woman and maternity centered. As noted at the outset of this chapter, gendered divisions of labor at home and in the workplace are changing (Medved & Rawlins, 2010). It is critical that the future research agenda not only broaden to explore the role of HRM in facilitating men's work-life balance, but also challenge the unitary categories of femininity and masculinity. As men continue to desire and take on more caregiving and domestic work at home, the workplace stereotypes of men as "ideal workers"—in other words, available to employers 24/7 without family responsibilities—continue to become less viable (Williams, 2000). Negotiations at home shape negotiations in the workplace, and future research must continue to connect both spheres of communication and relationships (Medved, 2004).

Finally, further investigation of communication and the construction of gender, race, and class are critical to HRM practices of work-life and are connected to issues of diversity. Most, if not all, communication work-life research focuses on the professional white-collar workplace. At the same time, low-income workers struggle in different, if not profoundly different, ways with managing caring and earning responsibilities (Council of Economic Advisors, 2010). If HRM professionals truly desire to create supportive work environments for all employees and to contribute to the bottom line of organizations, scholars interested in work-life issues of communication need to broaden their scope of investigation.

Bibliography

A Better Balance. (2010). *The business case for flexibility*. New York: A Better Balance.

Aumann, K., & Galinsky, E. (2009). *The state of health in the American workforce: Does having an effective workplace matter?* New York: Families and Work Institute.

Aumann, K., Galinsky, E., & Matos, K. (2011). *The new male mystique. National study of the changing workforce*. New York: Families and Work Institute.

Babcock, L., & Laschever, S. (2003). *Women don't ask: Negotiation and the gender divide*. Princeton, NJ: Princeton University Press.

Boston College Center for Work & Family. (2008). *Overcoming the implementation gap: How 20 leading companies are making flexibility work*. Boston: Boston College Center for Work & Family.

Boushey, H. (2011). The role of the government in work-family conflict. *Future of Children, 21*, 163–190.

Buzzanell, P.M., & Liu, M. (2007). It's "give and take": Maternity leave as a conflict management process. *Human Relations, 60*, 463–495.

Casper, W.J., & Harris, C. M. (2008). Work-life benefits and organizational attachment: Self-interest utility and signaling theory models. *Journal of Vocational Behavior, 72*(1), 95–109.

Casper, W.J., Weltman, D., & Swesiga, E. (2007). Beyond family friendly: The construct and measurement of singles-friendly work culture. *Journal of Vocational Behavior, 70*, 478–501.

Cheney, G., & Christensen, L. (2001). Organizational identity linkages between internal and external communication. In F. Jablin & L. Putnam (Eds.), *The new handbook of organizational communication: Advances in theory, research and method* (pp. 231–269). Thousand Oaks, CA: Sage.

Christensen, P. (1999). Toward a comprehensive work/life strategy. In S. Parasuraman & J. Greenhaus (Eds.), *Work and family: Challenges and choices for a changing world* (2nd ed., pp. 25–37). Westport, CT: Praeger.

Council of Economic Advisors. (2010). *Work-life balance and the economics of workplace flexibility*. Washington, DC: The White House.

Cowan, R.L., & Hoffman, M.F. (2008). The meaning of work/life: A corporate ideology of work/life balance. *Communication Quarterly, 56*, 227–246.

Daft, R.L., & Lengel, R.H. (1984). Information richness: A new approach to managerial behavior and organizational design. *Research in Organizational Behavior, 6*, 191–233.

Deetz, S.A., Tracy, S.J., & Simpson, J.L. (1999). *Leading organizations through transition: Communication and culture change.* Thousand Oaks, CA: Sage.

Dulk, L. Den, & Ruijter, J. de. (2008). Managing work-life policies: Disruption versus dependency arguments. *International Journal of Human Resource Management, 19*(7), 1222–1236.

Edmondson, A.C., & Detert, J. R. (2005). The role of speaking up in work-life balancing. In E. E. Kossek & S.J. Lambert (Eds.), *Work and life integration: Organizational, cultural and individual perspectives* (pp. 381–406). Mahwah, NJ: Taylor & Francis.

Fairhurst, G.T. (2011). *The power of framing: Creating the language of leadership.* San Francisco, CA: Jossey-Bass.

Fay, M.J., & Kline, S.L. (2011). Co-worker relationships and informal communication in high-intensity telecommuting. *Journal of Applied Communication Research, 39*, 144–163.

Flatley McGuire, J., Kenney, K., & Brashler, P. (2010). *Flexible work arrangements: The fact sheet.* Washington, DC: Georgetown University Law Center. Retrieved from: http://scholarship.law.georgetown.edu/legal/.

Friedman, D.E. (2002). *Workplace flexibility: A guide for companies.* New York: Families and Work Institute.

Friedman, D.E., & Galinsky, E. (1992). Work and family issues: A legitimate business case. In S. Zedeck (Ed.), *Work, families and organizations: Frontiers of industrial and organizational psychology* (pp. 168–207). San Francisco, CA: Jossey-Bass.

Fronner, K.L., & Roloff, M.E. (2010). Why teleworkers are more satisfied with their jobs than are office-based workers: When less contact is beneficial. *Journal of Applied Communication Research, 38*, 336–361.

Galinsky, E., & Bond, J.T. (2010). *The impact of the recession on employers.* New York: Families and Work Institute. Retrieved from http://familiesandwork.org/site/research/reports/Recession2009.pdf.

Galinsky, E., Sakai, K., & Wigton, T. (2011). Workplace flexibility: From research to action. *Future of Children, 21*, 141–161.

Gordon, M.E., & Miller, V.D. (2012). *Conversations about job performance: A communication perspective on the appraisal process.* New York: Business Expert Press.

Gornick, J.C., & Meyers, J.C. (2005). *Families that work: Policies for reconciling parenthood and employment.* New York: Russell Sage.

Hochschild, A.R. (1989). *The second shift.* New York: Avon Books.

Hoffman, M.F., & Cowan, R.L. (2008). The meaning of work/life: A corporate ideology of work/life balance. *Communication Quarterly, 56*(2), 227–246.

Hoffman, M.F., & Cowan, R.L. (2010). Be careful what you ask for: Structuration theory and work/life accommodation. *Communication Studies, 61*, 205–223.

Kelly, E.L., Kossek, E.E., Hammer, L.B., Durham, M., Bray, J., Chermack, K., Murphy, L.A., & Kaskubar, D. (2008). Getting there from here: Research on the effect of work-family initiatives on work-family conflict and business outcomes. *Academy of Management Annals, 2*, 305–349.

Kirby, E.L. (2000). Should I do as you say or as you do?: Mixed messages about work and family. *Electronic Journal of Communication, 10.* Retrieved from www.cios.org.remote.baruch.cuny.edu/EJCPUBLIC/010/3/010313.html.

Kirby, E.L., & Krone, K.J. (2002). "The policy exists but you can't really use it": Communication and the structuration of work-family policies. *Journal of Applied Communication Research, 30,* 50–77.

Kleinman, A. (2013, April 19). Marissa Mayer finally addresses work from home ban. *Huffington Post.* Retrieved from www.huffingtonpost.com/2013/04/19/marissa-mayer-work-from-home_n_3117352.html.

Kossek, E.E. (1989). The acceptance of human resource innovations by multiple stakeholders. *Personnel Psychology, 47*(2), 263–281.

Kossek, E.E. (2005). Workplace policies and practices to support work and families: Gaps in implementation and linkages to individual and organizational effectiveness. In S. Bianchi, L. Casper, & R. King (Eds.), *Work, family health and well-being* (pp. 97–116). Mahwah, NJ: Lawrence Erlbaum Associates.

Kossek, E.E., Bates, B.B., & Matthews, R.A. (2011). How work-family research can finally have an impact in organizations. *Industrial & Organizational Psychology, 4*(3), 352–369.

Kossek, E.E., & Nichol, V. (1992). The effects of on-site childcare on employee attitudes and performance. *Personnel Psychology, 45,* 485–509.

Kouzes, J.M., & Posner, B.Z. (2005). Leading in cynical times. *Journal of Management Inquiry, 14,* 357–364.

Liu, M., & Buzzanell, P. M. (2004). Negotiating maternity leave expectations: Perceived tensions between ethics of justice and care. *Journal of Business Communication, 41*(4), 323–349.

Matos, K., & Galinsky, E. (2012). *National study of employers.* New York: Families and Work Institute.

McCroskey, J.C., & Teven, J.J. (1999). Goodwill: A reexamination of the construct and its measurement. *Communication Monographs, 66,* 90–103.

Medved, C.E. (2004). The everyday accomplishment of work and family: Exploring practical actions in daily routines. *Communication Studies, 55,* 1–45.

Medved, C.E. (2010). Work and family communication. In S. Sweet & J. Casey (Eds.), *Work and family encyclopedia.* Chestnut Hill, MA: Sloan Work and Family Research Network. Retrieved from http://workfamily.sas.upenn.edu/wfrn-repo/object/3kb6k5cb4ft79l8c.

Medved, C.E., & Rawlins, W. K. (2010). At-home fathers and breadwinning mothers: Varieties in constructing work and family lives. *Women & Language, 34,* 9–39.

Meiners, E.B., & Boster, F.J. (2012). Integrative process in manager-employee negotiations: Relational and structural factors. *Journal of Applied Communication Research, 40,* 208–228.

MetLife (2006, July). *The MetLife caregiving costs study: Productivity losses to U.S. Businesses.* Westport, CT: MetLife Mature Market Institute and National Alliance for Caregiving. Retrieved from www.metlife.com/assets/cao/mmi/publications/studies/mmi-caregiver-cost-study-productivity.pdf.

Miller, V.D., & Jablin, F.M. (1991). Information seeking during organizational entry: Influences, tactics, and a model of the process. *Academy of Management Review, 16,* 92–120.

Miller, V.D., Jablin, F.M., Casey, M.K., Lamphear-Van Horn, M., & Ethington, C. (1996). The maternity leave as a role negotiation process. *Journal of Managerial Issues, 8,* 286–309.

Myers, K.K., Gaillaird, B.M., & Putnam, L.L. (2012). Reconsidering the concept of workplace flexibility: Is adaptability a better solution. In C. Salmon (Ed.), *Communication yearbook, 36* (pp. 195–230). Mahwah, NJ: Taylor & Francis.

O'Keefe, D.J. (1990). *Persuasion: Theory and research.* Los Angeles, CA: Sage.

Olufowote, J.O., Miller, V.D., & Wilson, S.R. (2005). The interactive effects of role change goals and relational exchanges on employee upward influence tactics. *Management Communication Quarterly, 18*(3), 385–403.

Peper, B., Den Dulk, L., & van Doorne-Huiskes, A. (2009). Work-family policies in a contradictory culture: A Dutch financial sector corporation. In S. Lewis, J. Brannen, & A. Nilson (Eds.), *Work, families, and organisations in transition: European perspectives* (pp. 113–128). Bristol: Policy Press.

Pitt-Catsouphes, M., Kossek, E.E., & Sweet, S. (Eds.) (2006). *The work and family handbook: Multidisciplinary perspectives, methods, and approaches.* Mahwah, NJ: Lawrence Erlbaum Associates.

Pounsford, M. (2007). Using storytelling, conversation and coaching to engage: How to initiate meaningful conversations inside your organization. *Strategic Communication Management, 11,* 32–35.

Rowan, K.E. (2003). Informing and explaining skills: Theory and research on informative communication. In J.O. Greene & B. Burleson (Eds.), *Handbook of communication and interaction skills* (pp. 403–438). Mahwah, NJ: Lawrence Erlbaum Associates.

Ryan, A.M., & Kossek, E.E. (2008). Work-life policy implementation: Breaking down or creating barriers to inclusiveness. *Human Resource Management, 47*(2), 295–310.

Saks, A.M. (2006). Antecedents and consequences of employee engagement. *Journal of Managerial Psychology, 21,* 600–619.

Street, R.L. (2003). Interpersonal communication skills in health care contexts. In J.O. Greene & B.R. Burleson (Eds.), *Handbook of communication and social interaction skills* (pp. 909–935). Mahwah, NJ: Lawrence Erlbaum Associates.

Ter Hoeven, C.L., Miller, V., Den Dulk, L., & Peper, B. (2012, May). *"The work must go on": The role of employee and managerial discourse in the implementation and restriction of work-life policy use.* Paper presented at the International Communication Association's 62nd Annual Conference, Phoenix, AZ.

Thompson, C.A., Beauvais, L.L., & Lyness, K.S. (1999). When work-family benefits are not enough: The influence of work-life culture, benefit utilization, organizational attachment, and work-life conflict. *Journal of Vocational Behavior, 54,* 392–415.

Tracy, S.J., & Rivera, K.D. (2010). Endorsing equity and applauding stay-at-home moms: How male voices on work-life reveal aversive sexism and flickers of transformation. *Management Communication Quarterly, 24,* 3–43.

Trevino, L.K., Daft, R.L., & Lengel, R.H. (1990). Understanding managers' media choices: A symbolic interactionist perspective. In J. Fulk & C. Steinfeld (Eds.), *Organizations and communication technology* (pp. 71–94). Newbury Park, CA: Sage.

Tucker, D.A., Yeow, P., & Viki, G.T. (2013). Communicating during organizational change using social accounts: The importance of ideological accounts. *Management Communication Quarterly, 27,* 184–209.

Ulrich, R. (1998). *Delivering results: A new mandate for human resource professionals.* Cambridge, MA: Harvard Business Review Press.

U.S. Department of Labor. (2013). *Wage and hour division: Family medical leave act.* Retrieved from http://www.dol.gov/whd/fmla/.

Welch, M., & Jackson, P.R. (2007). Rethinking internal communication: A stakeholder approach. *Corporate Communications, 12,* 177–198.

Williams, J.C. (2000). *Unbending gender: Why work and family conflict and what to do about it.* New York: Oxford University Press.

Williams, J.C. (2012). *Reshaping the work-family debate: Why men and class matter.* Cambridge, MA: Harvard University Press.

Wrench, J.S., McCroskey, J.C., Berletch, N., Powley, C., & Wehr, A. (2008). Organizational coaching as instructional communication. *Human Communication, 11,* 279–292.

SECTION SIX

MANAGING CONFLICT AND INCIVILITY FOR POSITIVE RELATIONSHIPS

Regardless of the industry or position, conflict is an omnipresent feature of the workplace. How we address conflict as employees, coworkers, and managers affects workplace environments in a multiplicity of ways. Conflict often reduces workplace satisfaction and productivity. Yet "conflict" can illuminate flaws in proposals and foster new approaches. The key lies in actively working to reduce *negative conflict*, such as bullying, and capitalize on the potential of conflict to advance progress toward workplace goals. Wiedmer contextualizes the challenges of conflict with a discussion of workplace bullying. While much attention over the last few years has highlighted bullying in schools and on social media, the same dynamics of bullying have persisted in the workplace for generations. Wiedmer gives specific attention to the role of employers in managing this specific manifestation of negative conflict. Hynes situates conflict as a distinctly communicative challenge and outlines five central strategies to manage conflict within given workplace roles. Finally, Porath, Foulk, and Erez take the research of the other two articles into consideration in denoting incivility as a form of everyday communication. Their research fills in some of the gaps within workplace conflict research to explain *why* incivility and other forms of conflict undermine factors such as job satisfaction and productivity. Together, these articles offer greater awareness of how conflict operates, its hidden costs, and pathways to maximize productive organizational and interpersonal relationships.

167

Consider the following questions when reading this section:

1. What might workplace bullying look like in practice? How do we know this is "bullying"?
2. What is the most important step employers might take to *proactively* reduce workplace bullying?
3. What factors determine the difference between *constructive* and *destructive* conflict?
4. Think about a conflict you have had in a workplace environment. Which strategy did you utilize to manage the conflict? What do you find to be the best means by which to approach possible negotiations in your target future workplace?
5. What are some of the hidden or lesser-known costs of workplace incivility, and how might we address these specific costs?
6. How might we address workplace incivility? How do these fit with those described by Wiedmer?

Key Terms and Concepts

- Bullying
- Conflict
- Accommodating
- Avoiding
- Compromising
- Forcing
- Collaborating
- Civility/incivility
- Cognitive resources

Workplace Bullying

Costly and Preventable

Terry L. Wiedmer

Workplace bullying is a pervasive practice by malicious individuals who seek power, control, domination, and subjugation. In businesses or schools, such bullying is an inefficient way of working that is both costly and preventable. Senior management and executives are ultimately responsible for creating and sustaining bully-free workplaces. Workplace bullies can be stopped if employees and employers work together to establish and enforce appropriate workplace policies and practices. This article presents information about workplace bullying, including its prevalence, targeted individuals, bullying behaviors, employer practices, and steps to prevent bullying. In the end, leadership and an environment of respect provide the ultimate formula for stopping workplace bullying.

Bullying occurs between and among people in all venues—in the home, community, and workplace. It is a pervasive, targeted, and planned effort that can be overtly obvious or can fly under the radar and is conducted by practiced and malicious individuals who seek power, control, domination, and subjugation. The impacts of such actions—in terms of finances, emotions, health, morale, and overall productivity—are destructive, and the ramifications are limitless (Mattice, 2009). Because no one is immune from the potential of being subjected to bullying in the workplace, this topic merits further review and analysis (Van Dusen, 2008).

To combat workplace bullying, often referred to as psychological harassment or violence (Workplace Bullying Institute [WBI], 2007), employers must have a full range of policies in place and means available to them to create and maintain a healthy workplace culture and climate. Although they are not generally for-profit endeavors, schools and school systems are purposeful businesses that share the same concerns and have the same responsibility to ensure that each employee works in a respectful environment and is not subjected to workplace bullies.

Workplace Bullying

According to the Workforce Bullying Institute (WBI), workplace bullying is

> the repeated, health-harming mistreatment of one or more persons (the targets) by one or more perpetrators that takes one or more of the following forms: verbal abuse; offensive conduct/behaviors (including nonverbal) which are threatening, humiliating, or intimidating; and work interference—sabotage—which prevents work from getting done. (Definition of Workplace Bullying, para. 1)

Bullies seek to induce harm, jeopardize one's career and job, and destroy interpersonal relationships. The behaviors of bullies harm people and ravage profits.

Prevalence of Workplace Bullying

Thirty-seven percent of U.S. workforce members report being bullied at work; this amounts to an estimated 54 million Americans, which translates to nearly the entire population of the states of Washington, Oregon, California, Nevada, Arizona, and Utah (Namie, 2007). These statistics are based on the August 2007 responses of 7,740 participants in the online WBI-Zogby U.S. Workplace Bullying Survey; the respondents comprised a sample representative of all American adults. The WBI-Zogby survey is the largest scientific study of bullying in the United States. Other key and depressing findings of the 2007 study included the following:

- Most bullies are bosses (72%);
- 60% of bullies are men;
- 57% of targets are women;
- Bullying is four times more prevalent than illegal forms of harassment;
- 62% of employers ignore or worsen the problem;
- 45% of targets suffer stress-related health problems;
- 40% of bullied individuals never tell their employers; and
- Only 3% of bullied people file lawsuits. (WBI, Key Findings, para. 2)

These workplace bullying activities resulted in the targets reporting stress-related health problems such as debilitating anxiety, panic attacks, clinical depression, and even post-traumatic stress (WBI).

Another significant finding of the WBI-Zogby survey was that, in 72% of cases, bullies had control over the targets' livelihood and consequently used this leverage to inflict pain or to block transfers, thus forcing employees to quit or lose their jobs (Namie, 2007). In addition to having to leave a job or a profession of choice, other reported economic impacts imposed by bullies included the target being forced to transfer (13%), being discharged without reasonable cause (24%), and quitting to address a decline in health and sanity (40%) (Namie, 2007). Controlling bullies seek to make targets resign, which results in unemployment, loss of health insurance, and the inability to seek medical attention. Accordingly, the bottom line is that all members of society pay for the consequences of unacceptable workplace behaviors and practices. According to the WBI, workplace bullying is thus a silent epidemic.

Profiles of Targets

The WBI (2007) reported that 61% of bullying occurs within the same gender, and 71% of female bullies target other women. In 2000, a WBI study found that veteran employees—often the best and brightest, not the weakest—are often selected to be targets (WBI, 2010). Bullies typically target individual(s) they perceive to pose a threat. Skilled targets are often sabotaged by insecure bully bosses who take credit for the work of the targets, who are thus not recognized or rewarded for their talents and contributions.

Based on findings from thousands of interviews in 2000, the WBI researchers confirmed workplace bullies typically target independent employees who refuse to be subservient. Furthermore, in 2010 WBI confirmed that targets were typically more technically skilled than the bullies and that they were the "go to" veteran employees from whom new workers sought guidance. Collectively, the targets were reportedly better liked, had more social skills, likely possessed higher emotional intelligence, and were appreciated by colleagues, customers, and management (bullies excluded) for the warmth and care they brought to the workplace (WBI, Who Gets Targeted). The principal weapons that bullying bosses and coworkers reportedly employed were alienating these targets from social interaction and withholding validation. As a result, coworkers often chose to separate themselves from the target out of fear of being the next victims (WBI, 2010).

Ethics and honesty are attributes often commonly possessed by targets. In particular, whistle blowers who expose illegal or fraudulent behaviors are most vulnerable to being bullied. Targets can be typified as morally superior to bullies due to their generally nonconfrontational, prosocial orientation focused on a desire to help, heal, teach, develop, and nurture others (Namie, 2007).

Practices of Employers and the Rights and Responsibilities of Targets

Employers have a moral and social responsibility to protect employees from bullying and to safeguard those who comprise their workforce. Employees need to be aware of bullying practices and knowledgeable about their rights and responsibilities, but ultimately managers and supervisors are the key players who are responsible for building and maintaining healthy and bully-free work cultures. When managers and supervisors commit time and effort to talk with their employees about the ecology of relationships in the workplace, employees better understand what factors foster the evolution of bullying. Such conversations can aid in policy refinement, improved employee guidance, and professional-development initiatives that contribute to a healthy and bully-free workplace.

Employees deserve and should be assured their place of employment is one where respect and civility prevail. Managers, supervisors, and other identified leaders of employees need to be foot soldiers to lead the fight against bullying—to identify bullies, to protect the bullied, and to intervene and stop bullying behaviors (Namie, 2007). Employees need to feel physically, emotionally, and socially safe and to believe they are valued and belong.

Practices of Bullies

Bullying is typically a series of calculated incidents that accumulate over time, carefully planned and executed by the bully to avoid legal grounds for grievance or disciplinary actions (Bully Online). Bullies may engage in some or all of the following behaviors toward their target(s):

- consciously undermine the position, status, worth, value, and potential;
- marginalize, ignore, overrule, and freeze out;
- set unrealistic (and even undesirable) goals, timelines, and expectations;
- distort, misrepresent, and twist anything said or done;
- single out, treat one differently from others, or ostracize;
- increase responsibility and simultaneously reduce authority;
- overload with work or have work taken away to trivialize existence;
- deny leave, even when provided for contractually;
- steal or plagiarize work and take credit for it;
- deny opportunities for training that are requisite for job performance; and
- coerce into leaving (constructive dismissal) through no fault of the target and activate early or ill-health retirement (Bully Online, para. 2).

Profile of the Typical Workplace Bully

Bullies engage in predictable and recurring practices to debase and debilitate their targets (Bully Online). Individuals who engage in such uncivil and amoral workplace bullying tactics demonstrate common elements and behaviors. Are any of these behaviors evident in your workplace? If so, you, too, may be subject to potentially being bullied. Workplace bullies often

- possess a Jekyll and Hyde nature (vindictive in private but charming in public);
- display self-assuredness and certitude to mask insecurity;
- portray self as wonderful, kind, caring, and compassionate, but actual behaviors contradict this self-crafted persona;

- cannot distinguish between leadership and bullying behaviors;
- counterattack and deny everything when asked to clarify;
- manipulate others through guilt;
- are obsessed with controlling others;
- use charm and behave in an appropriate manner when superiors or others are present;
- are convincing and compulsive liars in order to account for matters at hand; and
- excel at deception, lack a conscience, and are dysfunctional (Bully Online, para. 3).

At times every employee may demonstrate one or more of these behaviors. The key, however, is to monitor whether or not the behaviors are recurring and predictable with an intended outcome to cause harm. The target must document and record accurately when suspected bullying occurs should a need arise to stop bullying behaviors.

Stopping Bullying

To stop bullying in the workplace requires time, input, policy changes, and a company culture that does not tolerate bullies. To help managers and supervisors maintain a civilized workforce and handle bullying, Alsever (2008) outlined and recommended the following five-step process: (a) understand what constitutes bullying and recognize it in action, (b) act fast to show that the company will not tolerate bad behavior, (c) enforce a clear action plan, (d) devise a policy for a civilized workplace, and (e) screen for bullies in the recruiting process.

Serial violators need to be identified and stopped in their tracks. Policies, rules, and practices must be in place to make workplaces safe and conducive to workers producing at peak levels. Bullying hurts the bottom line through lost productivity, low morale, the departure of experienced workers, and higher health care costs for stressed-out victims (Ceridian Services, 2008, para. 12).

Chief executive officers, including school superintendents, can ill afford to mislead their supervisors, managers, and human resource personnel about the level of bullying in their workplaces. Efforts to cover up bullying may include no reporting, under-reporting, leveling no punishment, dismissal of the bullied, and promotion of the bully (WBI, How Bullying Happens). Left unaddressed, bullying can rapidly evolve into a serious workplace health issue.

Steps to Take

To reduce workplace bullying effectively, employees need to know that they are supported. The bottom line is that the employer's return on investment is dependent on the work produced in the workplace. If work is not completed successfully in a business, finances will suffer and the losses will inspire management to make adjustments. If workers in schools and school systems cannot be productive because of workplace bullying, the bottom line of student achievement is impacted. Thus, employers and school leaders need to take positive steps to address bullying with commitment and intensity.

First, put a policy in place. Second, address directly any reported or suspected bullying—regardless of who is reported. Third, identify resources and solutions and make them available to remedy a suspected problem. Those who manage and supervise employees ultimately represent and enforce workplace policies. They need to be competent and proactive in employee rights, as well as engage in leadership behaviors that create and enforce bully-free environments.

Put a Policy in Place

Workplace policies and procedures for addressing bullying may include disciplinary and legal consequences, additional supervision and oversight, training or counseling, and relationship-building activities. An extremely important aspect of policy and procedure is to have clear, detailed, and accurate documentation. Once reported, bullying incidents should be monitored and tracked over time to chronicle the incident reportage, steps taken, outcomes realized, and effectiveness of strategies employed. By tracking instances of transgression, employers can use the information gained to formulate preventative measures, identify alternative interventions, and guide professional development for all employees.

Employees and supervisors need to be aware of the most up-to-date policies and practices to ensure report assessment and implementation of appropriate actions. Timely implementation of policies is critical to initiate intervention, alert the parties involved, bring attention to the matter, monitor the situation, and address underlying, contributing problems. In extreme cases, it may be necessary to involve law enforcement officials.

Positive and trusting relationships among adults and the knowledge that a concern will be taken seriously are critical components to preventing and remedying bullying.

As part of policy, employers should incorporate regular and ongoing climate assessments for all employees in order to record their perceptions of workplace bullying, and the results of these assessments should be made public. Recognizing their responsibility to stop and prevent bullying, employers must ensure that policies are clearly outlined to mandate that managers and supervisors not only report bullying acts but also work quickly to protect bullied employee(s) from retaliation and further harm while resolving the situation.

Address Reported or Suspected Bullying Directly

A tremendous disconnect often occurs between what employees and employers believe to be the existence and degree of workplace bullying. To resolve this discrepancy, or at least narrow the divide, employers must encourage and enable all members of the workforce to report possible bullying incidents in a timely manner and, even more importantly, ensure an expeditious, fair, and ethical review and evaluation of suspected bullying incidences. They cannot allow a code of silence—often prevalent in bullying cases—to exist. Positive and trusting relationships among adults and the knowledge that a concern will be taken seriously are critical components to preventing and remedying bullying.

Employees must be able to go to a person(s) who can be trusted and who will respond to the matter in a concerned, proactive, and supportive way. Having such a trusted individual is key, because all too often the bully is the supervisor. In the case of schools, employee options may include going to a department chairperson, principal, human resource officer, or the superintendent. Multiple avenues are necessary if the bullying is endemic, or it will be nearly impossible to achieve recourse and resolution. Friends and coworkers of bullied individuals need to feel free and safe to speak up when they witness bullying behaviors, and employers have a responsibility to support employees in identifying and resolving troublesome behaviors without violence. Workplace cultural norms can either foster or eliminate bullying, depending on how superiors react to supported or suspected incidents. In short, unless actions are taken to address the underlying work culture and climate conditions that precipitated or allowed for bullying, such behaviors will continue.

Even more importantly, employers must carefully guard workplace climate by recognizing that bullying seldom occurs in isolation. Aggressive or bullying individuals typically seek out and befriend like individuals. When managers and supervisors model bullying behavior in the workplace, they unfortunately serve to normalize workplace-bullying behaviors. In such settings, when the managers or supervisors are the perpetrators and when they ignore or minimize the situation, employees report a diminished allegiance to and effort expended in their workplaces. Similarly, managers and supervisors are often less proactive and persistent in addressing and resolving bullying behavior among employees when human resource managers and chief executive officers are less focused on enforcing policies.

Identify Resources and Solutions

Employee training and awareness of anti-bullying policies and procedures that comprehensively address the issue of workplace bullying are key. The message must be clear wherever bullying behavior may occur—the office, lunchroom, parking lot, classroom, assembly line, cell phone, or the Internet—**it will not be tolerated**. Employers must establish and publicize systems to support employees and to address bullying behaviors and interpersonal conflicts. For example, rather than fighting, shutting down, or giving in to a bully, targets need to stay engaged and do their work. They need to maintain a calm and professional demeanor, remain engaged and focused, and plan ahead to deescalate a situation before it occurs (Ross, 2007–2009). The success of the school or business depends on all employees knowing where they can go for assistance and on their learning and practicing necessary skills to address workplace bullying.

A Respectful Workplace

Cade (2010), a workplace-bullying expert, identified three things leaders can do to create a respectful workplace where bullying is not allowed to exist: (a) show appreciation, (b) treat employees like insiders, and (c) demonstrate empathy for problems. She further suggested that bullying rarely exists when all workers honor each other as valuable; treat one another with dignity; communicate to include, not exclude or control; are heard by another and respond with courtesy and curiosity; acknowledge thoughts and feelings; ask—do not order or yell or swear; provide clear and informative answers to questions that are legitimately their business; know the right to receive encouragement and support; speak of others positively; and seek to connect and build communication for all parties as opposed to positioning for control (Cade, 2010, para. 2).

Everyone's Responsibility

Elimination of workplace bullying is the responsibility of all employees; however, senior management and executives are ultimately responsible for creating and sustaining bully-free workplaces. In school settings, key leaders such as superintendents, human resource officers, principals, supervisors, and department heads must guide the educational workforce to recognize and report bullying within their ranks. By launching united efforts, defining and implementing clear policies, putting model practices in place, and having the courage to stand up against bullies, individuals in all lines of work can stop workplace bullying. The simple formula of combining leadership with an environment of respect will contribute to the well-being of all employees and make an improved and healthy work climate and culture a reality.

References

Alsever, J. (2008, October 20). *How to handle a workplace bully*. Retrieved from http://www.bnet.com/article/how-to-handle-a-workplace-bully/242687

Bully Online. *United Kingdom National Workplace Bullying Advice Line*. Retrieved from http://www.bullyonline.org/workbully/amibeing.htm

Cade, V. (2010, July 7). *10-point assessment: What is respect?* Retrieved from http://www.bully-freeatwork.com/blog/?p=1289

Ceridian Services. (2008, August). The workplace bully and the bottom line. *Ceridian Connection*. Retrieved from http://www.ceridian.com/eap_article/1,6266,15757-69778,00.html

Mattice, C. (n.d.) What is workplace bullying? *No Workplace Bullies*. Retrieved from http://noworkplacebullies.com/

Mattice, C. (2009). *Successful learning organizations understand the power of positive workplaces*. Retrieved from http://noworkplacebullies.com/yahoo_site_admin/assets/docs/Kirkpatrick_Article.36120227.pdf

Namie, G. (2007, September). Workplace Bullying Institute & Zogby International. *U.S. Workplace Bullying Survey* [Electronic Version]. Retrieved from http://www.workplacebullying.org/docs/WBIsurvey2007.pdf

Ross, M. (2007–2009). *Workplace bullies: How to best the business bullies*. Retrieved from http://www.Kamaron.org/Dealing-With-The-Business-Customer-Bullies

VanDusen, A. (2008, March). *Ten signs you're being bullied at work*. Retrieved from http://forbes.com/2008/03/22/health-bullying-office-forbeslife-cx_avd_0324health.html

Workplace Bullying Institute. *Definition of workplace bullying*. Retrieved from http://www.workplacebullying.org/targets/problem/definition.html

Workplace Bullying Institute. *How bullying happens*. Retrieved from http://www.workplacebullying.org/targets/problem/why-bullies-bully.html

Workplace Bullying Institute. *Who gets targeted*. Retrieved from http://www.workplacebullying.org/targets/problem/who-gets-targeted.html

Workplace Bullying Institute. (2007). *Results of the WBI U.S. Workplace Survey*. Retrieved from http://www.workplacebullying.org/docs/WBIsurvey2007.pdf

Workplace Bullying Institute. (2010). *Frequently asked questions*. Retrieved from http://www.workplacebullying.org/faq.html

Strategies for Managing Conflict

Geraldine Hynes

"Getting it done" is all about daily workplace interactions. Continuing our examination of tough communication challenges that you face every day, this chapter looks at conflict. Included are strategies for managing clashes between you and your boss, you and your coworkers, and you and your subordinates.

We'll first distinguish between destructive and constructive conflict; you may be surprised to learn that conflict can benefit you and your company. Then we'll peek behind the curtain to learn why conflict is always such a strong presence, especially in diverse workplaces. Finally, and probably most important to you, we'll show you five strategies for dealing with conflict and explain when each one works best.

Tensions can run high at work. As a manager, you are likely to spend up to 35 percent of your time dealing with complaints and handling disruptions in your fast-paced, diverse work environment.[1] Conflict may range from a simple disagreement over a work procedure to an argument over priorities, to a work stoppage, and even to violence. The incidence of workplace violence continues to increase at an alarming rate. Violence is the number one cause of death on the job for women, and the number two cause for men. It's a manager's duty to protect workers from violence by developing intervention efforts.

When is conflict beneficial and when is it harmful? What causes conflict, anyway? What methods can you use to resolve conflict? Is any single method best? The following discussion answers these questions.

Pros and Cons of Workplace Conflict

Conflict generally is considered a negative influence that is destructive; however, it can be a positive influence if you manage it properly. Conflict forces you to analyze goals, it creates dialogue among employees, and it fosters creative solutions. It has been linked to organizational learning, and even to improved performance and productivity. Without conflict, employees and organizations would stagnate.

Conflict between diverse age groups is one example of how conflict can be positive. For the first time in U.S. history, four generations are working together. Conflict commonly is due to differences in their work style and philosophy. Older workers view "work" as a place—a location you go to at a specified time, such as 9 a.m. to 5 p.m. Younger workers tend to view "work" as something you do—anywhere, any time. They grew up in a digital world where information is always available. So it's easy for Boomers to conclude that Millennials who arrive at 9:30 a.m. are working less hard than they, who arrived at 8:30 a.m., not realizing that the younger generation may have already put in time at their home computers or smartphones while still in pajamas. To Millennials, rigid scheduling of work is unnecessary. Boomers can benefit from their younger coworkers by learning that much of today's work can be done in flextime for maximum efficiency.

Conflict may also foster creativity. It helps to overcome biases by forcing you out of your traditional ways of thinking. In this way, conflict promotes the unstructured thinking that lets you develop good, novel alternatives to difficult problems.[2]

In addition, decisions are better when there is open opposition and resistance. In one study, high-quality decisions occurred in 46 percent of the situations with strong worker resistance, but in only 19 percent of the situations where resistance was weak or nonexistent.[3]

Thus, if you are a manager who prides yourself on running a smooth ship, you may not be as effective as you think. The smooth ship may reflect suppressed conflict that could have potential benefit if allowed free play. In fact, the conflict might not be as harmful as suppressing it is.

BENEFITS OF CONFLICT:

- Forces goal analysis
- Creates dialogue among employees
- Fosters creative solutions
- Stimulates organizational learning
- Improves performance and productivity
- Prevents stagnation

Causes of Workplace Conflict

When you perceive conflict in the workplace, you may assume it's due to incompatible personalities. "Why can't everyone just get along?" you plead. But once you understand that the sources of conflict are often deeper than individual personality, then you will be able to select the right communication strategy for handling it.

The underlying causes of conflict are often the organization's hierarchy, ways of doing business, and a built-in opposition between units. Research shows that conflict increases with levels of hierarchy, standardization of jobs, and the number of workers.

The distribution of the limited resources available in an organization is another source of conflict. If resources were unlimited, few conflicts would arise, but this condition seldom exists. When resources are limited, and more than one person or group wants a share, conflict and competition develop.

Diverse goals are another source of organizational conflict. For instance, clashes may occur between Quality Assurance and Production in a manufacturing company. The goal of the quality control people is zero defects, while the goal of the production unit is filling the customers' orders on time. Conflicting goals and roles can also explain why a company's sales people routinely ignore the accounting staff's requests for expense receipts. Or why a shift foreman refuses to let his workers attend an employee development session offered by human resources. To reduce such traditional conflicts between functional units, managers should remind their people of the overarching goals, mission, and vision.

SOURCES OF CONFLICT:

- The organization's hierarchy
- Ways of doing business
- Built-in opposition between units
- Highly standardized jobs
- Large number of workers
- Distribution of limited resources
- Diverse goals

Strategies for Managing Conflict

Once you have pinpointed the sources of workplace conflict, you are ready to manage the conflict. This section offers strategies for managing conflict up the ladder of power and authority, across the ladder with peers, and down the ladder with subordinates. While reviewing these strategies, keep in mind that different conflict situations call for different strategies, so effective communication means that you match the strategy to the situation.

Managing Conflict with the Boss: Avoid

You might think that the best way to handle conflict with your boss is to avoid it. The avoidance or withdrawal strategy combines a low concern for production with a low concern for people. If you use this style a lot, you see conflict as useless. Rather than undergo the tension and frustration of conflict, you use avoidance simply to remove yourself from conflict situations, either physically or psychologically. You dislike tension, don't take sides in a disagreement among others, and feel little commitment to any decisions reached. This conflict management style is the second most popular among U.S. managers.

Avoidance doesn't need to be dramatic. You can avoid by ignoring a hurtful comment or quickly changing the subject when conversation begins to threaten. Another way to avoid is to place the responsibility for an issue back on your boss. A third way to withdraw is to use a simple response of "I'm looking into the matter," with the hopes that the boss will forget the issue.

The avoidance strategy is frequently used in large bureaucracies that have too many policies. Rather than tackling the conflict, you simply blame it on "policy." If you lack self-confidence in your communication abilities, you may hope the problem just disappears. However, following the dictum, "never complain, never explain," usually doesn't work in the long run. In fact, withdrawal has been negatively associated with knowledge of the boss's feelings and attitudes; open, upward communication; perceived helpfulness of the subordinate; and strength of the planning relationship. Thus, avoiding conflict with the boss doesn't usually make things better in critical managerial areas.[4]

Managing Conflict with the Boss and with Peers: Accommodate
The second type of conflict resolution is accommodating. You try to deal with conflict by giving in, hoping to make everyone happy. When using this approach, you emphasize maintaining relationships with bosses and coworkers, and you de-emphasize achieving productive goals. Since you are aiming for others' acceptance, you often give in to their desires in areas that conflict with your own. You use this style if you believe confrontation is destructive.

Typical attempts to accommodate may include such things as calling for a coffee break at a tense moment, breaking tension by cracking a joke, saying "you're right" when they're not, or engaging in some ritual show of togetherness such as an office birthday party. Since these efforts are likely to reduce feelings of conflict, they are better than simple avoidance. But handling conflict by giving in will probably have short-range effects. Just because someone does not experience a hostile or negative feeling does not mean the real cause of the conflict is resolved. In fact, accommodating is a camouflage approach that can break down at any time and create barriers to progress. Research has found that managers in low- or medium-performing organizations accommodate to reduce conflict more often than managers in high-performing organizations do.

In addition, accommodating hurts open communication with the boss and with participation in goal setting. Think of your latest performance review with your boss. Did you give in to the judgments of your work quality without discussion or pushback? If so, did the boss think you had accepted the judgments as fair and true? How did you feel afterward—motivated to work harder? Probably not.

Managing Conflict with Bosses and with Peers: Compromise
Compromise, the third strategy for conflict resolution up and across the ladder, assumes that half a loaf is better than none. Since compromise provides some gain for both sides rather than a unilateral victory or loss, you might judge this approach to be better than the other strategies just discussed.

Compromise is used when one of two conditions exists: (1) neither person thinks he/she can force their way on the other person or (2) one or both people believes winning may not be worth the cost in money, time, or energy. Compromise is often highly related to negotiating, which is a legitimate conflict resolution strategy in today's workplace. Compromising may make both parties think they won, but they may also both feel like losers. A negative overtone may develop in the working relationship, and any sense of trust may break down. While both people probably entered the negotiations with a cooperative attitude, a sense of competition may be the final outcome.

A second concern with compromise is that the person with the most information has the better position, usually the person who has a better network. This power of information may restrict open communication, often resulting in a lopsided compromise. A third factor is the principle of the least-interested party: The party that has the least interest in the outcome is the more powerful person in the negotiations. As a result, a coworker who has little concern about your welfare or the team's welfare may have the most influence in a compromise.

Managing Conflict with Subordinates: Force

The previous sections described traditional ways to approach conflict upward, that is, between you and your boss, and horizontally, between you and your peers at the same level of power. But what about conflict down the ladder, when you are experiencing conflict with your subordinates?

You use force when you need to meet production goals at all costs, without concern for the needs or acceptance of your subordinates or team. Losing is destructive because you think it reduces status, seems weak, and fosters a poor image. You must win no matter what, because winning gives you a sense of excitement and achievement. Not surprisingly, forcing is the number one conflict resolution strategy that U.S. managers use.

The forcing strategy will probably cause later conflicts, however. To see the negative effect this style may have, just think about the language managers use to describe conflict: beat the opposition, battle, fight, conquer, coerce, smash, nuke. Such language and imagery can result in long-lasting, emotional wounds.

While force can resolve immediate disputes, the long-term effects will probably include a loss of productivity. Forcing in conflict situations is negatively associated with adequacy of planning, helpfulness of the supervision, and participation in goal setting. The major result of forcing is that your employees are reluctant to carry out orders because they think that the ultimate resolution of the conflict will put them on the losing side of a win–lose position.

Interestingly, while little doubt exists that forcing has limited use, managers consider forcing to be their favorite backup strategy for dealing with conflict. Immediate compliance is misperceived as a long-term solution in these cases.

Managing Conflict with Anyone: Collaborate

So far, it may seem that no totally acceptable, productive strategy exists to manage conflict. I've discussed everything in terms of loss. Fortunately, this is not the case. Collaborating, the fifth strategy, is a win–win strategy for conflict. This complex and highly effective style requires skillful, strategic managerial communication, but it reaps a big dividend; thus, the remainder of this chapter centers on this strategy. Let's first describe the win–win strategy and then examine specific ways to use it.

The key to this strategy is that it follows a mutual problem-solving approach rather than a combative one. In contrast to managers who use accommodating, avoiding, compromising, or forcing, managers who collaborate assume that a high-quality, mutually acceptable solution is possible. Everyone directs energies toward defeating the problem and not each other.

Here are the five steps in the collaboration process:

1. *Define the problem.* The problem definition must be specific. A statement of the problem in a conflict situation is usually much more difficult than it seems, and most people jump to solutions before they clearly define the problem. Because of this, our inclination is to state the problem as a solution rather than as a goal, which results in ambiguous communication. The outcome may be increased conflict. One helpful strategy is to write out the problem statement clearly, so everyone can see it and agree on it. Or you can agree on a problem stated as a question. State goals in the form of group goals rather than your own goals.

2. *Analyze the problem.* Again, most people want to skip this step. After all, they may argue, they live with the problem. What is the point of spending more time wallowing in it? The answer is that by exploring the depths of the problem, by looking at its history, causes, effects, and extent, you can later come up with a solution that addresses more than symptoms, one that is more than a bandage. The analysis will address the root cause of the problem, thus improving the chances of being successful.

3. *Brainstorm alternatives.* Everyone involved in the conflict should offer potential solutions. One idea may stimulate other ideas. The more you communicate in an open, trusting environment, the greater the potential for finding effective solutions. Trust, of course, evaporates when an idea is criticized during a brainstorming session. As soon as someone says, "That's a terrible idea. It'll never work," who would be willing to take the risk of coming up with another idea? Make sure that you don't judge ideas prematurely.

4. *Develop criteria for a good solution.* These criteria, or standards, may already be in place and available. Other times, your boss will tell you what a good solution must look like. Occasionally, you and/or your team are allowed to develop your own criteria. The most common criteria for a good solution are:
   - It must be cheap.
   - It must be easy to do.
   - It must call for using resources already on hand.
   - It must be legal.
   - It must be in line with the company's mission or values.

5. *Evaluate the brainstormed alternatives using the criteria.* This is really the easiest step. By this time, you have reached agreement on the problem, and everyone has had a say about possible solutions. The best solution will appear naturally because it is the brainstormed alternative that matches your list of criteria.

> **STEPS IN THE COLLABORATION PROCESS:**
>
> 1. Define the problem
> 2. Analyze the problem
> 3. Brainstorm solutions
> 4. Develop criteria for a good solution
> 5. Find the best match

You might be asking, if collaborating is the best all-around strategy for resolving conflict, why don't we do it more often? The simple answer is that this process calls for two prerequisites: time and ability. You can't count on reaching consensus on a solution right away. Hearing everyone out takes time and patience, commodities that are rare in today's workplace. Secondly, the people have to know how to collaborate; they must be familiar with, and be willing to follow, the five steps described above.

Once I had a graduate student who managed the third shift in a manufacturing company. After attending my evening class from 6:00 to 9:00 p.m., Rob would head off to work from 11:00 p.m. to 7:00 a.m. Before class one evening, Rob told me that two of his subordinates had been locked in conflict for some time over a tools issue, and so he had tried using the collaborative strategy that I had taught in class. "How did it go?" I asked eagerly. Rob reported, "It didn't work." He had put his employees into the break room and said, "Come out when you two have reached an agreement." After an hour, they had returned to the line, saying they'd worked it out, but Rob said they hadn't used the process he had learned in class. When I asked what they had used, he told me, "Seniority." The worker who had been on the job longer got his way.

This example demonstrates the importance of training people on the steps in the collaboration strategy for conflict resolution. It's based on how we think when we are trying to rationally solve a problem, but participants must know and stick to the steps in the process for it to work.

Summary

To help you "get it done," this chapter focuses on strategies for managing conflict. Conflict is inevitable in the workplace, and it's even more powerful a factor when the workforce is diverse. You will be able to successfully deal with conflict by following the steps described here: read the situation to identify the source of the conflict, recognize whether the conflict is constructive or destructive, select the right strategy out of the toolbox, and then apply it. Table 6.2.1 will help you choose the right conflict resolution strategy.

TABLE 6.2.1   When to Use Each Conflict Resolution Strategy

Conflict Resolution Strategy	When It Works Best	Result
Avoiding	• There's little chance you'll get your way • The potential damage of addressing the conflict outweighs the benefits of resolution • People need a chance to cool down • Others are in a better position to resolve the conflict • The problem will go away by itself	I lose You lose
Accommodating	• Preserving harmony is important • Personal antagonism is the major source of conflict • The issue itself is unsolvable • You care more about the relationship than getting your way	I lose You win
Compromising	• Two opponents are equal in power • Temporary settlements on complex issues are needed • Opponents do not share goals • Forcing or problem solving won't work	I half win, half lose You half win, half lose
Forcing	• Quick, decisive action is needed, as in a crisis • A rule has to be enforced • You know you're right • You must protect yourself	I win You lose
Collaborating	• Both sets of concerns are too important to be compromised • It is important to work through hard feelings • Commitment to the resolution is important • A permanent solution is desired	I win You win

Notes

1 L.A. Erbert (2014). "Antagonistic and Non-Antagonistic Dialectical Contradictions in Organizational Conflict," *International Journal of Business Communication* 51, no. 2, pp. 138–58.

2 L. Putnam, S. Wilson (1988). "Argumentation and Bargaining Strategies as Discriminators of Integrative and Distributive Outcomes," in *Managing Conflict: An Interdisciplinary Approach*, ed. A. Rahim (New York, NY: Praeger Publishers), pp. 121–141.

3 R. Hoffman, E. Harburg, N.R.F. Meier (1962). "Differences and Disagreements as Factors in Creative Problem-Solving," *Journal of Abnormal and Social Psychology* 64, no. 2, pp. 206–24.

4 W.A. Donohue, M.E. Diez, R.B. Stahl (1983). "New Directions in Negotiations Research," in *Communication Yearbook* 7, ed. R.N. Bostrom (Beverly Hills, CA: Sage Publications), pp. 249–79.

How Incivility Hijacks Performance

It Robs Cognitive Resources, Increases Dysfunctional Behavior, and Infects Team Dynamics and Functioning

Christine L. Porath, Trevor Foulk, and Amir Erez

Recent surveys indicate that incivility is rampant and on the rise. According to a recent *Civility in America* poll, 70% of Americans believe that incivility has reached crisis proportions. Seventy-one percent believe civility has declined in recent years; and the majority expect the decline to continue. People in organizations and schools experience or witness incivility too often. Incivility is defined by Andersson and Pearson as the exchange of seemingly inconsequential, inconsiderate words and deeds that violate conventional norms of workplace conduct. It is important to note that incivility is all in the eyes of the beholder. It is not an objective phenomenon; it reflects people's interpretation about how actions make them feel.

In a study by Alan Rosenstein and Michelle O'Daniel, most of the 800 physician executives surveyed said that disruptive behavior happens in their hospitals at least once per month. Ten percent called it a daily occurrence and almost all believed that this bad behavior negatively affected their patients' care. What are the costs? Nearly one-fourth said that it led to actual harm to their patients. The news from doctors and nurses actually treating patients is even more frightening. Nearly three out of four identified bad behaviors within their teams that led to medical errors; more than one-fourth were convinced that these behaviors contributed to the deaths of their own patients.

How does this happen? Some evidence suggests that rudeness affects individual functioning. Research shows that targets of incivility suffer psychological distress, negative emotional effects, and job burnout. Targets may lose time and cognitive resources worrying about the uncivil interaction. However, an underlying assumption of this research is that a single uncivil incident is unlikely to trigger major consequences. Rather, an accumulated effect of frequent "daily hassles" is responsible for the harm.

Yet, several of our studies suggest that even a single, brief uncivil incident can cause an immediate reduction in people's performance. For example, we found that experiencing incivility hampered participants' ability to perform complex tasks and reduced their creativity. We also found that rudeness from customers reduced customer service representatives' ability to recall relevant information and perform analytical tasks. What's more, we found that the effects of incivility are not limited to those who experience incivility; witnesses of incivility showed a reduced capacity for solving complex problems and were much less creative.

Our research begs the question about how far-reaching the consequences of incivility stretch. Does working in an uncivil culture affect people's functioning? This also begs the question of *how* does incivility affect the performance of targets, witnesses, teams, or those around incivility? Is it possible, for example, that nurses, residents, or doctors who work in an uncivil context may be more prone to make errors?

Over the years we have found that rudeness makes people mad, sad, or even fearful. It also shows that people's motivation may plummet. People who experience or even witness incivility often reduce their effort and time at work. Yet, interestingly, we found that negative emotions or reduced motivation did not explain why performance tends to tank following incivility. Rather, we found that people get mentally tripped up. They do not seem to remember as well, cannot focus their attention, and do not work as well with others; and this affects their performance.

Building on these findings, we set out to test *how* incivility may reduce peoples' performance and cognitive functioning. We also examined how rudeness affected witnesses, teams, and even those simply "working around it."

In this article we share what we have learned over the years. We highlight the cognitive costs of bad behavior, and specifically discuss how incivility may instigate dysfunctional behavior, the contagious nature of incivility, and how incivility disrupts team dynamics. Finally, we share recommendations for what individuals should do to buffer the effects of incivility, as well as what organizations should do to manage incivility.

Cognitive Costs of Incivility

Over the years, we have uncovered considerable evidence that incivility is devastating to performance. While people admit to reducing their effort following encounters with incivility, our experiments have shown that a lack of motivation is not at the root of the performance losses. Just witnessing rudeness caused outcomes to falter by nearly half. Witnesses' reactions to brainstorming tasks were stifled. They stumbled at solving puzzles. External experts rated their deliverables as significantly less creative. These results led us to believe that rather than a reduction in effort being the cause of the performance issues we observed, some sort of cognitive disruption was impacting performance.

The question was—what was this cognitive disruption? We discovered that incivility was actually disrupting working memory. Working memory is a central component of the cognitive system. It is responsible for the rehearsal and storage of both verbal and visual information, and is also responsible for more in depth thought processes like decision-making and goal manage-ment. Digging deeper, we set out to uncover how incivility was impacting working memory by exploring its effect on the three separate functions of working memory. We started off looking at the effects of incivility on the verbal component of working memory. What did we learn? Those who witnessed rudeness performed 18% worse on the verbal tasks. Since processes associated with creativity draw upon this verbal function of working memory, participants' creativity was also impacted. They came up with 29% fewer creative ideas than those who had not witnessed rudeness. Experts rated their ideas as 23% less creative.

Building on these results, in another study we investigated whether incivility affects per-formance on visual tasks, which are also governed by working memory. This has important implications for how incivility may disrupt attention and cause people to "miss" critical informa-tion, often referred to as "inattentional blindness." Researchers Daniel Simons and Christopher Chabris have demonstrated that perception of visual information requires attention, and that when attention is diverted to other objects or tasks individuals often fail to perceive unexpected objects, even if people are right in front of their eyes for a significant amount of time.

We believed that since incivility tends to occupy one's mind, shifting the focus of attention to the uncivil event, it might contribute to inattentional blindness. To test this, we used Simon and Chabris' infamous "invisible gorilla" manipulation. During the task of counting basketball passes among a group, a person in gorilla suit walked through the screen. After viewing the complete video, participants were instructed to write down the tally for the number of passes made by the team they had been assigned to watch. Those who were primed with incivility were nearly five times less likely to notice anything unusual, including this "invisible" gorilla.

Finally, we explored whether incivility affected the central component of working memory respon-sible for problem solving, decision-making, and the planning of future actions. Those who experienced rudeness showed increases in both decision-making and physical move time for goal management activities, but not those that did not require goal management. These results help us to better pinpoint how incivility taxes working memory, and in doing so, decreases performance on complex tasks.

While those results suggested that actually experiencing incivility led to reduced cognitive performance, to test whether simply having incivility on your mind was detrimental, we con-ducted an experiment in which we primed people with incivility. We found that that even for those simply primed with incivility, working memory capacity suffered and performance declined on three separate tasks. Specifically, those in the uncivil condition recalled 17% less, performed 86% worse on the verbal tasks and came up with 38% fewer creative ideas than those who had not been primed with rudeness. Experts rated their ideas as 33% less creative. They also made 43% more math errors and 1.25 times more speed errors in the working memory task.

These priming results suggest that it is not simply witnessing an uncivil event that consumes cognitive resources, disrupts working memory, and harms performance. Rather, there seems to be something qualitatively disruptive about incivility in particular that elicits a response in people. Even subconscious triggers of incivility weigh on people's minds, taking a cognitive toll on working memory and subsequent performance. These results indicate that even if people are unaware of the effects of being around incivility, there are detrimental effects.

Taken together, these results show that incivility impairs working memory, which in turn negatively impacts both performance and creativity. Working memory has three main functions— the verbal function, the visual function, and the central function responsible for higher order cognitive tasks; incivility impairs all three. What's more, this effect occurs in the absence of a specific uncivil event; simply having incivility on one's mind has been shown to decrease working memory performance. This is important because it suggests that even being in a workplace that has a climate of incivility may impair workers' creativity and performance. Incivility robs people of cognitive resources, disrupts all three components of working memory, and ultimately hijacks performance.

Incivility Also Primes Dysfunctional Behavior

Beyond impairing working memory functioning, incivility influences cognitive functioning by priming dysfunctional thoughts. When asked what to do with a brick, participants who witnessed rudeness in all three of our studies—and those we have run previously—were more likely to create dysfunctional uses for a brick than those who did not witness rudeness. Participants in the rudeness condition wrote things like, "I'd like to smash the experimenter's face with a brick," as well as "break someone's nose," and "smash someone's fingers." Many stated that a brick could be used to "murder someone," "kill people," "attack someone," "beat someone up," "hurt someone," "torture someone," "throw at someone," "trip someone," "throw through a window," "sink a body in a river," and could be used as a weapon. Our experiments suggest that an isolated rude comment could provoke the urge to aggressively retaliate—or to take aggression out on someone. Participants who were exposed to rudeness not only produced more dysfunctional uses (which may be conscious or subconscious) but also tended to incorrectly reassemble the scrambled word "remdue" (which should have been assembled "demure") as "murder." Those in the rude condition were nine times more likely to write "murder." This kind of implicit measure is used by cognitive psychologists to uncover important facts about subconscious thinking processes.

Our findings suggest that an isolated rude comment could provoke conscious as well as subconscious aggressive thoughts that may cause individuals to behave in an aggressive manner. People who witness—or even work in an uncivil environment—may be more prone to lash out at others, to snap when responding to someone, or to take out frustrations on others without realizing it.

This suggests that incivility may spiral, as people display emotions or behaviors (even non-verbal) connected to such dysfunctional thoughts or behaviors. We believe that such reactions affect team functioning, the organization and its culture. In a *Fortune 100* manufacturer we worked with, the lead of an external consulting team presented their findings in a dismissive tone that set off one of the managers attending the meeting. Verbal exchanges between the presenter and the manager grew more personal until the manager challenged, "let's take it outside." The room full of "suits" marched out to the parking lot, where someone with a cooler head stepped in to prevent the fight. This is clearly atypical. But when incivility occurs, ill feelings and associated bad behaviors can escalate and spread until the entire environment seems nasty.

This type of contagion often occurs in teams. As depicted in ESPN's miniseries *The Bronx Is Burning*, on-and-off field incivilities within the 1977 New York Yankees eroded team dynamics. A three-way power struggle among owner George Steinbrenner, manager Billy Martin, and star Reggie Jackson evolved, generating numerous conflicts. Reggie Jackson caused enough friction among the team that members eventually refused to talk to him. Insults and incivilities escalated until Martin and Jackson had to be physically restrained from injuring each other.

Is Incivility Really Contagious?

To explore whether incivility could "infect" people, we conducted several studies to explore the contagious nature of incivility. The results of these studies showed that rudeness is indeed contagious, in that experiencing rudeness in one interaction causes individuals to be rude when they interact with others in the future. Digging deeper, we found the reason was that when people experience rudeness or incivility, they become more aware of incivility in their environment. Thus, if Tom is rude to me, I am more likely to notice rude cues from Jim in the future, and respond to Jim accordingly. This effect is less pronounced if Jim's actions are clear (if Jim is clearly being nice and polite, I am unlikely to believe he is being rude), but if Jim's actions are unclear, then my previous interaction with Tom taints the way I view the interaction with Jim. Research suggests that almost all interactions are at least somewhat ambiguous, meaning that almost all interactions are flavored by the tenor of prior interactions. This may be particularly true in today's corporate culture, where more and more communication is conducted via informal methods of communication like e-mail and text. Communicating in this manner may enhance the contagious nature of rudeness in an organization because it leaves communications somewhat ambiguous and open to interpretation.

The Impact of Incivility to the Team and Their Functioning

Beyond its ability to influence dysfunctional ideation and its contagious nature, rudeness may be particularly harmful in organizational settings because of its effects on teams. There are some types of threats that research has shown cause teams to become more cohesive and thus perform better. For example, when a team believes that their supervisor is unfair, they tend to band together in response to the shared threat. However, when teams experience incivility, the effect is exactly the opposite. When teams experience incivility, regardless of whether the incivility comes from inside the team or outside the team, it has catastrophic effects on the team's collaborative processes and severely impacts the way team members perform their tasks.

A nurse from a top hospital shared that when she called a physician who was not "in house" for a patient who was deteriorating, the physician said, "Do you know where I am? I am with my family and you are interrupting me. Find someone else to take care of your nonsense." The team member explained that, "I felt like I had done something wrong. I wanted to cry but knew my patient needed me. Being that this physician was close to the top of the chain, I really wasn't sure whom to call. It took me some time to recover, and my patient care was delayed. I felt like a horrible nurse that night. Moving forward, I was afraid to communicate with this physician, which presented a major issue because she and her team were assigned to many of my patients."

As this example illustrates, rudeness impairs team dynamics. Teammates no longer share information. They also fail to share the workload. In a recent study of 75 teams, those with high number of rude members reported work sharing behaviors that were 14% worse than other teams, and information sharing behaviors that were 9% worse than other teams. These findings hold even if the incivility is from an uncivil colleague outside the team: team functioning and performance suffer. In this context, teams that were exposed to rudeness experienced a 15% decrease in helping behaviors and a nearly 10% decrease in information sharing. Regardless of the source, teams are distracted. Whether teammates waste resources discussing the incident or how they might respond, replaying it in their minds, or avoiding the person, chances are the incident pulls them off track. The rude incident consumes resources that could have been focused toward more effective problem solving, task achievement, and customer or patient care.

How serious can this be? An anesthesiologist at a large university hospital in the southeast region of the United States communicated to us that when incivility is present in the operating room, it can have a tremendous effect on the team. Anesthesiologists, for example, not only have to constantly monitor the patient's condition, which is represented by a series of pings, beeps, and bleeps on various machines in the operating room, but also communicate this condition to the rest of the team so that they can successfully perform their functions. This process is tremendously taxing, and when there is incivility present this process is impaired. Each team member has a harder time performing his or her job, which subsequently impairs the way they communicate with and help other team members. In a situation like an OR (operating room), where a successful operation requires real time communication of tremendously detailed information, the consequences of distractions like incivility can be truly disastrous.

What Is Behind All These Losses?

In various experiments we have tried to pinpoint why incivility is so distracting. Why does it pull people and teams so off track? We have found evidence of at least three potential explanations: performance losses stem from conscious evaluations of the uncivil event, conscious processing of social information, and sub-conscious processes resulting from the perception of a social threat.

Perhaps the most obvious explanation for why incivility impairs performance is because it occupies individuals' conscious awareness. Compelling evidence suggests that when individuals experience incivility or any kind of social threat, they think about it. Because self-preservation is a fundamental human motive, any social experience that could be considered threatening tends to be consciously evaluated. Individuals think about the threat and evaluate its veracity, the potential consequences of the threat, and most important, potential reactions to the threat that would result in the least amount of harm. For example, research done with a large cellular communications provider in Israel found that when customer service representatives experienced incivility from customers, they had a harder time recalling details of the conversation with the customer because they spent mental energy thinking about the incivility. It is difficult to control this process. When people experience incivility, the process of consciously evaluating it seems to take precedence over primary tasks, even when an individual does not want to think about the rude incident. It tends to occupy them, even if they do not want it to.

A nurse in a top ranked research hospital in the northeast region of the United States shared how she called the surgeon because of the unexpected deterioration of his patient. The nurse was concerned about the planned discharge for this patient given the patient's state. The surgeon accused this nurse and the unit of not being "competent" to care for patients. The surgeon said that he would send all of his patients elsewhere from this point on. The nurse felt helpless as she knew her patient was in trouble and was trying to focus on the patient, not the uncivil tone and words from the surgeon. However, for the remainder of the day, the nurse was angry with the surgeon and spent time and mental energy thinking about the interaction. She admitted that she was distracted and irritable throughout the day, and that she did not perform as well because of this interaction with the surgeon. The discussion took her off track, and she struggled to focus on her other patients that day.

Another reason incivility may harm performance is that it presents people with an informational challenge. It may not be clear to the victim or a witness what the uncivil person "really" wants, why he or she is being rude, and how to respond. Instead of concentrating on the task at hand, the victim or the witness is likely to be focused by trying to understand what the source of the problem is and how to address it. As a result, incivility increases cognitive load and makes the task at hand more cognitively complex. In other words, it is possible that it is not only the emotional challenge described above, as people are upset by the event, that creates the cognitive distraction, but also the informational challenge that is presented by the uncivil person.

A vice president at a large bank recently recalled for us an incident in which she received what she considered to be an uncivil e-mail from a colleague from another country. "The most troubling part of the e-mail was that I wasn't sure what he meant—did he mean to come off like that, was he truly angry, or was I just misinterpreting it?" She elaborated, "I thought about it for a good amount of time after that—if I had known he was trying to be difficult it almost would have been better; at least then I would have known how to respond." Think about the last time you received a rude e-mail from someone. Often, the intention is not clear. You may have spent a significant part of the next hour or so ruminating over that e-mail. What did he/she want? Why did he/she treat me like that? This process of trying to evaluate the e-mail likely pulled at least part of your mental awareness away from the task at hand, and it is likely that task suffered as a result. Taken together these two mechanisms suggest that rudeness and incivility may have their effect on cognitive functioning and performance because people consciously ponder the event. These two mechanisms above (social threat and social information processing) may also interact with each other. Rudeness is on some level a social threat, but on another level the threat is ambiguous, so it may require cognitive resources to discern *if* there even is a threat.

Thus it may be that rudeness is particularly insidious because it is unclear how to react to it. If someone is "angry" with us or expresses "aggression" we know how to respond, and therefore it is not particularly cognitively taxing. Responses to rudeness are often not quite so clear. Did your teammate exclude you from the meeting with your boss because he is going behind your back, taking credit for the project you just busted your tail leading, or because he thinks he has a better relationship with him and can exert more influence garnering support for your project? You are steaming about it, and have played at least ten different scenarios through your mind. You have also wasted a ton of resources on how you handle this situation. Do you confront your teammate? When? How? Should you talk to a confidant on your team first to get her perspective and advice?

While both conscious evaluations of the event and the information challenge explanation assume that individuals are consciously thinking about the uncivil event, there is also evidence that suggests that automatic processes over which individuals have no control may also be responsible for performance impairment. Strong evidence from Joseph Ledoux and Antonio Damasio's neuroscience research suggests that the amygdala, located deep in the limbic system of the brain, is activated in the presence of even minor threats. When activated, the amygdala shifts attentional resources from higher processes to a more primitive flight or fight response. Incivility may disrupt cognition by automatically activating the primitive brain systems that communicate the fight or flight response rather than focusing on the cognitive task at hand. Since we are wired for survival, the priority is "self-protection." This process is *automatic*, meaning that individuals have no control over it, which implies that it cannot be stopped. Unlike the conscious evaluation of the event, this process has no conscious component—it is a primitive function designed to prepare people to respond to a threat. While this process is going on, individuals' attentional resources are likely devoted to the process, redirecting them away from the task at hand. Our ability to focus on the task takes a back seat, and performance suffers as a result. Try to remember how you felt the last time something surprising happened that really scared you. Were you able to concentrate on your work immediately? Most people cannot, because this automatic threat evaluation process is occurring and it draws attention to it, away from primary tasks. For some people, an uncivil interaction does just that.

Can Your Organization Afford These Losses?

Our findings may help explain why health care mistakes occur and patient care may suffer despite well-intentioned efforts. It is clear that incivility impairs individual's ability to think, even when individuals are not the targets. Witnessing incivility—or even being around it—triggers reactions in the brain, making it tougher to manage tasks and solve problems. Incivility increases the likelihood that people miss important information.

Not spotting the gorilla is one thing, but present a similar situation in a hospital and it can be fatal. A doctor detailed to us how a medical team at his west coast hospital administered the wrong treatment to a patient after an uncivil encounter with their supervising M.D. The necessary information was right there on the chart, but the team lacked the attention and awareness to take it into account. The patient died.

What is scary is that this medical story is far from unique. Other doctors and nurses have shared similar stories with us, and they urge us to spend time studying the health care industry because the costs are so high and way too prevalent.

Our team findings highlight how communication and helpfulness is often stifled following incivility. And, this reduces performance—and could help explain errors in the medical context.

Researcher Amy Edmondson and colleagues, and doctors such as Atul Gawande have highlighted that a climate of trust and respect, or psychological safety, benefits learning. Our study may offer some specifics about why this is the case. The implications of our research span far beyond health care, however. Employees whose work demands focus, problem solving, decision-making, creativity, or cognitive performance should be wary of incivility's impact. Beyond the workplace, our findings hold important implications for school settings. Students who are simply around an uncivil setting (e.g., classroom behavior, playground antics) may suffer negative cognitive effects and decreased performance. Given the relationship between working memory and learning, writing, language comprehension, and reasoning, we suspect that uncivil environments will reduce students' ability to be attentive, learn, and perform well. There may be a greater likelihood of dysfunctional behavior in uncivil environments as well.

Recommendations

Our results suggest that people may not realize that working in this environment may limit their potential and harm their functioning. They may be unaware that incivility is silently chipping away at their productivity, creativity, and well-being. Research by Richard Lazarus and Susan Folkman reveals that ordinary daily hassles considerably outstrip major life stressors and their impact on emotional, social, and work functioning. Incivility may be one such hassle, yet it may not be consciously acknowledged.

Individuals' Role in Buffering the Effects

Take Care of Yourself

Simply being aware of how distracting incivility is helpful. Recognize the toll that incivility is likely to take, and that your workplace effectiveness is likely to drop. Whether you are a target or are working in an uncivil environment, pay special attention to taking care of yourself. Surround yourself with friends and family members. Schedule time for relaxation and fun. Make time for activities where you feel a sense of thriving. Get into routines where you disengage from work (evenings, weekends, and vacations) and its strains. Thriving outside of the workplace can help rejuvenate you. It will help you bring a stronger, more vital self to work, where you will be more immune to the toxicity of incivility.

Reduce Your Exposure

Ideally people steer clear of incivility whenever possible, limiting their involvement with uncivil colleagues and organizations. Reduce your dependence on uncivil colleagues by seeking advice, information, and support from other teammates, peers, or leaders. You might strategically reduce your offenders' dependence on you by diverting his or her requests to other employees whenever possible. Schedule your work to limit your time (especially face-to-face) and exposure (using discretion on committee or projects).

Engage in Mindfulness

When around incivility, one should attempt to re-focus attention mindfully as best as possible. Mindfulness and meditation practices should enhance focus, particularly when dealing with emotions and stress stemming from incivility. Such practices should help people regulate their emotions, decreasing the likelihood of incivility spiraling, and increasing the chances that they will respond with emotional intelligence (versus saying or doing something that they might later regret).

The Organization's Role

While many recommendations for managing incivility are aimed at the target, our results shift the focus and onus to managers and organizations. Managers can limit incivility through recruiting and selection with an eye for civility, setting expectations, rewards and recognition, coaching and training. When incivility occurs, they cannot tolerate it. Managers must deal with it swiftly in order to limit the negative consequences.

Recruit and Select for Civility

Given the costs of incivility, it pays to invest in selecting civil employees. Do your homework. If in doubt, do not hire. Replacement costs soar quickly. A chief administrator told us how one highly talented, but uncivil, doctor cost his hospital millions. The chief administrator explained that had the hiring committee done its homework, it could have surfaced problems before hiring the offensive doctor: he had left a wake of complaints at his previous hospital. Here the offender spurred dissatisfaction among nurses and technicians. Their dissatisfaction sparked a lawsuit. Beyond the financial burden of the eventual settlement, the emotional toll was felt widely throughout the hospital.

Take a page from legendary basketball coach John Wooden's (at UCLA) notebook. Wooden surveyed people close to recruits (principal, opposing coaches, coach, etc.). He also used visits to screen for civility and character. In one case, when a talented player mouthed off to his mother, Wooden opted to pass on this blue chip recruit. Although this player went on to beat UCLA, Wooden stuck by his decision—for he did not want one bad apple to contaminate his team, and its values.

Choosing a civil workforce can only be as good as your candidate pool is. Use your network to attract better candidates. Tap friends, family members, colleagues, professional associations, former employees, consultants and search firms. Keep a database of excellent candidates who do not fit now, or who chose to work elsewhere for now. They also are an excellent source for referrals. Touching base with them, you may even find that their situation has changed and they are interested. One consulting firm we have worked with reports that they have landed some top employees in doing so—years after the initial contact.

Set Expectations and Norms for Civility

Leaders need to set expectations and norms for civility. Include civility as a value in the mission statement, highlighting the importance of how employees treat one another. Have a conversation about your goals for civility—and what individuals and the organization stand to gain from it. Give employees a voice in developing specific norms. You will gain support and empower employees to hold each other accountable for specific behaviors.

Establishing such expectations and norms provides a baseline for which organizations can measure, reward, and correct behavior.

Think creatively about how to encourage and promote civility. One bank we worked with formed a Civility Council to spearhead various initiatives.

Peer and Customer Recognition and Rewards

Use social network surveys or 360-degree feedback to track patterns of incivility; it may be helpful in rewarding and correcting behavior. How do people find working with others? Peers are the most underutilized source in reinforcing and rewarding behavior. Tap them and customers to reward civility.

Any Zappos employee at any level who sees a coworker doing something special can award a "Wow," which includes cash awards of up to $50. All recipients of "Wow" are automatically eligible for Zappos coveted "Hero" awards, which are selected by the top executives. Those chosen receive a covered "Hero" parking spot for a month, a $150 Zappos gift card and a hero's cape.

The National Security Agency (NSA) has a Civility Wall of Fame in which employees nominate candidates. They recognize one star each month. In addition to being featured on their Wall of Fame at headquarters, they are recognized on the company webpage with their photo, story and details of what scored them the award. NP Medical has employees nominate employees for living their positive values (including civility). At their quarterly meetings, they talk about the nominations, tell stories about the positive exemplars, and distribute prizes. Alaska Airlines has a nifty Above and Beyond program ($500 and name in company magazine) in which customers nominate employees they see living the Alaska Spirit.

In these organizations, the stories of the specifics behaviors and values the person enacts reinforce civil behavior.

Coach for Civility

Porath found that a quarter of uncivil employees blame their organizations for not providing them with interpersonal skills training. Investing in training is wise. There are many possibilities. Organizations that she has worked with have sent their doctors to charm school, their attorneys to anger management classes, their sales people to negotiation courses, and employees to stress management, civility, and diversity training sessions. Research has shown that such training can make a difference.

Coaches can also help uncover potential incivility through surveying and interviewing those with whom they work, and may shadow you at meetings and events to pick up on subtleties. This information can be used to guide improvement.

Do Not Tolerate Incivility

Leaders need to signal that the organization will not tolerate bad behavior. Employees who fail to comply with established norms are given fair notice about their behavior—along with clear direction about what needs to change. They must be dealt with swiftly. Failure to do so results in cynicism about the organization and its values—and costs mount. Avoid transferring uncivil employees, as this contaminates other teams and areas. Although letting talented but toxic employees go feels costly, it can generate faith in leaders and sends a strong signal about the organization's values. Think about the employees you may retain in taking such actions—or the extra cognitive resources, motivation, focus, engagement, and commitment you gain from so many other employees.

Conclusion

We hope our results raise awareness about the costs of incivility—the cognitive toll it takes on people, sneakily robbing them of resources, disrupting working memory, prompting dysfunctional thoughts and ultimately hijacking performance. What's more, incivility is contagious. Anyone can be a carrier. Given this, it is no wonder that incivility tends to impact team functioning and performance. Overall our findings imply that this incivility contagion is much larger than was realized and that it could carry major consequences for people, organizations, and society.

Selected Bibliography

For information on the costs of incivility and benefits of civility, see our book (with C. Pearson), *The Cost of Bad Behavior—How Incivility Damages Your Business and What You Can Do about It (Penguin: Portfolio, 2009)*. The article also draws from our articles, "The Price of Incivility: Lack of Respect in the Workplace Hurts Morale—and the Bottom Line," *Harvard Business Review*, 2013, 91 (January–February), 114–121: "The Effects of Civility on Advice, Leadership, and Performance," *Journal of Applied Psychology (in press)*, and "The Cost of Bad Behavior," *Organizational Dynamics*, 2010, 39, 64–71.

For other incivility articles that the reader might find informative, see C.L. Porath and A. Erez, "Does Rudeness Matter? The Effects of Rude Behavior on Task Performance and Helpfulness," *Academy of Management Journal*, 2007, 50, 1181–1197; C.L. Porath and A. Erez, "Overlooked but

Not Untouched: How Incivility Reduces Onlookers' Performance on Routine and Creative Tasks," *Organizational Behavior and Human Decision Processes*, 2009, 109, 29–44; T. Foulk, A.H. Woolum, A. Erez, in press, "Catching Rudeness Is Like Catching a Cold: The Contagion Effects of Low-Intensity Negative Behaviors," *Journal of Applied Psychology.*

For more information about civility and how to manage for it, see Robert Sutton, *The No Asshole Rule* (NY: Warner Books, 2007).

For the Civility in America survey cited, see http://www.webershandwick.com/news/article/civility-in-america-2013-incivility-has-reached-crisis-levels. For related research cited in our paper, see A. Damasio, *Descartes' Error: Emotion, Reason, and the Human Brain* (Penguin Books: New York, 1995); A.C. Edmondson, R.M. Bohmer, and G.P. Pisano, "Disrupted Routines: Team Learning and New Technology Implementation in Hospitals," *Administrative Science Quarterly*, 2001, 46, 685–716; A. Gawande, "The Learning Curve," *The New Yorker*, 2002, 77(45), 52–61; R.S. Lazarus and S. Folkman, "*Stress, Appraisal, and Coping* (Springer: New York, 1984); A. Rosenstein, and M. Daniel, "A Survey of the Impact of Disruptive Behaviors and Communication Defects on Patient Safety," *Joint Commission Journal on Quality and Patient Safety*, 2008, 34, 464–471; and S. Sitkin, and R. Hackman, "Developing Team Leadership: An Interview with Coach Mike Krzyzewski," *Academy of Management Learning and Education*, 2011, 10 (3), 494–501.

SECTION SEVEN

COMMUNICATING AS A LEADER AND LEADING THROUGH COMMUNICATION

M ost of us often think of leadership and communication as distinct features of an organization, yet they are inextricably linked. Studies show that leaders in a business spend a sizable amount of time communicating with their employees. In fact, the entire organizational culture flows from those in leadership positions and is normalized through communicative interactions. Leaders communicate the values and mission that guide the operations of an organization. This section explores such influences on organizational culture, as well as day-to-day communicative interactions in the workplace, from the perspective of professionals and communication consultants. Straus begins the section with a discussion of "facilitative leadership." Straus starts from the assumption that leaders have a "profound effect on the cultures" of organizations. Instead of following the traditional top-down organizational model, Straus describes a leadership model that drives collaborative teamwork to advance not only productivity but also a culture of rewarding interaction. Such collaboration is important for large projects and regular interactions like meetings. These necessary communicative interactions stand out as one of the most hated communication forums in the workplace. Booher continues the discussion of facilitative leadership in meetings, focusing on how we relate to one another in meetings. All meeting participants can contribute to a facilitative environment by being a good participant. Booher walks students through what it means to be a productive group member and how to avoid the potential drawbacks of participants dividing into "dominators" and "passives" in how each communicates ideas. Moreover, Booher offers concrete steps and examples to help manage these difficulties. Viator, Dalton, and Harp round out this section with a discussion of mentoring relationships. Although specific to CPAs, their lessons provide universal advice for executing an essential and underutilized role of leadership communication.

Consider the following questions when reading this section:

1. How does facilitative leadership differ from traditional top-down models of leadership?
2. How might leaders employ facilitative leadership in meetings for class or business projects?
3. If you arrived at a new job that included a structured mentoring program, what features would you find most important for your performance?
4. What does it mean to be a mentor or engage in mentoring within your target future workplace?
5. What distinguishes a good meeting from a bad meeting? How can leaders turn less productive meetings into ones that are more productive?

Key Terms and Concepts

- Collaboration
- Facilitation
- Facilitative leadership
- Stakeholder involvement
- Consensus building
- Stakeholder buy-in
- Process design
- Uncharacteristic symbolic acts
- Mentor(ing)
- Protégé
- Dominators
- Passives

Facilitative Leadership

David A. Straus

Leaders have a profound effect on the cultures of their organizations and communities. The support of leadership is essential if an organization or community is to build a collaborative environment and implement the five principles of collaboration.

These truths became clear to me when I facilitated a retreat in Northern California for a city manager and his staff. The retreat was designed, in part, to allow the staff to surface problems that affected everyone, and then to collaboratively develop solutions to those problems. In the preretreat planning session, the city manager expressed considerable enthusiasm and support for this kind of collaborative problem solving. During the retreat, we hit a snag when the participants had some difficulty brainstorming potential problems to work on. They seemed to feel very inhibited and couldn't come up with many good examples.

What was needed at that point was for the city manager to assure his staff that it was OK to be honest about any problems that existed, be they small or large, and to encourage them to think openly and "outside the box." Instead, the manager stood up and delivered one of the most uncollaborative leadership messages I've ever witnessed. "You are a talented group," he began. "I hired you because you are good problem solvers, and I have given you the authority to deal with the problems of your own departments. So if you have a problem for us to work on, it had better be a serious problem or else you are not doing your job."

Here I was, asking the staff to brainstorm—to throw out ideas without concern for their value—while their manager was telling them they were in trouble if they did! It was a memorable illustration of how *not* to foster collaboration.

Harnessing the power of collaborative action requires a different model of leadership than the classic "command-and-control" model, in which the leader solves problems, makes decisions, and issues orders unilaterally. Indeed, the old model is antithetical to building a collaborative culture.

To harness the power of collaborative action, you must become a *facilitative leader*. A facilitative leader is one who engages relevant stakeholders in solving problems collaboratively and works to build a more collaborative culture in his or her organization or community. A facilitative leader has the usual positional power to act unilaterally, but chooses instead to work with others when appropriate to find win-win solutions to important issues.

Each of the five principles contains a message for you as a leader. *Stakeholder involvement* suggests that you as a decision maker engage other stakeholders in solving problems and making decisions. *Consensus building* suggests that you work for agreement on a definition of the problem and for alignment on a vision before advocating solutions. *Process design* suggests that part of your role as a leader is to convene, promote, and support collaborative action throughout your organization or community, and insist on clear, well-designed process maps for each collaborative effort. *Facilitation* suggests that you get out of the way and let someone else facilitate your meetings. And *group memory* suggests that you prevent common meeting problems by getting someone to create a record of your meetings on chart pad paper.

This chapter builds on the leadership messages of those five principles and sets forth a practical model for facilitative leadership. It looks at the role of leadership in supporting collaborative action in a group, organization, or community. The chapter is addressed primarily toward leaders and decision makers. But whether or not you are currently a manager in your organization or an elected or appointed official in your community, you most likely have opportunities to lead and influence the people around you. So, no matter what your title, you can play an important leadership role in assisting your group, organization, or community to learn to be more collaborative.

This chapter focuses on four skill sets essential to facilitative leadership:

- Choosing when and how much collaboration is appropriate
- Being consistent in your words and actions
- Supporting and promoting collaborative action
- Creating a collaborative culture

Choosing When and How Much Collaboration Is Appropriate

Many leaders, once they understand the advantages of collaborative action, believe that all decisions should be made by consensus. Sometimes they even abdicate their responsibilities as leaders completely and become passive members of their team. Obviously, that's *not* what we advocate! Collaboration needn't be used on every minor decision and problem, and it's not a way for you to avoid your duties as a manager and decision maker. As a facilitative leader, you retain all of your decision-making responsibilities. The art of facilitative leadership, then, involves making conscious choices about how much collaboration is appropriate for each decision. After

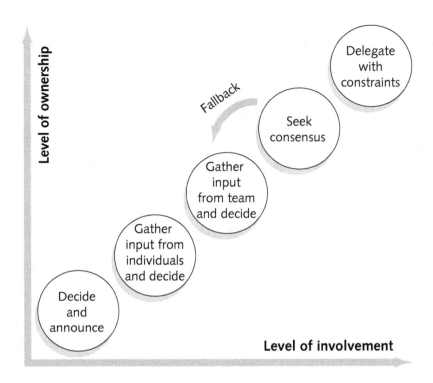

FIGURE 7.1.1 Levels of Involvement in Decision Making

all, there are many levels of involvement between making a decision unilaterally and delegating it to an individual or group below you. To help clarify these levels of involvement, my colleagues at Interaction Associates and I developed the model in Figure 7.1.1.

In this figure, the horizontal axis represents "level of involvement" and the vertical axis represents "level of ownership." As you move up the circles from left to right, the decision-making processes require more stakeholder involvement and inspire in stakeholders a greater sense of ownership of the decision. Let's examine briefly each of these decision-making options.

Decide and Announce

As a facilitative leader, you don't need to make decisions by consensus all the time. It's often completely appropriate for you to make a decision with little or no input and then announce your decision to the rest of your group, organization, or community. These are the times when strength and will are necessary—when you have to bite the proverbial bullet and make a decision. It may be that the situation is something of an emergency and requires immediate action. There's no time to get people together to talk about it. Or, the decision may involve being consistent with your agreed-upon core values and strategies. For example, you might have to state strongly: "We will implement our stated policy of seeking diversity in all hiring decisions." There may even be times when, paradoxically, you have to be authoritarian about being collaborative: "I insist that this issue be resolved collaboratively."

The great advantage of the decide-and-announce option, of course, is speed. You can make the decision quickly and begin to implement it immediately. The disadvantages of this approach read like the arguments *for* collaboration:

- Stakeholders may have the power to block your decision, or at least resist its implementation.
- The decision won't be as good without the input of others.
- It may take a long time to sell your decision to stakeholders, and you may meet with resistance from others just because they weren't consulted.
- You've made a commitment to involve stakeholders in decisions that affect their lives and your "decide-and-announce" decision appears to violate that commitment.

If you have to make a decide-and-announce decision, try to frame your decision in its context, explaining the underlying rationale for it and how the criteria you used are consistent with the established vision, mission, values, and strategies of your organization or community.

Gather Input from Individuals and Decide

Stakeholder involvement, as we've learned, is one of the key principles of collaboration. But it's possible to involve stakeholders without having them meet face-to-face. Sometimes it may be appropriate, and more efficient, to contact key stakeholders individually to gather input from them before making your decision. That way, the stakeholders will feel included, and you'll have the benefit of their advice. This option works best for those decisions that are clearly yours to make, but for which input may be helpful to you—as in the case of personnel issues, for example.

But be careful. If you choose to ignore stakeholders' advice, they may feel resentful and less likely to be direct with you the next time you seek their opinions. During your conversations with them, try to be clear that you are not seeking consensus, but that you do value their input. If possible, explain the criteria you will be using to make your decision, and let them know when and how they will be informed of it.

Gather Input from the Team and Decide

There is something powerful about discussing ideas openly in a group. Everyone hears the same ideas raised and has a chance to consider and respond to those ideas, and everyone learns how others feel about an issue. As a decision maker, you have the option, short of direct consensus building, to convene a meeting and solicit input on a decision that you will make later on your own. Perhaps the decision is too trivial (e.g., the location of the new copier) or too pressing (e.g., whether to bid on a specific contract) to take the time to work for consensus. However, you may believe it's important for participants to hear each other's ideas and to witness that you as decision maker have heard them.

The one danger with this option is that the group may clearly favor a particular course of action, and you may choose later to do something different. If this happens, you may bring about greater resistance than if you had just consulted people individually. So, if your mind is already made up, don't hold an information-gathering session. And when you do choose this option, you may want to inform stakeholders that you reserve the right to disagree with them, and that you will base your decision not only on their ideas but on external factors as well. You should also let participants know when you will be making your decision and how you will inform them of it.

Seek Consensus

By now, the definition and benefits of consensus should be clear. The five principles of collaboration I presented (stakeholder involvement, consensus building, process design, facilitation, and group memory) all advocate for the advantages of this decision-making option. And remember: There is a clear fallback if consensus can't be reached. You, as formal decision maker, must approve of the final decision. You can't be outvoted. If you disagree with an emerging consensus decision, you can just say so, and (unless the group can convince you otherwise) that option will be abandoned.

This is a good place to stress an important point: It takes personal strength and maturity to be a good facilitative leader. Making a decision by consensus involves being open and honest, and therefore exposed and vulnerable. Your problem-solving processes and the content of your thinking are visible for everyone to observe. People will see your humanity—your heuristic mistakes as well as your intelligent solutions. A more autocratic leader can hide behind his or her office door, go through the messiness of human problem solving, and then present a proposal in its final, polished form. A facilitative leader must feel comfortable revealing what he or she knows and doesn't know and not be afraid of looking "stupid." Fortunately, the benefits of being a collaborative leader are tremendous. Being collaborative builds teamwork, strengthens relationships and trust, and transfers skills and knowledge to your team members. It's worth the risks.

Many leaders fear that if they opt for a facilitated, consensus-based process, they will end up being the lone voice in support of a particular option. I have rarely seen this happen. If the issues are complex and several reasonable options exist, usually more than one person will advocate for each solution. If you get to a point at which the group is divided between two or more options and time is running out, often your direct reports will be more than willing to pass the decision back to you. They will understand better how difficult the decision is and how hard it would be to reach consensus, and they will know you have heard all the different points of view. In fact, the members of your team may be relieved to have you make the final decision.

Whether or not consensus is reached, you will advance the cause of collaborative action by striving for it. If consensus is reached, your decision will be based on this consensus, and stakeholders will feel empowered and proud to have taken part in the process. If consensus isn't reached, you will have demonstrated your commitment to collaborative decision making, and your team will most likely support whatever you decide.

Delegate Decisions with Constraints

As a leader, one of the best ways to build a collaborative culture in your organization or community is to get out of the way and turn the responsibility for making a decision over to the appropriate stakeholders. If you have built alignment on the important issues of vision, mission, values, and strategy, you should be able to trust others to make good decisions.

You can do several things to ensure successful delegation. First, be clear about the boundaries of the decision—in other words, the constraints in terms of dollars, time, resources, etc. Be explicit about the charge or task and any criteria that an acceptable solution must meet. Also, if your formal approval of the decision is necessary, insist on reviewing a map of the decision-making process to ensure that there are checkpoints at the end of each phase. In this way, you, as a stakeholder, can be part of the agreement-building process and approve the group's definition and analysis of the problem before they work to find solutions. Delegation does not mean abdication. With good process design, you can efficiently and effectively support a group to address an issue while still being part of the final decision.

Which Option to Use When

So, how do you know when to use which decision-making option? It's impossible to give a precise answer to that question, because so much depends on the context and the specifics of the decision you are trying to make. But you can weigh a number of factors to help you decide:

- **Stakeholder Buy-In.** How much do key stakeholders need to be involved so that they can confidently support the implementation of the decision?
- **Available Time.** How much time can be spent making the decision?
- **Importance of the Decision.** How important is the issue to the people in your organization or community?
- **Needed Information.** Who has information or expertise that can contribute to a quality decision?
- **Capability.** How capable and experienced are people in operating as decision makers or as a decision-making team?
- **Teamwork Opportunity.** What is the potential value of using this opportunity to create a stronger team?

So, to review, one skill necessary for facilitative leadership is the ability to make conscious choices about the appropriate level of involvement required for each issue or decision as it arises. As the level of trust grows in your group, organization, or community, your "followers" will become more willing to have you make decisions on their behalf. And you, in turn, will feel more trust in delegating decisions to them.

Making Your Words and Actions Congruent

What you do as a leader has as much effect as—if not more than—what you say. If you want to build a more collaborative culture, you must begin by acting collaboratively. Your words and actions must be congruent. How you run your meetings, how you interact with your top team, even which pronouns you use ("we" vs. "I") all send a message to your people about whether or not you are serious about teamwork and collaboration—whether you really intend to change how your group or organization works, or whether your actions are window dressing. When you first start being more facilitative in your leadership style, your symbolic acts, especially your uncharacteristic symbolic acts, may be the most powerful tools you have.

Uncharacteristic Symbolic Acts

Uncharacteristic symbolic acts are just what they sound like—actions you take or decisions you make as a leader that startle people into realizing that you intend to change the way you lead. I remember two great examples of symbolic acts from our consulting work with Jack Telnak, head of the design division at Ford Motor Company.

At the time, Jack realized he needed to communicate the message that truck designers were just as important to the company as car designers. (In fact, trucks were much more profitable to produce.) As a prerogative of his position, Jack got to drive home a different vehicle every evening in order to check out the competition. All of the employees in the division watched to see what kind of machine was stationed in Jack's parking space. He had traditionally chosen sexy foreign cars like Jaguars and Porsches. Imagine the impact and the symbolic message when, for a change, a series of different model trucks was parked where only luxury automobiles had been before. By this simple symbolic act, Jack sent a powerful message to his employees: Truck design is as important to us as car design.

Jack made another symbolic move when he initiated the collaborative effort to shorten the design cycle for new vehicles. Jack had come to realize that the design process was taking far too long, and that something radical had to be done to get the other senior vice presidents to realize it as well. In their meetings together, the senior VPs always worked hard to make their own divisions look good and to cover up any problems. At a key meeting, then, Jack stood up and publicly "shot himself in the foot." "Our design and engineering process is taking us too long," he said, "and here is how my design division is contributing to the problem." Jack went on to list ways in which the design process was being drawn out longer than absolutely necessary. But Jack continued, "I don't think we are the only ones. What do you think you all contribute to this mess?" Then, following Jack's uncharacteristic lead, other VPs began to admit their responsibility for the problem. At that point, Jack suggested forming a cross-functional committee to analyze the problem and return with some recommendations. With that one uncharacteristic act, he launched what turned out to be a critical and very successful collaborative effort in process redesign.

Being Facilitative in Meetings

Systems change only through the constant reinforcement and demonstrated success of the desired behaviors, attitudes, and values. Your task as a facilitative leader is to demonstrate the power of collaborative action whenever and wherever you can. One important venue is your own meetings. Where you sit, how you set up the room, who facilitates the meeting, and how and when you participate all send important clues to the members of your team about whether or not you are interested in open and honest discussion and true collaboration.

One powerful symbolic act is to simply rearrange the chairs—to get rid of your conference table, arrange the chairs in a U-shape, and tack flipcharts to the walls. The rearrangement of the meeting space will communicate that the focus is not on you as the leader, but on some common task.

Ask someone else to facilitate—or at least record—your meetings. Having someone else facilitate, as I've discussed, gets you out of the dual role of process leader and content leader, and removes from you the burden of having to worry about meeting logistics. You'll find that the constructive give-and-take with the facilitator is very liberating, allowing you to focus on the issues and advocate for your ideas, without dominating the group in your enthusiasm.

You can also demonstrate the power of collaboration by learning to be a good participant in a meeting—by practicing effective facilitative interventions and preventions, even when you are not facilitating. Facilitative preventions include such actions as getting agreement on outcomes, the agenda, meeting roles, decision making, and ground rules before leaping into the substantive discussion. A simple facilitative request such as, "Let's agree on how we are going to address this issue before we leap in," can be very effective and models good collaborative behavior. Then, during the meeting you can demonstrate facilitative interventions by, for example, asking open-ended questions, redirecting questions rather than always answering them, listening and paraphrasing, and refocusing the discussion when participants get off track.

Supporting and Promoting Collaborative Action

It's been something of a cliché to say that managers do things right; leaders do the right things. We would say that *facilitative leaders get the right people to collaborate on the right things*. Many people in leadership positions feel responsible for producing answers to organizational issues themselves. But you will rarely get it right by yourself, and even if you do, making decisions on your own is disempowering for your organization.

Your role as a facilitative leader is to focus the energies of your organization on the most strategic issues, not to solve them yourself. Your role is to get the right people working on the right problems, with the right processes and resources. To do this, there are several powerful tools at your disposal: you can convene, promote, design, charter, and support collaborative processes. Let's look at each of these tools separately.

Convene

One of the most powerful ways in which you can use your positional power as a leader is to convene. You can say, "Please come to a meeting I'm holding to address this important issue," and people will come—particularly if those people are your subordinates. That's one of the great features of a hierarchy—clarity about who has more decision-making power than whom. But even if the invitees are not your subordinates, the prestige of your office or your organization may be plenty of incentive to attract the people you want to come to a specific meeting. Sometimes just publishing a list of the other invitees can entice some people to come—people who don't want to be left out of something important.

Former President Jimmy Carter uses his position as former president of the United States very effectively to apply nonadversarial processes to address some of the world's most pressing problems. Using the venue of the Carter Center in Atlanta, Carter has for more than a decade been convening meetings to address such issues as Latin American debt and U.S. competitiveness. Carter sometimes will invite other international figures and former presidents to co-convene with him, to avoid any appearance of bias. He often uses professional facilitators or mediators to run these meetings. He invites participants to put aside prepared speeches and work with him informally and off-the-record to explore new solutions to intractable problems.

The format of these collaborative, facilitated work sessions is often new to the world leaders who attend, but, as I have witnessed, Carter's own modeling of facilitative behaviors and his active promoting of the values of openness and cooperation have been enough to bring together the right people to address issues in new, more constructive ways. Carter has clearly found that he can be more effective by applying collaborative processes than by trying to advocate for his own solutions.

Promote

As President Carter has demonstrated, convening is only the first step you must take as a facilitative leader. Next, you must use your position to promote the power of collaborative action, to advocate for addressing a given problem cooperatively, rather than adversarially. Instead of trying to sell stakeholders on your solution to a problem, you need to invite them to join you in a collaborative process. You can use your position to promote collaborative action and, like a master in judo, focus the energy of the group on the right problem by means of a well-designed collaborative process. Furthermore, you can invite the participants to work with you to design the process itself. You can use the full moral force of your role as a leader to promote—or even present as a condition for your participation—the values of teamwork, inclusion, and collaboration.

Alex Plinio used this intervention effectively during the first meeting of stakeholders he convened at the beginning of the Newark Collaboration Group. At a strategic moment, Alex jumped in with an impassioned plea for the creation of a public-private partnership and the initiation of a collaborative, long-range planning process. He invited participants to join him in a self-selected process design group to explore how this might be done. Convene, advocate for collaboration, and then model facilitative behaviors by working with key stakeholders to design a planning process collaboratively: Alex Plinio demonstrated all these important practices of facilitative leadership in this one critical meeting in Newark.

Design

Groups can tolerate only a certain level of ambiguity and chaos before a situation becomes dysfunctional. It would be intolerable in most cases for a leader to say, "I don't know what our strategy will be and I don't even know how we are going to develop one." However, it is acceptable, and often advisable, for a leader to say, "I don't know exactly what our final strategy will be, but here is the process by which we are going to build that strategy together." It's a question of degrees of freedom. You can and must, as a facilitative leader, be open-ended about responses to critical problems, turning the issues back to your organization to solve. But you also must insist on clear process maps for getting from here to there. People need to know when and how they will be involved. You, as a leader, need to know who is responsible for managing a process, who is going to be involved, and when the process will be completed. A process map, as we have seen, is a powerful tool for focusing the energies of your organization or community in a manageable collaborative effort. It's a way to reduce ambiguity but still keep the content of a decision open until it has been fully discussed by all relevant stakeholders.

So one of the levers you have as a facilitative leader is to require that a process map be designed for each important collaborative effort and that the key stakeholders, including you, agree to the map, with its milestones and deliverables, before the substantive discussions begin. Process maps are tools for ensuring that collaborative processes are open, visible, and inclusive before such efforts progress too far.

Charter

Typically, a core team or task force forms the center of a collaborative project. The first phase of many efforts involves assembling the team and agreeing on the work plan, including the process map. It's important for you, as a facilitative leader, to also require that the team work with you to develop and agree to an explicit charter before work begins. A charter should clarify such issues as shared and meaningful purpose, specific and challenging goals, clear roles, common and collaborative approach, and complementary skills and resources. (See page 226 in Additional Models.) It allows you to be sure that the right problem is being addressed by the right people, in the right way, even though you may only be involved in the process at a few checkpoints.

Support

To guarantee the success of a collaborative project once it's chartered and launched, you must actively support it. Your support as a leader can be crucial. Just showing up at approval meetings can have a powerful impact, demonstrating that the project is important and worthy of your valuable time. Obviously, your facilitative behaviors at these meetings can also reinforce the collaborative culture—you should listen more than speak, be respectful and appreciative of the effort that has been made, and contribute your own thoughts, as appropriate. You can also support a project by clearing the way through bureaucratic hurdles and making timely decisions that reinforce and speed up a project.

General Electric's "work out" process is a good example of leaders effectively supporting and resourcing a collaborative effort. In this process, decision makers and relevant stakeholders are assembled in one place with a limited amount of time. After prioritizing a list of key issues, work groups are formed with the charge of returning in a few hours with some recommendations. While the senior decision makers may not be involved in the subgroups, they return in person to listen to the reports and make decisions on the spot. It's clear from their presence and actions that the process is "for real" and that the work groups' recommendations will be acted upon.

You can also provide essential support for a project in more traditional ways, such as by providing release time, appropriate staffing and facilities, technology, process and technical assistance, skill development for the team, and funding for travel. Just designing a process and launching a task force is not enough. If you do not provide the project with the necessary resources, you might as well not get it started at all. Delivering critical support is another lever of the facilitative leader.

Lead the Process of Cultural Change

If you want to build a collaborative environment, one capable of responding quickly in this rapidly changing world of global markets, then you must lead the process of cultural change. The cultures of groups and organizations are finely crafted systems—even in their dysfunctionality. Everyone colludes in maintaining the existing culture, even though many may complain vociferously. Everyone gets something out of the way things are, even if it is just predictability. No one is more essential for changing the culture than you, the leader.

Systemic change poses several significant challenges to you as a leader and agent of change. Much as people may complain about the old system, people are naturally afraid of change. The old and familiar is less threatening than the new and unpredictable. We have found that some of the most vocal critics of the old are also the most resistant to adopting new attitudes and behaviors. And change is difficult, time consuming, and sometimes painful. A system undergoing change may function more poorly for a while before it improves. For example, when you are learning to use a new or upgraded word-processing program, writing documents using the new program may take longer and be more difficult than using the old one—though after a while it should go faster and be more efficient. Similarly, when an autocratic system tries to become more collaborative, for a while things will seem to be a mess. There will seem to be more conflict rather than less as many of the old issues bubble to the surface and as everyone wants to be involved in everything. It takes a tremendous amount of courage and conviction to lead your system through such a change. When your organization or community hits a rough spot or crisis, there will be a strong tendency to fall back to the old ways of doing things. This is just when your commitment to and modeling of the new ways of doing things is most important. At these strategic moments, if you meet and work through the challenges collaboratively, you will have taken a great step in building a collaborative environment.

Most processes of cultural change progress through three phases. The first phase involves describing what exists today: accurately describing and acknowledging responsibility for the current norms, values, and behaviors. If the members of your organization don't recognize and understand the problem, they won't support the changes you want to make. You must participate with your team in a process of looking at how things actually work—not at your professed values and procedures, but at the unwritten rules of the road. To get at the current norms, we often ask the question this way: "If you were briefing a new member of your team about how to get along, how to fit in, what would you tell him or her about how to succeed—how not to rock the boat?" This often elicits smiles from the group and makes it OK to discuss things that are usually left unsaid.

Some of the norms and values may be positive—you may want to hold on to them. Others may be clearly destructive and not in keeping with the culture you would like to build. Your move as a facilitative leader is not only to make it comfortable for people to discuss the current culture but, more importantly, to acknowledge your role in having kept things the way they are. It's important to model openness and vulnerability, to be able to take responsibility for how you have colluded in maintaining the negative aspects of the current culture. If you can't do this yourself, you can't expect your direct reports to be brave enough to assume responsibility for their own role in the situation in your presence.

A good example of this kind of facilitative leadership style was modeled by the president of a hospital for which I did consulting work. Hospitals are notorious for the adversarial relationships that exist between administrators and physicians. In this particular hospital, everyone (president, physicians, administrators, nurses, even the board) complained about the institution's very autocratic, command-and-control culture and about the open warfare between the president and the division chiefs (who were physicians). After some coaching, the president openly admitted to his physician chiefs that in some ways he liked the fighting—it kept him in control and kept the chiefs from acquiring too much power. Besides, he could tolerate it because he only had to meet with them for two hours each month.

The division chiefs subsequently admitted that they also colluded in maintaining the system. By conducting one-on-one budget negotiations with the president instead of working collaboratively with other divisions, each chief thought he could make a better deal for his division and didn't have to worry about trade-offs with other divisions. Both the president and the division chiefs confessed to each other that they would have to give up these perceived benefits if they were to move to a more collaborative culture, one they agreed they needed in order to survive in a rapidly changing, competitive external environment.

The second phase of cultural change is often the easiest: agreeing on the new norms and behaviors toward which you want to move. If you have done a good job of uncovering what doesn't work in your current culture, you already have an idea of what you want in the new one. At this point, it's totally appropriate for you to use your positional power to advocate for values supporting collaborative action: respect for human dignity, and the right of appropriate stakeholder involvement. For many leaders, these values become nonnegotiable, absolute musts.

The third phase is the most difficult: adopting, modeling, and reinforcing the new values and behaviors to the point where they become the new norms. During the early period of this phase, the change process is most vulnerable. Everyone is watching for whether the change will stick—whether it's something that will last or just a passing fancy. The person they will watch the most will be you. If you are really trying to model the new, more collaborative behaviors, if you are "walking the talk," then the message will spread through the organization that a serious change is taking place. When you fail (as everyone does at some point), if you can laugh at yourself and acknowledge how difficult it is to change behaviors, this, too, will support the effort. Likewise, if you can acknowledge and celebrate change in others, you will reinforce the effort as a whole. It is particularly in times of crisis that organizational systems tend to snap back to old norms. During these time of stress, leaders must stay the course if they want the change to succeed.

Conclusion

This chapter has touched on those leadership skill sets that most directly relate to supporting collaborative action and building collaborative cultures. (For an overview of our complete model of the seven practices of facilitative leadership, please refer to the Resources section.) The key message is that collaboration requires a new model of leadership—facilitative leadership—which is essential for building collaborative cultures in organizations and communities. Leaders have a profound impact on organizational cultures. Collaborative cultures can't be nurtured without the support and congruent actions of their leaders.

How to Be a Successful Mentor

Managing Challenges, Avoiding Pitfalls, and Recognizing Benefits

Ralph E. Viator, Derek Dalton, and Nancy Harp

In recent years, public accounting firms and other organizations have recognized that mentoring junior-level accountants promotes long-term growth and success. As a result, most firms encourage experienced personnel to engage in mentoring activities. Many organizations use highly structured, formal programs to facilitate the mentoring process and match potential mentors with potential protégés. CPAs who have been asked to serve as formally assigned mentors or are considering informally mentoring lower-level employees should ask themselves whether they are aware of the potential challenges and pitfalls of mentoring and, more importantly, whether they know how to navigate around them. The discussion below identifies the roles that mentors perform, offers specific suggestions for managing mentoring challenges and avoiding mentoring pitfalls, and explores the personal benefits that CPAs can enjoy by becoming true mentors.

Being a True Mentor

True mentors provide their protégés with both career support and social support. Individuals who decide to become mentors can provide career support by assigning protégés challenging tasks and then coaching them during those tasks. Furthermore, when protégés are ready for advancement, mentors can help them develop relationships with higher ranking personnel; at the same time, they can shield protégés from organizational politics and provide them with insight into organizational changes.

True mentors can provide social support for their protégés through open and candid conversations about goals and career aspirations, fears and anxieties, and potential work-family conflicts. By providing acceptance and confirmation, mentors enable

protégés to take risks and venture onto new paths. Social support also includes providing assurance to protégés that mentors will support them even if they make mistakes. In essence, a true mentor serves as a confidant, friend, and trusted advisor.

Challenges of Mentoring

Numerous challenges can arise during the mentoring process that might result from differences between mentors and protégés. The following sections examine some of these potential issues.

Gender Differences

In the case of female protégés, mentors can provide unique guidance and support in many ways, including promoting women's success and advancement within the organization, facilitating women's connections to informal networks, increasing female protégés' exposure to top clients and high-profile engagements, and reassuring them that they can advance within the organization and the profession. Such reassurance is not trivial, given that women represent only 21% of all partners in public accounting firms (*2011 Trends in the Supply of Accounting Graduates and the Demand for Public Accounting Recruits*, AICPA, www.aicpa.org/InterestAreas/AccountingEducation/NewsAndPublications/DownloadableDocuments/2011TrendsReport.pdf) and 9% of CFOs at *Fortune* 500 companies (Marielle Segarra, "Women CFOs: Still at 9%," CFO.com, June 22, 2011, www.cfonet.com/article.cfm/14581369).

National and regional public accounting firms clearly recognize the importance of mentoring in retaining and promoting women in public accounting. For example, Deloitte's Women's Initiative (WIN) hosts more than 400 professional development, networking, and mentoring events each year (*Unleashing Potential: Women's Initiative Annual Report*, Deloitte, http://www.deloitte.com/assets/Dcom-UnitedStates/Local%20Assets/Documents/WAR_sm%20FINAL.pdf). Although business organizations aggressively pursue policies for hiring, retaining, and promoting women (Herminia Ibara, Nancy M. Carter, and Christine Silva, "Why Men Still Get More Promotions Than Women," *Harvard Business Review*, September 2010), the low percentage of women at the highest organizational levels might cause young female professional accountants to wonder whether they can really make it to the level of senior executive. As mentors, CPAs can help young female professionals evaluate their strengths and weaknesses, examine their desire for promotion and increased responsibility, and, when appropriate, provide encouragement.

Career advancement is not the only possible outcome of a successful mentoring relationship, however; mentoring can also lead to strong personal relationships that provide protégés with much-needed social support.

Career advancement is not the only possible outcome of a successful mentoring relationship, however; mentoring can also lead to strong personal relationships that provide protégés with much-needed social support. For example, high-quality mentoring relationships can assist protégés (both male and female) in balancing work and family issues or adjusting to life as a professional accountant. Academic research has shown that, in some cases, women prefer strong, supportive relationships, regardless of whether the relationship facilitates career advancement, such as being assigned high-profile engagements or obtaining accelerated promotions (Carol McKeen and Merridee Bujaki, "Gender and Mentoring: Issues, Effects, and Opportunities," *The Handbook of Mentoring at Work: Theory, Research, and Practice,* Sage Publications, 2007). Therefore, when serving as mentors, CPAs should keep in mind that sometimes male and female protégés view successful mentoring relationships differently. But open, supportive personal relationships can be intrinsically satisfying to both a protégé and a mentor, regardless of the protégé's career aspirations (Joyce K. Fletcher and Belle Rose Ragins, "Stone Center Relational Cultural Theory: A Window on Relational Mentoring," *The Handbook of Mentoring at Work: Theory, Research, and Practice*, Sage Publications, 2007).

Racial Diversity

The workforce in the United States is becoming more diverse. In 2000, ethnic minorities (primarily African Americans, Hispanics, and Asian Americans) represented 29% of the workforce and 19% of all professional positions. By 2010, however, those percentages increased, and ethnic minorities constituted 35% of the workforce and 25% of all professional positions ("Job Patterns for Minorities and Women in Private Industry," U.S. Equal Employment Opportunity Commission, http://eeoc.gov/eeoc/statistics/employment/jobpat-eeo1/). Furthermore, ethnic minorities accounted for 21% of all employees in public accounting firms (3% African American,

4% Hispanic, 11% Asian American, and 3% other) but only 6% of all public accounting partners in 2010 (AICPA 2011).

The growth of ethnic minorities as a percentage of the U.S. workforce provides senior employees with the opportunity to enhance diversity in the workplace by mentoring ethnic-minority protégés. Because white professionals currently hold the vast majority of senior-level positions (partners, senior executives, and managers), they can provide ethnic minorities with substantive career support by providing challenging assignments, coaching protégés through assignments, sponsoring protégés for promotions, and providing exposure and visibility to protégés—as well as protection from organizational politics. Yet, one specific question lingers: can senior-level white professionals provide ethnic minorities with the necessary social support? David A. Thomas, a distinguished African American business professor who retired from Harvard University, noted the following in a coauthored essay:

> People of color often develop two complementary networks: one set of relationships with Whites who may provide access to resources and opportunities and another set of relationships with people of color who provide psychosocial and emotional support. Whites, on the other hand, don't have to include people who are racially different from them within their networks. ... For people of color, same-race and interracial mentoring serve very different purposes. (Stacy Blake-Beard, Audrey Murrell, and David A. Thomas, "Unfinished Business: The Impact of Race on Understanding Mentoring Relationships," *The Handbook of Mentoring at Work: Theory, Research, and Practice*, Sage Publications, 2007)

Given this insight, encouraging ethnic minority professionals to develop relationships with multiple mentors is reasonable advice. CPAs can encourage ethnic-minority protégés to stay in touch with same-race mentors at other office locations or at their own organizational level. Some accounting firms specifically encourage the development of these connections internally through firm-organized groups. For example, PricewaterhouseCoopers' groups are known as "Minority Circles" and Deloitte's groups are known as "Business Resource Groups" (BRG), such as the "Hispanic/Latino(a) Employee Network & Allies BRG." If a firm does not have internal organized groups, CPAs can encourage minority protégés to join national support groups, such as the National Association of Black Accountants, the Association of Latino Professionals in Finance and Accounting, and Ascend (Pan-Asian Leaders). Encouraging ethnic minorities to join firm-specific or national support groups is a good human resources practice, and it demonstrates a sincere interest in employees' professional development.

Work-Family Conflicts

It's easy to promote the concept of work-family balance, but it's difficult to actually find that balance. Most professionals want a job that they find both interesting and challenging, as well as time to enjoy with friends and family. Talented and well-educated individuals are attracted to the accounting profession because of career opportunities, financial rewards, and the personal satisfaction derived from meaningful work; however, young accounting professionals often quickly discover that obtaining these goals requires working long days, spending weekends completing assignments, traveling to client locations, attending training seminars, and studying emerging issues. All of these activities require spending time away from family and friends.

Each protégé is likely to respond differently to these demands. Some might question whether the time commitment is worth it; others might find satisfaction from challenging projects, regardless of the time spent on them. CPA mentors should recognize that their values might differ from protégés' values regarding the relative importance of work versus personal time. In addition, CPAs should ask themselves some basic questions regarding work-family issues.

First, is a protégé's family role similar to or different from a mentor's own family role? Protégés will likely differ in their responsibility concerning child-rearing tasks, household maintenance, and time spent with extended family. Perhaps career advancement is one of the mentor's top goals, but it might not be of paramount importance to some protégés. Mentors must ask themselves whether they can provide guidance that recognizes the differences, as well as the similarities, between their own career aspirations and their protégés' aspirations. Mentors should identify advice that they can give protégés who want to succeed at the firm or company, but who also have a strong desire to protect time spent with family and friends.

Second, mentors must determine whether they are willing to share personal experiences related to work-family conflict with protégés. For example, mentors must ask themselves whether they are willing to reveal how they handled specific conflicts and the consequences of their actions. Third, mentors must acknowledge whether they are willing to help protégés identify their personal values and recognize the importance of those values. Perhaps a protégé wants to focus on succeeding with the firm or company; a true mentor can help this protégé understand both the positive and negative consequences of those values. Alternatively, a protégé might value time spent with friends more than time spent at the office. Once again, a true mentor can help the protégé understand the potential consequences of those values.

ADDITIONAL READING

Lillian T. Eby, Jaime R. Durley, Sarah C. Evans, and Belle Rose Ragins, "Mentors' Perceptions of Negative Mentoring Experiences: Scale Development and Nomological Validation," *Journal of Applied Psychology*, March 2008.

Lillian T. Eby and Stacy E. McManus, "The Protégé's Role in Negative Mentoring Experiences," *Journal of Vocational Behavior*, October 2004.

Jeffrey H. Greenhaus and Romila Singh, "Mentoring and the Work-Family Interface," *The Handbook of Mentoring at Work: Theory, Research, and Practice*, Sage Publications, 2007.

Belle Rose Ragins and Terri A. Scandura, "Burden or Blessing? Expected Costs and Benefits of Being a Mentor," *Journal of Organizational Behavior*, July 1999.

Avoiding Pitfalls

Challenges don't only occur as a result of disparate qualities in a mentor-protégé relationship. Sometimes, obstacles can arise from a protégé's poor performance or lack of independence. The following sections discuss several pitfalls that CPAs might encounter during the mentoring process.

Protégé Performance Problems: Technical and Interpersonal Skills

Unfortunately, not all protégés will meet their stated career goals. Some protégés lack technical skills that cannot be acquired through additional training or coaching. Others lack the interpersonal skills needed to interact effectively with team members, client personnel, or top management. Thus, when serving as mentors, CPAs should critically assess protégés' stated career goals against their personal strengths and weaknesses. A change in career goals is sometimes the best solution, and a true mentor can guide protégés through those changes. For example, an accounting protégé who has an outstanding personality but weak analytical skills might blossom by working in human resources, running professional training programs, or even recruiting other young professionals to the organization.

Protégé Performance Problems: Willingness to Learn

One of the most valuable traits that potential protégés can possess is a willingness to learn. Talented young professional accountants sometimes appear uneager to learn new skills, tackle new projects, or initiate new ways of getting the job done. Perhaps these employees simply need a mentor who is willing to tell it to them straight by describing other employees who failed to demonstrate on-the-job learning and, subsequently, did not receive expected promotions or pay raises. To avoid mentoring protégés who lack a willingness to learn, CPAs should observe whether potential protégés respond positively to recommendations encouraging the development of new skills.

Bad Reflection

A real risk in mentoring junior-level accountants is that they might ultimately underperform or fail to meet the organization's expectations. Although this failure may be attributed strictly to a protégé's lack of technical skills, the negative outcomes could become associated with their mentors. Such associations, while certainly unfair, are a reality that potential mentors must acknowledge and address. Thus, CPAs should exercise careful judgment when evaluating potential protégés' current and future performance.

Self-Destructive Behavior

In a world filled with a variety of opportunities and temptations, some protégés engage in self-destructive behavior, such as alcohol or drug abuse, or have harmful personal relationships. Often, it is difficult to distinguish protégés who handle themselves well at social gatherings from those who eventually overindulge in alcohol and embarrass themselves. To minimize the odds of encountering such problems, CPAs should carefully evaluate protégés' potential for self-destructive behavior. They should avoid glossing over the issue with excuses such as, "Oh, he's just having fun." Instead, mentors should have candid conversations with protégés, informing them of the potential consequences of their actions and, perhaps, including examples of other employees who drank excessively at social gatherings and developed bad reputations within the organization.

Too Reliant or Time-Consuming

True mentoring implies that CPAs will eventually release protégés to function independently; however, some protégés have trouble finishing tasks by themselves and continue to rely unnecessarily on their mentors. In these circumstances, mentors must be prepared to have candid conversations with their protégés. CPAs should explain that protégés are expected to demonstrate more self-reliance when solving problems in order to advance in the organization.

Benefits of Mentoring

Given the substantial commitment required to be a true mentor, why would any professional accountant willingly mentor others? The reason is simple: serving as a true mentor can offer significant personal benefits to CPAs.

Improved Job Performance

CPAs who currently supervise young accountants should decide whether they perceive themselves as the accountants' supervisor, mentor, or both. By recognizing that part of their job includes mentoring protégés, CPAs can view the time spent developing protégés' talents as an investment ranther than an expense. CPAs can develop protégés' talents by assigning them challenging tasks and coaching them as they perform those tasks. As protégés develop new skills, their mentors will eventually be able to turn more work over to them and focus on other issues, such as client relations and engagement planning. In the long term, devoting time to mentoring protégés can improve a mentor's job performance as well.

Recognition by Others

As protégés become more competent and reliable, mentors will be seen as someone who can get the job done. A protégé's success can reflect positively on a mentor, earning additional respect from higher ranking managers or partners.

> *The benefits of mentoring can outweigh the costs, but CPAs considering mentoring should keep in mind that the benefits are sometimes intrinsic rather than extrinsic.*

Loyal Support Base

True mentoring relationships take time to develop, but once a commitment is established and protégés have demonstrated on-the-job competency, a personal bond generally develops between the mentor and the protégé. This bond is extremely valuable, and mentors often discover that protégés will become some of the mentor's most loyal supporters, providing assistance when difficult situations arise.

Potential Clients

Strong connections with protégés who eventually leave the organization can provide CPAs with excellent future networking and business opportunities. For example, a protégé might eventually work at a company that a CPA's firm is targeting as a potential client. If protégés communicate a positive view of their mentor wherever they go, then the CPA is more likely to develop positive relationships with individuals outside of her own firm or company.

Intrinsically Rewarding

Mentors often describe the satisfaction they receive from passing along their insights and wisdom. As CPAs assume additional responsibilities, whether in public accounting, industry, or government, they acquire unique perspectives on organizational operations and real-world decision making. Such insights are extremely valuable and, at the same time, unavailable in training seminars or professional textbooks. By purposefully mentoring junior-level accountants, mentors have the opportunity to pass along their knowledge, as well as guidance that they acquired from their own former mentors.

Rejuvenating Experiences

Historically, mentors tend to identify and select protégés who appear to be younger versions of themselves. When evaluating potential protégés, CPAs might recognize a passion and motivation that they possessed when they first entered the profession. Perhaps they might see someone who has potential, but simply lacks the guidance and advice that they needed when they began their careers. By connecting with potential protégés, CPAs can literally reconnect with their younger selves and feel rejuvenated.

Additional Advice

True mentors provide protégés with social support in addition to career support. Successful mentoring requires an understanding of how to navigate the challenges posed by mentor-protégé differences, with respect to gender, ethnicity, work-family conflict, and career aspirations. Mentors must learn how to avoid pitfalls by critically evaluating protégés. The benefits of mentoring can outweigh the costs, but CPAs considering mentoring should keep in mind that the benefits are sometimes intrinsic (such as the personal satisfaction obtained from helping protégés align their abilities with their goals) rather than extrinsic (the financial rewards that can accrue when protégés assume positions of responsibility and enable mentors to expand their practices or businesses).

Ralph E. Viator, PhD, is a Clark & Lois Webster Professor of accounting at Rawls College of Business, Texas Tech University, Lubbock, Tex. Derek Dalton, PhD, CPA, is an assistant professor in the college of business and behavioral science at Clemson University, Clemson, S.C. Nancy Harp, CPA, is a PhD candidate, also at Rawls College of Business, Texas Tech University.

Meet Like You Mean Business

Diana Booher

You will never see eye-to-eye if you never meet face-to-face.
—Warren Buffett, Businessman, Investor, and Philanthropist

When you attend a meeting as a participant rather than as a facilitator, you produce value by contributing to the outcome—not simply by your presence. Although that may sound obvious, it's not: I've sat through meetings in which a few attendees played with their devices, worked on other projects, or left the room repeatedly to take other calls.

Such behavior is a mistake. **If you show up physically, be present mentally.** If the meeting leader fails to facilitate, understand the meeting process and follow the flow well enough so that you can step into the gap and demonstrate your leadership skills as you guide a productive discussion. Of course, don't make a big play to "take over" the facilitator role. But as a meeting participant, you can do much to steer the discussion by being familiar with meeting processes: brainstorming alternatives, analyzing potential solutions, building consensus, deciding, summarizing, transitioning to new topics, and so forth.

The meeting communication roles and strategies that follow increase your chances to end with results, not excuses because you weren't *the* leader in charge.

Rein in a Rambling Discussion

As Charles Kettering, the famed inventor and head of research for General Motors, once stated, "A problem well stated is a problem half-solved." As a strong meeting contributor, reel in an unwieldy discussion to respond to the question before the group.

If no clear question or well-defined problem has been posed, consider that your challenge: State it succinctly for the group's focus.

Analyze Where the Discussion Needs to Go

You have many choices to structure your discussion: From status quo to goal. From problem to solution. From need to criteria to options to decision. From pro/con analysis of options to decision. From opportunity to creation of new ideas to decisive action. If the meeting leader lags behind, you can suggest a structure for the group to follow. Most inexperienced facilitators will gladly allow you to help move the discussion along as opposed to drifting uncomfortably in a free-for-all situation.

Decide When to Offer Your Opinion First

If you intend to move ahead with your idea but want input or validation, don't set yourself up to be shot down with statements like: "I plan to do X next quarter. Anybody have a problem with that?"

> If you **show up** physically, **be present** mentally.

Or: "I'm going to be changing the policy on X to allow Y. Everybody okay with that?" Such phrasing makes some people uncomfortable. They'll need chutzpah to raise an objection or give negative feedback in front of a group—especially when the statements sound as if the decision has already been made.

Rephrase to get candid feedback: "I plan to do X next quarter. What challenges and obstacles do you think I need to prepare for?" Or: "I'm *thinking* about changing the policy on X to allow Y. I know everyone won't agree. What pushback do you anticipate I'll get?" This last rewording sounds particularly open, as if you're waiting for input before making a final decision.

Understand also that this phrasing communicates your strong opinion and that you are conceding little or no decision authority to the group. If that's your intent, let the group know that at the beginning rather than mislead them about their input on the issue.

Decide When to Offer Your Opinion Last

If your group includes members who seem timid about expressing themselves on controversial issues, you may want to offer your comments last. Toss out an open-ended question on your topic. Ask followup questions. Allow plenty of silence after people answer your questions or give input. People tend to fill silence with more information. (I've found this technique invaluable in interviewing job applicants. An original 20-second answer can turn into a valuable five-minute disclosure.)

If you'd like to share your own input about a topic, you can always do that after others have voiced theirs.

Create a Safe Environment

In an ideal world, all meeting attendees would play nice. They would arrive on time, put away their devices, tune in to the discussion, contribute passionately, listen to their colleagues' opinions, understand the logical flow of the commentary, resolve conflict amicably, leave fully committed to the group's decisions, and be accountable for any assigned follow-up action.

But meetings may unfold similar to encounters on the playground: Passive and dominating attendees annoy each other and complicate the process. So why not simply let the passives fade into the woodwork and let the dominators take over the game board? Several reasons:

- Dominators answer every question before others have time to respond to the challenge, analyze issues, and think for themselves.
- Dominators often ramble and repeat themselves, creating boredom and impatience among the group members.
- Dominators monopolize and prevent other ideas and solutions from surfacing.
- The biased opinion of one or two dominant personalities may not represent the group as a whole, and, as a result, decisions and actions may not accurately reflect the group's thinking—or yours.
- Passives frequently complain later that they've had no opportunity for input.
- Passives often fail to engage and lend their support to important initiatives.
- Passives deprive others of their expertise.

So what's your role as a participant? You serve in much the same capacity as a panelist at a forum or industry conference. Your goal, along with that of the facilitator, is to create an environment in which everyone has a chance to contribute. That often means putting some controls on the dominator. You can:

Accept comments from the dominator without yielding the floor. Giving verbal pats on the back typically encourages the person to keep talking and explaining. (Examples of verbal pats on the back: "That's an idea. Others?" "Good idea." "I like that." "That could work.") *Withholding such pats* can extinguish the dominator's input.

Acknowledge a contribution with body language only—eye contact, a smile, a nod, an open palm—and then turn to someone else for another contribution.

Call on others by name to jump into the discussion: "Jaime, what do you think about X?"

Play traffic cop with a verbal cue: "Let's hear from several people on this issue." "Somebody from Legal—what do you think about the proposed change?" Or: "I'd like to hear everyone weigh in on this issue. What do the rest of you think?"

Play traffic cop with your body language or voice. Simply break eye contact, and divert attention elsewhere in the room. If on a teleconference, break the dominator's train of thought during a long ramble by asking a question: "Julie, excuse me for interrupting here. Let me ask you a question about what you just said." Then ask a short-answer question. That distraction typically breaks the ramble and gives you opportunity to regain the floor after the person's short answer.

Call the dominator by name: "Tyler, before we get on another track here, I'd like us to spend more time discussing how to …" Calling a person's name puts him or her on the spot in a gentle way to relinquish the floor—and refocuses discussion quickly to avoid embarrassing anyone.

To sum up: Being a meeting participant dropout and playing word games on your smartphone or responding to email is not the answer to meaningless meetings. Instead, contribute value by paying attention to process and rescuing an inept facilitator. Counter group-think and create a level playing field for all to participate productively. Real leaders take the initiative when the stakes are high.

SECTION EIGHT

COMMUNICATION SKILLS FOR INTERVIEWS

To conclude this collection, section 8 presents one of the most important communicative interactions within business communication. Students might consider two phases of business communication: obtaining employment and executing employment. Davis and Hererra discuss interviewing from the perspective of the interviewer. What defines a "good" interview, and what are the various responsibilities of the interviewer? Students should find this perspective helpful in preparing for their own interviews. It never hurts to know what the other side is thinking! Berk continues this discussion by identifying some of those specific types of questions that might throw off candidates during the interview. "What is your spirit animal?" has found its way into more than one interview! How would you react? What if you did not know the answer to a question and drew a blank? Berk offers several tips to ace these questions and more by presenting difficult (yet still common) interview questions, followed by several potential ways in which to respond. Moreover, Berk offers commentary on most of the potential questions that describes *how* to articulate these answers in the best possible manner.

Consider the following questions when reading this section:

1. What difficulties have you encountered in previous interviews?
2. What types of questions might be inappropriate for an interviewer to ask?
3. How might interviewers make sure they do not ask inappropriate questions?

4. How might you answer a question that you do not have enough information to answer accurately as stated?
5. "If you could be an eagle, bear, or fish, which animal would you choose?"
6. "If you were a type of cereal, what would you be?"
7. As a potential job candidate, what will make you stand out from other candidates with the exact same basic skills set?

Key Terms and Concepts

- Task interviews
- Stress interviews
- Behavioral interviews
- Technical questions
- Nontechnical questions
- Sticky-situation questions

Preparing for the Job Interview

The Interviewer's Responsibility

Charles E. Davis and Anthony Herrera

"What would you do if I gave you an elephant?" "What do you think of the artwork hanging on this wall?" "If you were a dog, what kind of dog would you be?" These are actual questions that candidates report having been asked in job interviews. But how will answers to these questions help you make an intelligent hiring decision? If you can't answer that question, then you shouldn't be asking the others.

Research confirms what common knowledge suggests—interviews are one of the most commonly used and well-liked tools for selecting employees. Yet most interviewers never receive training on conducting an effective interview. Instead, they fly by the seat of their pants, blissfully ignorant of the fact that they don't know what they are doing or why they are asking the questions on their list—assuming they have thought enough in advance to make a list of questions.

The interview questions on the previous page were reported in Ann Howard, Scott Erker, and Neal Bruce's 2007 white paper, "Slugging Through the War for Talent." Their research showed that training increases the interviewer's confidence in his or her interviewing ability (see Figure 8.1.1). Knowing that, it seems that educating interviewers on how best to conduct an employment interview will result in better identification of the best candidate to fill a particular job opening. This article provides you with basic information on how to prepare for and conduct an effective interview.

The key to hiring success is identifying the candidate with the greatest level of "fit" with the job and organization. A candidate's fit with the job may be assessed partially through a résumé or skills testing. But the fit with the organization's values, norms, and culture is best assessed through a face-to-face interview that's structured to accomplish three goals. First, the interviewer must communicate the organization's values, norms, and culture to the candidate. Second, the interviewer must assess

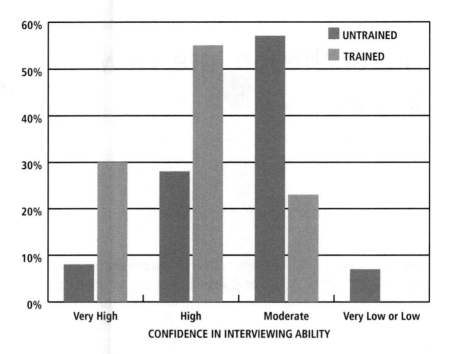

FIGURE 8.1.1 Training Increases Interviewer Confidence

Source: Ann Howard, Scott Erker, and Neal Bruce, "Slugging Through the War for Talent," Development Dimensions International, Inc., 2007. Reprinted with permission from Development Dimensions International, Inc.

the candidate's values, work ethic, and, to some degree, skills and knowledge. Finally, both the interviewer and the candidate must determine the degree of organizational fit.

Why is it important to identify and hire a candidate with a high degree of organizational fit? It's because a bad hire is a costly mistake. In a recent CareerBuilder survey, 41% of the responding companies estimated that a bad hiring mistake cost them more than $25,000, while 24% reported an estimated cost of more than $50,000. The respondents also reported additional negative impacts other than the direct monetary costs, as Table 8.1.1 shows.

Types of Interviews

There are three basic interview approaches: task interviews, stress interviews, and behavioral interviews. Each type assesses a different set of skills, so you need to match the purpose of your interview with the type of interview.

In a task interview, the candidate is asked to perform a task or solve a problem. Questions asked during the interview might be similar to "How many stoplights are there in Manhattan?" In this example, the actual answer isn't as important as how the candidate developed his or her answer. An extended task interview model might assign a candidate to work on an actual short-term project as a member of an existing team. The assignment facilitates an assessment

TABLE 8.1.1   Negative Impacts of a Bad Hire

Impact	% of Companies Experiencing the Impact
Lost worker productivity	39%
Lost time to recruit and train replacement worker	39%
Negative impact on employee morale	33%
Negative impact on client solutions	19%
Lost sales to customers	11%
Legal proceedings	9%

Source: CareerBuilder.com, "Nearly Seven in Ten Businesses Affected by a Bad Hire in the Past Year, According to CareerBuilder Survey," December 13, 2012, www.careerbuilder.com/share/aboutus/pressreleasesdetail.aspx?sd=12%2f13%2f2012&siteid=cbpr&sc_cmp1=cb_pr730_&id=pr730&ed=12%2f31%2f2012.

of how the candidate solves a particular task and interacts with team members. Task interviews are useful for positions where interviewers are trying to assess a candidate's analytical and problem-solving skills, such as consulting or investment banking positions.

A stress interview is useful for assessing how a candidate reacts in stressful situations. In this type of interview, the interviewer may use long periods of silence between questions and answers, ask leading questions, or frequently interrupt the candidate. Questions may be similar to "I've interviewed five candidates with more experience than you, so why should I hire you instead?" When delivered with an accusatory or harsh vocal tone, such questions will create a heightened level of stress for the candidate. Stress interviews are best used for positions that require employees to function under highly stressful conditions, such as collection agents and customer service representatives. Be careful if you choose to use stress interviews, however, as candidates might be offended or bothered by the antagonistic nature of the questioning and will decide not to work for the company even when there's a high level of organizational fit on other components. This is particularly true for entry-level-position candidates in areas such as accounting and finance.

In a behavioral interview, the interviewer attempts to discern how a candidate will behave and react in a particular situation. The candidate is asked to recall a situation he or she has experienced and is then asked a question related to that experience. The candidate's response is used as a predictor of future performance or behavior. Since an employee's behavior influences job performance in many ways, behavioral interviews are useful in a variety of settings from entry-level positions to senior-executive positions. Questions in a behavioral interview will be similar to "Think of a time when you were involved in a project that required attention to details. How did you make sure all the details were covered?"

Research shows that people provide more information and details about their behavior when asked to explain their past behaviors. This additional information helps interviewers make better, more-informed hiring decisions. And while behavioral interview questions can also be structured around hypothetical situations, research shows that interviews based on actual experiences are more valid than those using hypothetical situations.

The Interviewer's Two Tasks

The ultimate goal of the interview is to identify the candidate who best matches the organization's culture and needs and to have that candidate accept the employment offer. This means that you as the interviewer have to accomplish two tasks during the interview: a buy task and a sell task.

As a buyer of talent, you must focus on assessing how well a candidate's skills, knowledge, and personality match the demands of the position. This match is determined by asking job-related, behavior-based questions during the interview. If planned systematically before the interview, these questions will provide sufficient information for making the appropriate determination. Of course, the focus on job-related questions means that questions such as the one about the elephant posed at the beginning of this article should be avoided ... unless, of course, you're interviewing someone for a zookeeper position. If you want to tap into the candidate's creativity or ability to think fast on his or her feet, spend some time before the interview thinking about how to use well-designed, behavior-based questions to make that assessment.

The second task you must complete during the interview is to sell the company and the position to the candidate. The information you provide will allow the candidate to assess whether he or she will fit in and be successful in the position. As an interviewer, you can do a fantastic job of assessing employee fit from the company's perspective, but if you don't successfully sell the company and position to the candidate, he or she won't accept your job offer.

Recognizing the two goals of an interview, it's important to balance the session between the two tasks. Failure to appropriately plan an interview strategy commonly leads to accomplishing just one of the tasks, which results in an incomplete interview. Spend too much time on the buy task, and the candidate can't assess the degree of cultural fit with the organization. If you spend too much time on the sell task, you won't have a good understanding of the candidate's qualifications. Either way, the interview process would fail, and the likelihood of making a good hiring decision is reduced. Table 8.1.2 provides points on how to complete both the buy and sell sides of the interview.

Planning the "Buy" Task

Begin planning for the interview by considering the buy task. Answering the following two questions will give you a good starting point:

1.   What are the company's values?
2.   What core competencies must the candidate possess to achieve a high degree of organizational fit?

TABLE 8.1.2   Interviewer Tasks

	Buy	**Sell**
DO	• Ask job-related questions to help ensure quality of hires and reduce potential for legal trouble. • Structure your interview to target pertinent information and limit faking. • Ask behavior-based questions to get specific information about past actions; especially important for high-level, complex positions.	• Sell what the applicant wants to buy: a job and organization that fit personal needs. • Be nice, warm, friendly, and humorous. • Be fair, and keep the process consistent among all candidates.
DON'T	• Wander by asking irrelevant, inappropriate, or personal questions. • Stroke your ego by talking about yourself rather than the candidate or you won't learn enough about the person.	• Devalue candidate by being late, uninterested, preoccupied, or unprepared. • Withhold information about the job or the organization. • Grill the candidate, which can cause stress and repel the person.

Source: Ann Howard and Johanna Johnson, "If You Were a Tree, What Kind Would You Be?" Development Dimensions International, Inc., 2008, p. 9. Reprinted with permission from Development Dimensions International, Inc.

While you may be tempted to develop a long list of characteristics, try to limit it to four or five key critical values and competencies. These critical competencies may be overarching and may encompass several of the values and competencies from your longer list. Answers to these questions will vary from company to company and from position to position, but common examples include leadership, time management, communication skills, interpersonal skills, and a focus on customer service.

Next, use the list of critical competencies to help you develop the questions you'll ask to assess a candidate's degree of organizational fit. Remember to address both the company's values and the required job competencies. Otherwise, you could end up like the capital management firm we know of. The company has a strong culture in which worker actions are monitored closely—employees are expected to be at their desks at all times and are given specific break times. A search firm recommended a candidate who possessed the desired high level of technical skills and financial modeling skills, but the firm failed to assess the candidate's fit with the strong culture. Once hired, the candidate couldn't conform to the culture and left the company after a short time.

For each of the critical competencies, create two or three interview questions that will lead the candidate to respond with answers that will help you evaluate whether he or she possesses that particular value or core competency. The result will be a list of eight to 15 interview questions that you can use.

Suppose that leadership is a core competency of the position you're trying to fill. You need to develop two or three questions that will elicit answers that reveal a candidate's leadership style and ability. You might consider asking the following:

1. Describe a time when you had to lead a team to achieve an outcome. What was your role? How did you resolve conflict among the team members?
2. Think about a time when your team members disagreed with a decision you made. How did you react to the disagreement?
3. Reflect on a recent team that you led. Give me an example of how you motivated the team members to accomplish a goal you set for the team.

Planning the buy portion of the interview may seem like a relatively easy task, but it's vital. If you skip this step or devote very little effort to it, you'll likely end up with interview questions that fail to generate the answers you need to adequately assess the candidate, and you'll have failed at the buy task.

Planning the "Sell" Task

Interviewers know that they must complete the buy task, even if they don't know how to go about it. The sell task, however, often gets overlooked. It's common for untrained interviewers to never think about it at all. They assume that if the candidate has made the effort to apply for a position with the organization, then that person has already decided that the organization is a good fit and there's no need to sell the organization to the candidate during the interview. But don't make this mistake—there's always more selling that can be done to ensure that the candidate can assess the degree of fit and feel comfortable accepting an employment offer. You don't want to end up losing your top candidate just because you failed at the sell task.

In working with college students, we frequently see instances where firms fail to adequately complete the sell side of the hiring process. The firms do a great job deciding which candidates they want to hire, but they frequently don't do enough to differentiate their firm from similar firms that are competing for the same candidate, thereby failing at the sell side and not landing their targets.

There are two parts to the sell task: selling the organization and selling the position. A candidate needs to be able to assess his or her fit with both. Executing these two sell tasks successfully will give your organization the best chance that the candidate you've identified as the best fit will accept an employment offer.

A good way to begin planning your sell task is by considering what makes your organization unique. These characteristics are the factors that set your organization apart from others in the candidate's mind. Of course, you want these characteristics to be those that are valued by the candidate, so consider the following areas:

1. Work environment—Is the environment casual or formal? What makes it a fun place to work?

2. Organization culture—Are flexible work schedules acceptable and supported? Are work projects challenging and varied?
3. Compensation and benefits—Is the position's salary competitive with your peers' salary levels? What benefits are offered (such as vacation, personal leave, retirement)?

Next, consider how your organization develops its employees. The best job candidates are looking for organizations that are willing to invest in their personal and professional development. It won't be enough to just tell candidates about your training, mentoring, and coaching programs. You'll have to sell these programs to the candidates by describing how current employees are flourishing in the organization because of these programs.

Finally, think about how you can sell the specific position. Determine how the person in the position will contribute in meaningful ways to the organization. Develop an understanding of the position's visibility within the organization and how the candidate will gain face time with key employees in other groups and divisions, including senior management. This visibility analysis will help you illustrate how the successful candidate can build his or her skill set and professional network.

If you want to master the sell task, you must first understand the candidate. Ask the candidate directly what he or she values in an employer and a position. Once you know what the candidate is seeking, you can develop your sell effort to highlight how the organization and position meet those needs. For example, if the candidate values a variety of projects, you'll emphasize how many projects the candidate will work on at one time and how frequently the project assignments will change.

Putting It All Together

The scheduled interview time has arrived. You've planned the interview and developed a set of appropriate questions to help you assess the candidate's skills. The candidate has researched your organization and is ready to answer your questions. You're ready to listen to the candidate's responses for clues on how to sell the organization and the position to the candidate.

Take a deep breath, relax, and welcome the candidate. Establish a friendly yet professional atmosphere, and ask your first question. The rest of the interview will fall into place, and you'll be well on your way to identifying the best candidate for the position and making a successful hire.

How to Ace the Most Challenging Job Interview Questions

Avoid Awkward Moments during an Interview by Preparing for the Toughest Questions in Advance

Beth A. Berk

> *Be prepared to define what a challenge means to you, as well as what your goals and expectations for professional advancement are.*

In today's job market it is not uncommon for CPAs to have opportunities to choose from. Yet interviewing is still an important skill to master. Excelling on job interviews can mean the difference between landing your dream job and settling for one that's good though not ideal.

During an interview, you may be asked a question that triggers an unexpected reaction or response. You may find yourself answering awkwardly or being unable to think of anything to say. Being properly prepared can help you when you're put on the spot. Here are a few of the more challenging interview questions you may be asked and suggestions for how best to respond.

The question: Why are you looking to leave your current job? (Or why did you leave your last job?)

How to answer: It depends upon your reason for leaving. Some good responses include:

- **"I came across an amazing opportunity that is (was) too good to pass up."** As long as you have been in your current (or prior) role for a few years, the hiring professional should find this answer acceptable—especially if he or she is the one offering the opportunity.

- **"I wasn't being challenged enough in my last role"** or **"There aren't enough opportunities for advancement at my current job."** In this case, be prepared to define what a challenge means to you, as well as what your goals and expectations for professional advancement are. That way, if the role you're interviewing for isn't a match for your expectations, the interviewer will (hopefully) let you know, and you can rule that job out.

- **"There isn't enough flexibility in my schedule."** This is an acceptable answer, but be sure the job you're interviewing for can provide the kind of schedule you need.
- **"My salary isn't commensurate with my skills and experience."** In this case, do some research into what the market rate is in your area for someone with your background to make sure your expectations are not out of line with reality. Also, don't bring up your financial obligations: Mentioning your bills, rent, or college loans can make the interviewer think you're only interested in the job because it pays more.
- **"It was just time to move on."** If this is the case, explain why. Perhaps recent layoffs sparked fears that your job may be in jeopardy, or the company and/or your role changed significantly due to a merger or acquisition.

The question: Having to state your salary requirements without knowing the salary range.
How to answer: If asked about your current or last salary, state that you are seeking a market rate for the role for which you are being considered based on your education, certifications, experience, and skills. If your skills are in high demand, say so tactfully. Don't forget to consider the cost of living and your employer's location (i.e., city vs. suburbs), especially if you're relocating.

If you must provide an amount or range, let the interviewer know when you last received a raise and what your base salary was apart from bonuses and other benefits. If you think your requirements may be higher than what the employer wishes to pay, tell the interviewer that you are flexible about salary if you think an employer is a good fit.

The question: Being asked about a sticky situation, such as being fired for cause or a time when you were asked to compromise your ethics.
How to answer: Stick to relaying facts that can be verified by others (e.g., references, prior supervisors, or peers). Keep in mind that a hiring professional may know someone you worked with at a prior job and ask that person about you. Try not to sound accusatory or derogatory about the other people or companies involved. If necessary, write down your answers, and practice saying them in front of a mirror or to family and friends, paying close attention to your nonverbal expressions and tone of voice. If a sticky situation recently happened and you are still emotional about it, consider postponing interviews for a short while.

The question: What is your greatest weakness?
How to answer: Before an interview, think about times in your life when you received constructive criticism and what you did thereafter. Tell the story of one of these incidents if you're asked about your greatest weakness. If you can't come up with a particular incident, think about one of your traits that could be viewed as both an asset and a liability. For example, being detail-oriented can mean that you sometimes pay too much attention to details that aren't important, but it can also mean that you don't let anything vital slip by you. You may also want to mention steps you've taken to improve, such as working with a coach or mentor.

IN BRIEF

- When an interviewer asks about your salary requirements, a sticky situation in your past, or the reason for leaving your current job, it's best to answer honestly yet diplomatically.
- To prepare for being asked about your greatest weakness, think of an anecdote about how you used constructive criticism to improve yourself. Alternatively, you can mention a weakness that can also be viewed as a strength.
- If you're asked a question you can't answer on the spot, don't bluff. Ask for more time to think about it, and then be sure to follow up.

The question: Any technical question you don't know how to answer.

How to answer: If you get a technical question about a topic you have never dealt with or haven't dealt with in a long time, state that fact to the interviewer. Giving an answer for the sake of giving an answer, or answering incorrectly, most likely will not get you the job. You may want to describe how you would go about finding the answer if on the job, or say that you are willing to learn what you don't know—and on your own time if necessary.

> *Giving an answer for the sake of giving an answer, or answering incorrectly, on a technical question most likely will not get you the job.*

The question: Any nontechnical question where you just draw a blank.

How to answer: In this situation, the worst thing to do is to avoid answering the question. Instead, be honest and state that you are not sure how to respond. If you simply need more time, say that it is a good question and you'd like to think about it further before providing an answer. And if you haven't come up with an answer by the end of the interview, tell the interviewer that you will get back to him or her, specifying a time frame (later in the day, tomorrow, etc.) and how you'll reply (telephone or email). Then make sure you follow through.

Lastly, be sure to convey why you want the job and are qualified for it. Hopefully, having answered all questions asked during the interview, you've made this evident in more ways than one. Good luck!

CONCLUSION

As students move from the classroom to the workforce, having strong communication competence can make the difference in both securing desired employment and having success within employment. Yet business and professional communication operates within and beyond just the workplace. This book explored communicative interactions within business and professional environments through a relational perspective. Viewing these interactions as *relational* necessarily requires attention to aspects typically overlooked by traditional texts. This approach aligns with growing concerns from businesses that current applicants lack the "soft skills".

If relationships form the pretext for communication, then understanding those relational aspects of communication within business and professional environments provides the basis for success. The articles and essays included in this volume were selected to highlight various intersections of social existence, professionalism, image, diversity, and more within business communication. Many of these influences converge in specific communicative environments.

Given all of this, students should finish this volume with an understanding of the fundamental influences that shape and are shaped by communication within business and professional environments. Whether students end up as sales representatives, nonprofit executives, farmers, public servants, attorneys, chefs, or teachers, the lessons included in this volume will aid students broadly in navigating the often difficult terrain of interacting with coworkers, managers, bosses, and customers. Analyzing business and professional communication through a relational perspective allows students to create a "toolbox" from which they can access these many tools to construct the messages that best lead toward successful communication. Good luck!

ABOUT THE AUTHOR

William James Taylor is the assistant director of debate and instructor in communication studies at Kansas State University, where he teaches courses in argumentation, debate, small-group communication, and business communication. His teaching and research efforts include argumentation, "organizational & relational communication," and food studies.

CPSIA information can be obtained
at www.ICGtesting.com
Printed in the USA
LVHW060908180723
752713LV00012B/49